One from the Many

The Global Economy Since 1850

CHRISTOPHER M. MEISSNER

OXFORD
UNIVERSITY PRESS

OXFORD
UNIVERSITY PRESS

Oxford University Press is a department of the University of Oxford. It furthers
the University's objective of excellence in research, scholarship, and education
by publishing worldwide. Oxford is a registered trade mark of Oxford University
Press in the UK and certain other countries.

Published in the United States of America by Oxford University Press
198 Madison Avenue, New York, NY 10016, United States of America.

© Oxford University Press 2024

CIP data is on file at the Library of Congress

ISBN 978–0–19–775931–8 (pbk.)
ISBN 978–0–19–992446–2 (hbk.)

DOI: 10.1093/oso/9780199924462.001.0001

Paperback printed by Sheridan Books, Inc., United States of America
Hardback printed by Bridgeport National Bindery, Inc., United States of America

For LD

Contents

Preface

This book briefly introduces some key topics in the long-run history of the global economy. The focus is largely on three areas of analysis, international trade, capital/financial flows, and movement of people, encompassing three periods: 1850–1914, 1918–1938, and 1945–present. The first and last periods represent the major waves of "globalization." The middle period, between the two world wars, or the interwar period, witnessed a retreat of globalization and global economic depression. Economists define globalization as sustained intensification in international flows of trade, finance, and workers.

The focus is on these issues since the early 1800s, when astounding technological advances and unprecedented political changes laid the foundation for a new epoch in the history of the global economy. These changes continue to shape the global economy today, strongly determine overall well-being and the standard of living, and continuously affect political debates. As this book is being written, issues like Brexit and the election of Donald Trump to the US presidency herald for some the impending end of globalization. This book places these and other recent debates in historical context, making the case that the past matters for the future of the global economy. Moreover, evidence from the very long run suggests that the global economy can and will survive, despite the latest round of setbacks.

The first objective of this book is to provide a broad overview and account of globalization over the long run for those unfamiliar with the basics. The second objective is to help the reader understand better the costs and benefits of globalization. Does globalization make countries richer and wealthier? Does it reduce or raise economic risk and uncertainty? Which countries, factors of production, industries, or interest groups "win" and which "lose" from globalization? How does globalization impinge on and interact with nations' economic policy choices?

To help formulate an informed opinion about these issues, a long-run, comprehensive view of the global economy is necessary. For readers already familiar with these issues, the book aims to serve as a fundamental reference and concise reminder of the evolution of the global economy since 1850. The book unapologetically relies heavily, but not exclusively, on a neo-classical, some might say orthodox, approach to economic interactions. Concepts based on this paradigm feature heavily in this book. Hypotheses generated by recent research in this tradition feature throughout the book. These predictions are compared to the data. Along the way, associated non-quantitative historical evidence is included. In this way, the book follows a comparative historical approach. It is important to remember that many decisions and outcomes are political and not mediated directly by the market. Therefore, the book cannot, and does not, totally neglect the "political economy" of globalization.

By the end of this book, the reader will have gained a greater appreciation for the conditions under which the global economy succeeds and fails in the short and long run. The reader is invited to explore the long-run evolution of the global economy, an entity unto itself, apart from the national economies that make it up. One global economy emerges and emanates from the many national economies.[1]

The title of this book, *One from the Many*, acknowledges that the global economy derives from a large multiplicity of economic (and political) interactions between nations (and other economic actors/agents), all of which add up to a global economy. The global economy is an entity unto itself. It can be, and should be, analyzed as such, lest the systemic forces which matter for humanity and the planet itself go unrecognized. The global economy has a "life unto itself."

---

[1] The motto of Alfred Marshall's influential book *Industry and Trade* is "The many in the one, the one in the many." Readers (and numismatists) will also note the resemblance and relation to the American motto "E pluribus unum."

Acknowledgments

This book has been on slow-cook mode since about 2008. It began a little after moving back to California and joining the faculty of economics at the University of California, Davis. At UC Davis I had the privilege of assuming the duty of teaching two classes covering the economic history of the global economy, one at the undergraduate level and another at the graduate level. Regularly lecturing to 180 undergraduate students at a time, I have enjoyed an ample audience with which to share and develop this economic history of the global economy. Over time, I have attempted to make the curriculum relevant and timely and to cover standard topics in comparative economic history that I firmly believe all economics students should learn at some point. The students at UC Davis have been good sports, and without their presence, this book would not be what it has become.

Moving back to California after a six-year hiatus at Cambridge University was also a fantastic opportunity to re-join a vibrant community of economic historians, historians, and economists who had an interest in global economic history and the global economy. I have learned so much from so many scholars in this great state over the years. Over the last decade-and-a-half, my colleagues Greg Clark, Katherine Eriksson, Peter Lindert, Alan Olmstead, Santiago Pérez, Eric Rauchway, and Alan M. Taylor have been treating me daily to world-class interactions in seminars, in the hallway, at the water cooler, during many trips to Peet's coffee, and over many fine meals.

Between 1996 and 2001, I received excellent PhD training at UC Berkeley, learning a great deal about global economic history (and so much more) from Brad DeLong and Barry Eichengreen. The classes for which I served as a teaching assistant for Professors DeLong and Eichengreen laid a strong foundation for this book. Throughout these early years, I had the opportunity to learn from and receive encouragement from numerous other people at Berkeley, including Carlos Arteta, Matias Barenstein, Mark Carlson, Susan Carter, Andrea De Michelis, Jan De Vries, Gabriel Demombynes, Julian Di Giovanni, Rui Esteves, Fabio Ghironi, Galina Hale, Tim Hatton, David Huffman, Drew Keeling, Marc Meundler, Kris James Mitchener, Ernesto López-Córdova, Ian McLean, Marcelo Moreira, Petra Moser,

Maurice Obstfeld, Martha Olney, Phil Oreopoulos, Hélène Rey, Christina Romer, David Romer, Gary Richardson, Andrew Rose, Jay Shambaugh, Jean Philippe Stijns, Tobias Straumann, Richard Sutch, Chang Tai-Hsieh, and Eric Verhoogen.

The wider (and sizeable) economic history community in California has, over the years, been extraordinarily beneficial too. The All-UC group in economic history, and its legendary conferences in which faculty and graduate students from California and the rest of the world participated, nourished my intellectual journey with incredible insights and outstanding camaraderie. A number of co-authors, graduate students, and other colleagues who have been associated with the UC Davis Economics program have been essential in helping me teach, collaborate, and accumulate knowledge, for which I am grateful. These include Lety Arroyo-Abad, Paul Bergin, Beau Bressler, Doug Campbell, Jeff Cheung, Dan Díaz-Vidal, Robert Feenstra, Rowena Grey, Sun Go, Yu (Max) Hao, David Jacks, Yuzuru Kumon, Mingxi Li, Zhixian (Peter) Lin, Dan Liu, Gabriel Mathy, Dennis Novy, John Parman, Sarah Quincy, Kathryn Russ, Camila Saez, Rivka Shenhav, and Stephen Sun.

I have received helpful comments on early drafts of this book from many undergraduate students (too many to name). To the students in my honors classes, I thank you for helping me to improve my writing, clarify my thoughts, and avoid other stylistic issues. Students in larger classes have, as mentioned, been willing to hear me out and given me feedback on the approach developed here—often voting with their feet when not impressed. Michael Bordo, my long-time co-author and friend, provided detailed and extremely helpful comments on a draft of this book. If I have strayed and failed to incorporate his many constructive comments, it is my failure alone. I thank Alan M. Taylor for pestering me to finish this book in a timely fashion and for sharing so many nuggets of knowledge and wisdom with me over the years. Haoze (Anson) Li did superb work tracking down data and improving the appearance of nearly all the figures and tables, for which I am forever grateful. I also thank, without implicating, four anonymous reviewers of this manuscript and my early proposal for many insightful comments.

Many others have played a role, in many and varied ways, in my professional and intellectual formation. The probably incomplete list of those whose direct or indirect influence may be visible somewhere in this book include Ran Abramitzky, Philipp Ager, Toke Aidt, Bob Allen, Marc Badia-Miró, Stephane Becuwe, Bertrand Blancheton, Fred Boehmke, Dan Bogart, Steve Broadberry, Lawrence Broz, Pablo Bustelo, Nick Crafts, Bill Collins, Anna Carreras, Leah

Boustan, Guillaume Daudin, Marc Dincecco, Dave Donaldson, Giovanni Federico, Price Fishback, Jeff Frieden, Gregori Galofré-Vila, Claudia Goldin, Tim Guinnane, Eric Hilt, Josh Hausman, Michael Huberman, Doug Irwin, Harold James, Peter Sandholt Jensen, Davis Kedrosky, Sukko Kim, Wilfried Kisling, Alex Klein, Michael W. Klein, Markus Lampe, Naomi Lamoreaux, Debin Ma, Dierdre McCloskey, Joel Mokyr, Aldo Musacchio, Douglass C. North, Nathan Nunn, Kim Oosterlinck, Pseudoerasmus, Nuria Puig-Raposo, Albrecht Ritschl, James Robinson, Joan Rosés, Steve Redding, Angela Redish, Jean Laurent Rosenthal, Emma Rothschild, Peter Rousseau, Mare Sarr, Paul Sharp, Catherine Schenk, Moritz Schularick, Ken Sokoloff, Solomos Solomou, David Stuckler, Nathan Sussman, Tim Swanson, Richard Sylla, John Tang, Peter Temin, Hans-Joachim Voth, Marc Weidenmier, and Nikolaus Wolf. I thank these scholars for all their contributions to economics and economic history from which I have learned so much.

A special shout out goes to three of my economic history heroes: Larry Neal, Kevin O'Rourke, and Jeff Williamson, whose big economic history energy and massive contributions to the field have always been inspirational. These three scholars are giants in the field of Cliometric-style, global economic history. It has been my good fortune to interact with them over the years.

1

Introduction

Globalization is part of what makes us human. Trade and exchange are fundamentally human activities and unique to the species. Globalization, a process of economic *integration* and interconnection, has increased inexorably over the very long run. Globalization is a persistent economic process. Consumers, firms, governments, and organizations benefit from greater integration. Nations tend to prosper when integration is higher. Integration between countries is like a new technology. It has the capacity to give us more of what we want while using fewer resources. The process of globalization can recede at times. But, on a long-enough timeline, it has always seemed to make a comeback. Until *Homo sapiens* goes extinct, globalization will continue.

For most of human history, integration has been undeniably present. Over the last twelve thousand years, since the neo-lithic revolution and the advent of agriculture, groups of humans have become increasingly integrated. In the last two hundred years, globalization has accelerated. Integration has advanced more than it had done in all of human history. There is little chance of going permanently backward. The technologies that enable integration are continuously improving and widely adopted as they appear. Trade and integration, resting on cooperative behavior and highly complex social interaction, are fundamental to human behavior.

Nevertheless, history shows that the most frequent setbacks for integration are humanly devised constraints such as policies and laws. This might seem to contradict the idea that globalization is unlikely to go backward, but then again, humans are also fundamentally full of internal contradictions. Individual and societal choices are not always as rational nor as far-sighted as basic analytical models often assume. Often we learn from our mistakes, and the process of integration can be understood as a process whereby humans learn to do more of it over the long run as its benefits are revealed, as humans' ability to organize complex systems evolves, and as the costs of limiting integration become apparent.

Integration can be, and has been, slowed and reversed temporarily by special interest groups, entrepreneurial politicians, and labor movements.

One from the Many. Christopher M. Meissner, Oxford University Press. © Oxford University Press 2024.
DOI: 10.1093/oso/9780199924462.003.0001

There are three general reasons for this. First, some of these want to protect privileges—what economists call *rents* or *super-normal profits*. Monopolist suppliers are surely threatened by increased foreign competition. Second, some of them seek redress for the difficult changes required by greater integration. New competition and interaction can imply significant and costly adjustments to ways of work and life. Frequently, integration forces us to refocus our efforts on what we are best at *in relative, terms* which often only comes at a significant short-run transitional cost. Third, values and preferences are often not shared universally. The apparent loss of sovereignty accompanying integration can squash integration. For instance, American health and safety standards currently allow application of chlorine products to food-grade processed poultry to avoid microbial infections, but European standards do not. American consumers generally do not worry about "chlorinated chicken," but some European consumers and their vocal political representatives are ostensibly vociferously against the idea.[1]

What Is the Global Economy?

This book studies international markets for products and commodities, capital, and labor. These are the primary focus of research in international economics. Herein lies a long-run account of their growth and impact on people's lives. Since about 1850, the level of integration between once-separate markets has increased dramatically. Figures 1.1, 1.2 and 1.3 show the record on how integration proceeded in goods markets, capital markets, and labor markets. When these indicators turn upward, we say that these markets are becoming more integrated. Based on these figures, economists highlight two periods of "globalization" since the 1850s. These are the period from 1850 until 1914 and the period from 1950 until the present. We call these moments "periods of globalization" because integration concurrently increased in all three types of markets, significantly transforming local markets into global markets. When local markets are affected by events and outcomes in foreign markets, then markets are said to be *integrated*.

The global economy, a complex system built up from the many local markets (hence the title of this book) has a life unto itself—one separate from the domestic economies that are its foundation. Understanding its evolution

---

[1] "Cabinet Is Split as Gove Vows to Ban US Chicken," *The Times of London*, July 27, 2017.

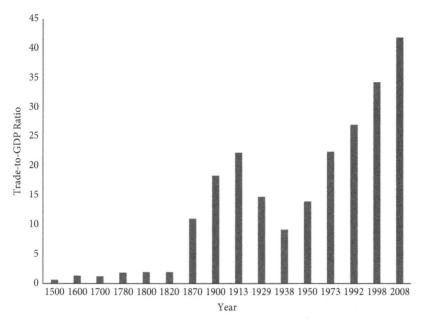

Figure 1.1 Ratio of World Trade to World GDP, 1500–2008
Sources: 1500–1820: author's calculations based on data underlying Estevadeordal, Frantz, and Taylor (2003); 1870–2008: author's calculations from data underlying Jacks, Meissner, and Novy (2008)

since 1850 and the legacy of past choices illuminates the future and helps us understand where we are today. Trade partners yesterday are much likelier to be our trade partners today. The places that Europeans colonized as far back as five hundred years ago trade more closely today with those European countries, although they long ago ceased to be controlled by Europeans. Moreover, they are often likely to be poorer if they were heavily exploited for their commodities and minerals in the 19th century. Regions in West Africa, terrorized by the Atlantic slave trade in the 17th through the early 19th centuries, are today poorer than other regions less affected by these historical events. Oppositely, the Chinese government designated some cities as trading or "treaty ports" in the 19th century; they were partially governed by Europeans, and are today more prosperous and vibrant than similar uncolonized cities.[2] Immigrant flows are heavily, though not exclusively, determined by the location choices of those in the past. Asian immigration to the

---

[2] See Jia (2014).

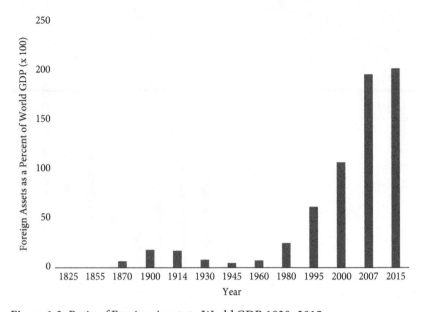

Figure 1.2 Ratio of Foreign Assets to World GDP, 1820–2015

Source: 1820–2000: Obstfeld and Taylor (2005); 2007–2015: author's calculations based on data from Lane and Milesi-Ferretti (2017) and World Bank (2021)

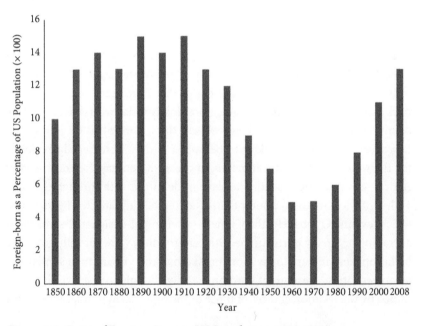

Figure 1.3 Ratio of Foreign-Born to US Population, 1850–2008

Source: 1850–1990: Gibson and Lennon (1999); 2000–2008: based on Kandel (2011)

United States is relatively larger in the western United States, and especially California, than in other regions. Italy and Spain today have stronger economic (and soccer) linkages with Argentina than they do with New Zealand and South Korea. Capital flows and the associated crises of the past still cast a shadow on how policy today is conducted.

This book aims to demonstrate how these markets mattered for economic growth and for other important outcomes such as the purchasing power of consumers, exposure to financial crises, and the amount of autonomy a country can exercise. These areas of study are where much of the recent research in economics, economic history, and international relations has focused, and the aim is to provide a survey of what we know about these areas over the long run based on the efforts of a new generation of scholarship and research.

Why Study the Global Economy?

Most economists believe that free international trade provides overall gains for the countries involved. This is a theoretical result that is also generally supported in the data. The argument forms the foundation for a large amount of scientific research on the connections between economic growth, development, and the international economy. A simple intuition underlies the assertion. Voluntary trade and exchange allocate scarce resources to their most efficient use when the opportunity for trade arises. Trade is more likely to occur when a mutually beneficial outcome is feasible. When countries engage in trade across borders, they specialize in the production of goods that use the resources (e.g., land, skilled or unskilled labor, minerals, capital) that they have in (relative) abundance, or in which they are relatively skilled or efficient at producing. For example, Australia is a net exporter of minerals, Saudi Arabia exports petroleum, China exports manufactured goods using labor intensively to assemble them from imported parts, and Germany exports high-quality durable goods and machinery using high-skilled labor and advanced machinery. This is the essence and articulation of *comparative advantage*, a concept first clearly enunciated by British economist David Ricardo (1772–1823).

The barriers to trade, also referred to as *trade costs*, determine the "gains from trade." When communication improves, shipping technologies advance, tariffs fall, or uncertainty in the economic environment declines, trade costs are lower. Consequently, international trade expands and factors of production are allocated more efficiently. Consumers obtain products at lower cost due to a more efficient allocation of production. Consumers also access a wider range of products not previously available when trade barriers were high. The economic environment becomes more competitive, eroding monopoly power, again acting to lower prices for consumers. On the supply-side, the least productive firms are likely to exit, leaving more productive firms with higher revenues and greater incentives to invest and upgrade their technologies.

Similar forces affect the movement of labor and capital. Improvements in transportation and communication make it easier to travel long distances and for investors to know about risks and rewards of foreign markets. Workers from low-wage economies move to high-wage regions when they can overcome the financial constraints involved in moving and when artificial barriers like immigration restrictions are eliminated. In the late 20th and early 21st century, nurses from less developed countries but with valuable skills sought higher wages in advanced countries precisely where the demand for their services was high. Multinational corporations have, over recent decades, relocated production to offshore facilities and invested abroad to take advantage of low-cost inputs (labor, capital, resources), or to be closer to local markets and so to save on transportation costs and to "jump" tariff barriers. Managerial teams and their know-how often accompany the physical machinery which offers a means for technology transfer.

International capital flows depend on barriers to such investment, including communication technologies and government restrictions on foreign investment. Legal limitations on foreign investment are known as "capital controls." As better information becomes available, or as governments "liberalize" their financial sector, capital (i.e., accumulated savings) flows to where saving is low and capital is "scarce." The addition to the pool of local savings enhances the productivity of local factors of production and allows entrepreneurs to finance projects they were unable to fund themselves. Investors seize the opportunity to earn higher returns and "diversify" their portfolios. Diversification allows investors to insure themselves against negative shocks in their home markets.

As we will see, the textbook examples given above are generally thought to raise economic growth and welfare. However, while they are informative examples, they are also largely theoretical abstractions. The historical record shows that trade often *does* make the parties involved better off by allowing for higher incomes and increased productivity. Still, the long-run record also tells us that trade, capital, and labor markets are neither necessary nor sufficient for raising economic growth or improving well-being. Moreover, there are costs.

Often the costs of globalization are related to the "distributional issue." Who gains from globalization? In fact, the gains from openness and integration are not necessarily equally distributed. Incumbent producers may suffer as global competition increases. In recent years, a policy concern has been the loss of emigrant nurses. These emigrants may give advantage to the receiving countries, but the sending countries are left with a scarcity of nurses and now must pay higher wages to induce more people to go into nursing. Capital flows bring the potential for heightened financial instability, especially when governments mismanage these flows or are not prepared to alter their policies in an environment of global integration.

Non-voluntary exchanges and power relationships can also be important. Human history shows that empire and military or political power also matter. Many decisions have been made for individuals and nations over time without recourse to the invisible hand of the market. In the 19th century, European colonization of Africa and Asia had a decisive impact on the allocation of resources. The trans-Atlantic slave trade, a tragic episode, also left an economic legacy on the entire global economy. Wars, alliances, treaties, and policy paradigms have an impact on decisions throughout the period of analysis.

Accordingly, this book attempts to help make sense of a wide swath of economic, historic, and political research to illustrate when globalization increases economic growth and well-being, when it is neutral or was a subsidiary force, and when it may have hurt long-term prospects for economic growth and well-being. This more cautious view may not always totally jive with the conventional view espoused in mainstream economics courses and textbooks. Care is taken in the pages that follow to illustrate where, when, and under what circumstances globalization hindered growth and stability and when it helped.

The Importance of Interdependence

Finally, the issue of interdependence is inseparable from integration. Global markets are, by definition, about connections between disparate local markets. What happens in one region, country, or market can have an important impact on another market. Contrary to the view that "all politics is local," it is quite reasonable to argue that globalization forces local policies to become entwined and dependent on policies and economic activity in the rest of the world.

Trade policy is a political decision about the acceptable level of tariffs and non-tariff barriers. These policy choices are a function of the relative strength of local interest groups who stand to gain or lose from the global economy. But local forces affect the global economy itself. If trading partners raise tariffs, then perhaps other countries will want to retaliate. Trade wars attempt to punish another nation for perceived economic injury. Trade wars occurred frequently in the 19th century. Retaliatory action to re-balance the economy was common during the Great Depression in the 1930s. They seemed to make a comeback with the Trump administration. However, disputes about "unfair" trade practices occurred well before Trump became president. Today, the World Trade Organization (WTO), a *multilateral* institution, attempts to negotiate settlements between countries with trade disputes.

At times, there are positive incentives that make globalization more palatable. Reciprocal tariff concessions, foreign aid, and foreign investment can all help build the global economy. This notion guided American trade policy from the mid-1930s and shaped the global economy throughout the post–World War II period. "Reciprocity" was also common in the 19th century. The threats for trade incentives to be withdrawn in the case of bad behavior actually increased cooperation.

Non-discrimination in trade policy is another policy tool that historically boosted the global economy both in recent decades and in history. The rapid rise of the "unconditional Most-Favored Nation" (MFN) clause in trade treaties after 1860 came about after Britain and France signed the Cobden–Chevalier Treaty. In 1860 these two nations offered each other lower tariffs and removed trade restrictions between each other. Importantly, the Cobden–Chevalier Treaty also featured the MFN clause, which was non-discriminatory. The clause stipulated that any concession France or Britain extended to other countries would automatically be applied to the original signatories. Fearing a decrease in British and French demand, other nations quickly signed similar deals with these two nations.

The reopening of the United States to freer trade after 1934 with the Reciprocal Trade Agreements Act (RTAA) also brought significant strategic cooperation. With high tariffs, on the order of 30% to 40%, and facing high tariffs across the world since the start of the Depression, US producers lost foreign market share and revenue. President Roosevelt's answer was to offer access to US markets in exchange for better access to foreign markets.

This trend continued in the years that followed World War II under the aegis of the General Agreement on Trade and Tariffs (GATT). By the late 20th century, tariffs in economically advanced countries had fallen to negligible levels. The rise of a negotiated multi-lateral system featuring unconditional "most-favored nation" clauses and non-discrimination in the successive rounds of negotiation in the GATT yielded global cooperation on free trade.

Still more examples of strategic interdependence come to mind. When foreign nations devalued their exchange rates to spur economic recovery in the Great Depression of the 1930s, other nations retaliated often by devaluing their currencies as well or implementing trade barriers. This instability allegedly shifted the pain of the Depression onto trading partners, since a devalued currency would boost exports for the devaluing nation and lower demand for foreign products.

After World War II, the United States offered reconstruction assistance to Europe via the Marshall Plan, but only as long as the Europeans avoided the policies most at odds with American interests and beliefs about the market economy. From 1957, when the Treaty of Rome was signed, European nations have drawn themselves closer together, eventually creating a European Union (EU). The EU binds member economies together in a dizzying number of ways. EU-wide regulations on health, safety and hygiene, working conditions, financial regulations, and fiscal policy are examples. These examples stoked indignation among many voters in the United Kingdom. The vote to leave the EU in July 2016, also known as "Brexit," was partly a rejection of deep integration. Many voters believed the EU, the European Commission, and other member nations had gone too far in telling Britons how their economy should be run. Regional agreements focused on greater economic cooperation, including, the Association of Southeast Asian Nations (ASEAN) group, Mercosur, and the North American Free Trade Agreement (NAFTA). The G-7, G-20, Paris Club, the Bretton Woods institutions (World Bank, International Monetary Fund), the GATT, the WTO, the Food and Agriculture Organization (FAO) are all important in the headlines on a daily basis.

Today, many people accuse the global economy of leading to a labor or environmental "race to the bottom." The argument suggests that nations lower regulations to attract polluting firms and firms that "exploit" labor. The bottom line is allegedly more important to firms than the social costs of environmental degradation or labor market instability. As it turns out, higher labor standards were sometimes actually a product of intensified globalization in the late 19th century. Shared global governance and the upside to strategic interaction—cooperation—have both played their role in shaping these outcomes in the global economy since 1850.[3] Various attempts at international "cooperation" such as the Bank for International Settlements (BIS) in the 1930s, the European Payments Union (EPU), and innumerable treaties designed to cover intellectual property rights, protect the environment, and uphold minimum regulatory standards in corporate governance and labor relations will be analyzed. Cooperation is fundamental to the human species, but so is conflict. The global economy is a result of cooperation as much as conflict.

Important also is a sense of how interdependence can affect the stability or instability of the economies involved. We seek to trace the historical progress of economic interaction and governance between nations. All these aspects of the global economy have profound effects on domestic economies by affecting the pace of economic growth, risk and uncertainty, the distribution of income, and ultimately welfare.

Perhaps the thorniest area in this analysis is "interdependence." When there are spillovers, people's preferences about the "right" amount of autonomy matter. Often these preferences are revealed through surveys, referenda, or through the political system. People's preferences can, of course, be subverted or ignored by anti-competitive political systems or by bad actors seeking to exert influence on others. The most interesting aspect of interdependence is arguably whether those who are free to decide to go further with integration actually choose to do so. The limits to globalization depend as much on this sentiment as on the technological constraints imposed by the laws of physics and engineering. We will come back to the policy issues of trade wars, financial crises, and migration near the end after a thorough introduction to the long run of the global economy.

The Relevance of History for Globalization

History is of fundamental importance to the global economy. Where we are today depends on the past. This concept is known as "path dependence."

---

[3] See Huberman (2012) on trade and labor standards in history.

It can be understood in many ways. Perhaps the most famous example of path dependence concerns the layout on the computer keyboard I am using right now to write these words. QWERTY is the arrangement, on modern keyboards, for the first six letters of the top row. Why? After all, there are other arrangements of letters that would improve typing speed, including the Dvorak keyboard. To condense a long story, what matters is that most of us have trained on a QWERTY keyboard.[4] Since this is so, employers and manufacturers of devices with keyboards provide QWERTY layouts. Any alternative layout would meet with very low demand. On the other hand, since most keyboards sold today are QWERTY, most people who learn to type do so on a QWERTY layout. They know that typing ability on alternative keyboards will not be very useful when QWERTY predominates. Other examples, include the use of platforms and standards, which become entrenched due to first-mover advantages. Everything from Facebook to measurement and industry standards, faces a certain amount of "lock-in" and dependence on history.

As with the keyboard, so goes the global economy. Where we are today depends on what has happened in the past. A large shock to the trade environment like the Cobden–Chevalier Treaty of 1860 generated the spread of a free trade network. It was hard for small countries to deviate from the network. The Great Depression led to stringent limits on international capital movements after World War II. Events yesterday shape people's expectations about the future. European colonization of Africa and the exploitative Atlantic slave trade of the 18th and early 19th centuries made an impact on how the newly sovereign nations after de-colonization were governed. Countries' incomes are lower today where extraction, plundering, and the slave trade were strongest. Clearly, people's expectations about what might happen in the future are heavily influenced by similar past experiences. The past matters for the global economy.

A Brief Overview

The exploration of the global economy in this book covers the period from roughly 10000 BCE to about 1850 CE very rapidly. This short introduction to the ancient- and modern-era economies up to 1850 serves to illustrate that

---

[4] See David (1985).

progress was slow in terms of achieving integration prior to the mid-19th century. The impact on local economies was significant at times, but nowhere near as large as it would be later.

The number of years discussed per page decelerates dramatically after a quick, initial tour through over twelve millennia of human history. Most of the book is devoted to the years after the mid-19th century until the present. The principal reason is that numerous technological and policy changes emerged in the mid-19th century, strongly transforming the nature of the global economy. For instance, shipping and communication technologies witnessed transformative innovations from the early 19th century. In trade policy, we see greater intellectual support for and more industrial interests favoring free trade, lower tariffs, and reductions in other trade barriers across Europe. The speed with which nations dismantled the "Mercantilist" regime varied, but global trade and market integration exploded after 1850 like it never had done before in the history of mankind. European colonization of Africa and South Asia, and independence of the American colonies, brought free trade to the entire globe. Trade treaties were forcefully imposed, even in the absence of outright colonization, in East Asia, notably in Japan and mainland China. Meanwhile, an unprecedented level of international capital flows to Latin America, and to Eastern and Southern Europe led naturally to greater trade and integration. Massive levels of migration also led to a global labor market.

World War I disrupted much of this progress. In the so-called inter-war period, 1919 to 1938, an attempt was made to resurrect globalization. Trade grew, but tariffs and trade policy became more restrictive. Capital flows, once a force for stability, became drivers of financial crises and economic calamities. Migration also declined dramatically as countries in the New World, once open to European migrants, imposed legal barriers to the movements of people. The Great Depression of the 1930s illustrates that lower integration is associated with lower standards of living.

After World War II, the world attempted, once again, to achieve economic prosperity and growth. The global economy was recognized as a driver of this prosperity in Western market economies. Economists realized, however, that serious modifications to policies had to be implemented. Capital flows were severely limited following World War II, and migration was meager compared to the 19th century. Trade grew strongly, however, from the 1950s among the most advanced market-based economies. Trade policy became less restrictive and container shipping emerged. Eventually, by the 1970s, global capital flows resumed. Migration rates rose again, as the global airline industry expanded, communications improved, civil wars erupted, and labor shortages in certain sectors expanded. The globalization of the late 20th century was "superficially similar" to but dramatically different from the 19th century in terms of production patterns and complexity. In trade, offshoring has huge implications for how the gains from international trade are distributed. In capital markets, the interconnections between globally active financial institutions and governments have altered how policy is made and also affected financial stability. Since the late 1990s, globalization has been significantly influenced by a sequence of important policy changes in China dating back to the 1970s. The decades between the 1980s and present have been called "hyper-globalization."

Long-Run Economic Growth

For literally 99.9% of the 200,000 years *Homo sapiens* has existed, material living standards were extremely low. For this 99.9% of the time, 99.9% of all humans lived at a subsistence level or worse. Before the advent of agriculture in about 10,000 BCE, humans hunted animals and gathered plants to sustain themselves. Population density was extremely low and societal organization was ostensibly similar across the world.

With the advent of agriculture, humans became more sedentary. Local economies developed "surplus" production beyond what would provide bare minimum subsistence. The surplus became unevenly distributed, and a small, ruling, elite class of powerful people emerged. These people generally lived at much higher standards of living than the average person. Some evidence even points to the idea that most people's living conditions worsened, since they now had to work harder than before. The trade-off appears to have been for greater certainty about caloric intake and for greater protection from nature and other, not-so-friendly, groups of people. The ancient civilizations in Mesopotamia and the Yangtze delta, some of the first civilizations to discover agriculture, built strong empires with massive armies. In this period, new technologies that advanced productive capability were either not widely applied or else were met with significant increases in population. Population growth quickly eliminated the added gains to production capability, driving per capita incomes back down to near subsistence. This is called the "Malthusian" trap after British economist Robert Malthus (1766–1834).

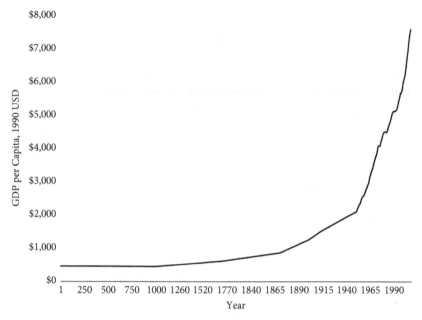

Figure 1.4 World GDP per capita 1 CE–2008 CE
Source: Bolt et al. (2018)

Beginning in the 18th century, however, scientific advances together with institutional changes generated, for the first time, "modern economic growth." The hallmark of modern economic growth is sustained advances in the level of per capita income. The harnessing of nature's abundant energy sources to improve mechanical efficiency and many other new technologies mattered for humans' well-being. This "industrial revolution" generated a new surplus. To ensure that the ruling class did not simply appropriate the gains that could be garnered from such advances, nations found ways to limit and constrain the elite class. A new, middle class emerged, heavily engaged in trade, innovation, and business. Figure 1.4 shows that these advances led to unprecedented rises in per capita incomes after about 1800.

The historical record (Figure 1.5) shows that not all societies were initially equally successful at growing their economies. Northwestern Europeans and eventually the United States were the first places to reap the advantages of these technological, social, and political changes. Asia, Africa, and Latin America fell behind these leaders, creating a "great divergence" between regions that for most of human history had been roughly all equal in terms of living standards. Between 1980 and the 2020s, the blink-of-an-eye in

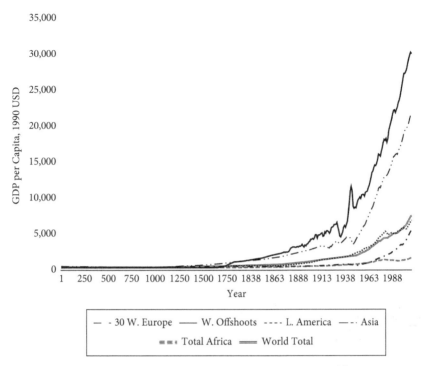

Figure 1.5 Real GDP per capita 1 CE–2008 CE, 5 Regions + World
Source: Bolt et al. (2018)

proportion to two hundred thousand years of human history, there has been dramatic convergence in living standards. The proportion of the world's population living in extreme poverty in the 1950s was about 75%. In the 1970s it was on the order of 45%. By 2015 the share had fallen to about 10%.[5]

While many people in the world are still relatively poor, in the decades following the 1980s many have seen a dramatic closing of the gap between the most advanced countries and the less developed countries. Globalization is unlikely to be the main cause of this convergence, but it has certainly not impeded convergence. Consider an example. North Korea, a country largely closed to international integration, has a per capita income of about $3.50 per day. South Korea, an export powerhouse and modern economy, has a per capita income of almost $82 per day (i.e., $30,000 annually). It would be

[5] The definition of "extreme poverty" used is someone who lives on $1 per day. This threshold has recently been raised to $1.90 per day.

hard to argue that being closed off has been economically beneficial, and oppositely, it would be hard to argue that openness to international integration has been harmful.

Learning Methods and Objectives

In the rest of this book, the reader will explore the very long-run evolution of the global economy. For four periods (600 BCE–1850, 1850–1914, 1919–1938, and 1945–present), we will explore integration in trade, capital, and labor markets. We will rely heavily on the scientific research of previous historians and economic historians who have collected data and tracked archival records to paint relevant and accurate pictures of the past.

Our objective when discovering these data is to study two main questions. The first is a narrow question and can be answered by period. What impact did integration have on local economies within each period? Specifically, we will examine the impact on economic growth and well-being whenever and wherever possible. Which interest groups gained and which ones were worse off from globalization? How were the gains from the global economy distributed within and across nations? How did these forces feed back into the system to affect the trajectory of the global economy?

The second big question is this: how long will globalization continue? It will be necessary to understand the very long run to answer this question. Early humans engaged in trade, and since the Neolithic revolution, we have seen examples of trade over progressively longer distances.[6] Trade was once restricted to a small number of high-value-to-weight products. But humans have progressively learned to trade even very low-value-to-weight products (e.g., wheat or water). Again, the 19th century was a watershed thanks to the new technologies. These new technologies transformed not only the ways people consumed and traded commodities, but where they lived, how they invested their hard-earned savings, and ultimately how much control they would have over their own destinies.

The process of globalization, based fundamentally on technologies and the strong human urge to trade, has been relentless over the long run. While the level of integration and people's enthusiasm for it has witnessed cyclical

---

[6] Interesting and highly readable references for the very long run are Harari (2015) and Diamond (1997).

downturns, been the target of political backlash, and been obliterated by the ravages of wars, it has kept coming back. The coming chapters will sketch the contours of the process of economic globalization right up to the present. By then, the reader will be able to look at modern debates about the future of globalization with the benefit of an historical viewpoint. The reader will then also be able to appreciate just how inexorable the process of globalization is and always will be. This survey also aims to illustrate that in order to understand the global economy as a system and its impact at the local level, more than just the study of any individual economy in isolation is required.

2

The Very Long Run

10,000 BCE–1820 CE

Humans have always traded. Former science editor for *The Economist* Matt Ridley believes that exchange and trade differentiate humans from all other living species. Voluntary, mutually beneficial exchanges raise well-being and expand the consumption possibilities of those that undertake them. Exchange promotes productivity. Producers generate more value per unit of time as they become more specialized. This chapter aims to introduce, the long, run history of such activity.

Over the very long run (i.e., the last twelve thousand years), the global economy has always been expanding. Long-distance trade is a principal human activity. So has globalization been present since the dawn of humanity? When exactly did globalization begin? Was it in Roman times or before? Did the Arab caliphates create globalization? Some authors speak of the *Pax Mongolica* led by Genghis Khan and his golden horde. At his peak, Genghis Khan controlled a wide swath of the Eurasian landmass, stimulating overland trade and interaction between far-flung regions. Certainly, these empires were associated with some form of globalization, but none of them was on the scale of what was witnessed after 1850.

Some historians argue that the advent of the global economy coincides with the voyages of European discovery and conquest in the late 15th century. The evidence certainly shows a rise in long-distance movement of people, ideas, germs, and crops after that date. Peppers, potatoes, and tomatoes, all native to the Americas, would eventually become part of the diet all the way from India to East Asia and beyond.[1] Consumption of Asian and tropical goods became more prevalent in Western Europe. Still, deep market integration on a broad scale remained elusive until the mid-19th century. As is evident, it remains important to understand the limits of

---

[1] See Nunn and Qian (2010) for an introduction to the movement and adoption of various foods like capsicum pepper and tomato to places outside of the Americas, where they originated.

One from the Many. Christopher M. Meissner, Oxford University Press. © Oxford University Press 2024.
DOI: 10.1093/oso/9780199924462.003.0002

globalization prior to 1850 and to be aware of the massive transformation that occurred after 1850.

The Ancient Economies

From earliest times, humans have traded. Recorded human history and archaeological evidence from before the advent of writing clearly reveal this. Sumerians, Carthaginians, and Phoenicians engaged in long-distance trade. The ancient Greeks established city-states that depended integrally on hinterland agriculture for survival. Basic goods, food, and raw materials were traded for territorial protection and for other urban consumables.

Research by generations of historians on the Roman Empire reveals significant evidence of active long-distance trade. From the first century BC, until its lethargic decline, the Roman Empire enjoyed the benefits of a highly organized and integrated economy. At its height, Roman territory stretched across Western Europe, northern Africa, and into western and central Asia. The Roman Empire used central Asian overland trade routes to engage in commerce with the ancient societies of China. Parallel to what was happening in the Mediterranean basin and western Eurasia, the dynasties of China also facilitated and engaged in long-distance trade in East Asia.

The Roman Empire facilitated crucial imports of food and other commodities to the hundreds of thousands of urban residents in Rome. From the West and the South, the olive groves of the river Guadalquivir, and the Maghreb, provided the multipurpose staple olive oil. This oil was used for food preparation but also for fuel, lighting, and even medicinal and cosmetic applications. Wheat, fish, nails, precious metals, and other minerals were transported and sold far from where they originated.

The Roman Empire, capitalizing on the fundamental desires of humans to exchange, provided an institutional framework and defensive umbrella, under which trade could flourish. Contractual and informational problems were solved via the Roman legal system. Money and credit, the necessary media of exchange, and grease for the wheels of commerce were also part of the Roman economy. Goods traveled by sea and river on elaborate boats. Lacking refrigeration technology, merchants transported fish across long distances in boats equipped with immense holding tanks. Evidence shows that movements in grain prices on the Italian peninsula were highly correlated with those in northern Egypt, which lies more than over 1,500 kilometers from Rome.

The legendary Roman road network provided the basic infrastructure to accommodate inland movement of merchandise. The roadways connected Roman military outposts across Western Europe. Research shows that these roads were not the most-efficient road network possible, but they did manage to avoid the most rugged terrain, thereby saving on transportation costs. These massive Roman investments are still present today. The Roman road network is still visible in the routes followed by the expressways and high-speed railway network in France, for instance. It has even been argued that vestiges of the Roman urban network persist in France. Guy Michaels and Ferdinand Rauch report that sixteen of the twenty largest cities in France today are located near, or on, urban settlements from Roman times.[2]

Of course, not even the mighty Roman Empire could overcome the constraint of distance. Given the technology circa 301 CE, the average cost of shipping 1 kilogram of wheat 1,000 kilometers was 0.67 denarii, compared to a daily salary of a farm worker of 25 denarii.[3] Shipping was time and labor intensive. One estimate shows that a 60-kilometer overland shipment took six days and required the labor input of six men. Shipping by land with a wagon was 52 times more expensive than shipping by sea. Shipping by river was 5 (downstream) to 10 (upstream) times more costly than ocean freight.

After the Romans, a succession of civilizations and groups that were preoccupied with long-distance trade and exchange appeared in Europe. The Vikings, hailing from the colder northern climes of Northern Europe, managed to settle parts of Sicily, the British Isles, and significant territory along the Volga River. While the Vikings evidently did not find much of interest in North America, which they reached somewhere around 1000 CE, they did carry on a lively trade between northern and southern routes across Europe. Again, sea prowess and the use of force to settle contractual disputes often lubricated the wheels of commerce. The Vikings, famous for their looting and marauding, illustrate some of the ways that exchange between nations can provide winners and losers.

The Rise of Islam and Eurasia

The rise of Islam in the 7th century CE strongly promoted new global trade networks. Caravans were sent westward from the Arab homelands, plying

---

[2] See Michaels and Rauch (2018).
[3] See Scheidel (2014).

the Sahara Desert and regularly embarking in Timbuktu and points beyond. In the East, Arab traders successfully established outputs in South Asia, including the Indian subcontinent, the Indonesian archipelago, and even all the way to mainland China.

Arab traders took advantage of large price discrepancies between localities in order to make significant profits. Such price discrepancies existed due to an inability to produce goods efficiently in one locality compared with another. In this case, one particularly profitable trade for the Arabs was facilitating the European and Near Eastern consumption of the scarce luxuries of East and Southeast Asia. For those customers most willing to pay in Europe and the Near East, such luxuries added to the variety of their consumption. Fine silks, spices, and many other rare luxury items could not be produced in Europe and hence locals were willing to pay a premium over the origin prices in Asia. Indeed, the Arabs specialized in bringing such goods from halfway across the world and reselling them to Venetian and Genoan merchants. The Venetians and Genoans would purchase these products and trade them onward to northwestern Europe for a handsome profit.

The Arabs excelled at trade because the Islamic Caliphates and Islam itself provided contractual security. Military prowess and religious and cultural linkages made trade more secure. The Arab traders were also geographically privileged since the caliphates were centered in the Middle East—an area between Europe and Asia known as a "chokepoint." The only alternative was the costly overland route traversing the deserts of central Asia.

This more northern route, now commonly referred to as the "Silk Road," experienced its efflorescence from about the late 13th century, when the Mongols led by Genghis Khan created a pathway for such east–west trade. The Pax Mongolica, famous for cementing the reputation of the Silk Road, provided an umbrella of security and stability that allowed trade to flourish. Successive dynasties in China also eked out a large area of economic operation in East Asia. What is curious about this is that from about 1425 the Chinese ostensibly *chose* not to engage in long-distance trade themselves, despite the capacity to do so. Zheng He was the Chinese admiral of the world's largest and most impressive fleet. He commanded over 300 ships, which were staffed by 28,000 sailors. His fleet reached the horn of Africa between 1405 and 1420 in the "voyages to the western oceans." Surprisingly, superior shipbuilding technology, navigational prowess, and organizational capacity failed to ensure that the Chinese would dominate this vast area. The decision was political. By 1435 the emperor, and his inner circle, declined to participate in a large-scale territorial conquest; nor did they favor ongoing trade with these regions. Instead, the Chinese continued to rely on Muslim "middlemen" who offered western silver for Asian luxury goods. The Chinese preferred to focus on creating a large network of inland canals and river ways that integrated domestic markets.

By the 1500s, China, under the Ming dynasty, was arguably the most prosperous and most technologically sophisticated region in the world. This dominance would not last forever. Soon the Europeans would embark on their "voyages of discovery," ultimately leading to a "great divergence." Northwestern Europe raised its living standards rapidly after the 1500s, overtaking Chinese per capita income by the 18th century.

The Age of European Conquest

Beginning in the 15th century, Europeans made rapid advances in sailing and navigation. One goal was to short-circuit Muslim middlemen and their Venetian partners in order to take a larger slice of the profit from trading with Asia. The Portuguese mission to displace this monopoly ultimately failed. By the 1500s, Portuguese merchants could only claim about half of all trade between Europe and Asia. By the 17th century, Dutch merchants from the Dutch East India Company (also known by its Dutch acronym, VOC for Vereenigde Oostindische Compagnie) effectively controlled much of the trade between northern Europe and Asia. The British East India Company carved markets out of the Mughal Empires in India and monopolized the trade between the subcontinent and England. Spain restricted trade in its American colonies such that all cargo had to pass through Spanish ports and to be carried by Spanish vessels. Markups (i.e., the price ratio between Europe and Asia) on spices and other precious commodities failed to fall significantly until the early 1800s due to this continued lack of strong competition (Figure 2.1).

One way economists define integration is by the price difference (or ratio) between the consumer and the supplier of a good. Figure 2.2 illustrates how the trade-cost wedge mattered for these differences. The demand function for the product is graphed as line D while the supply of the product is represented by line S. There is a trade-cost wedge, measured by line segment ab, since the product costs more in the destination market than in the origin

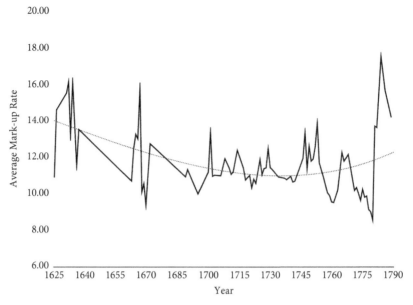

Figure 2.1 Average Price Ratio "Markups" for Pepper, Clove, and Mace, Amsterdam versus Asia, 1608–1800

Source: Author's calculations from data underlying de Zwart (2016)

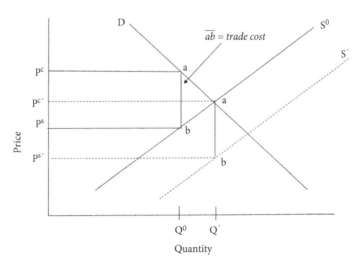

Figure 2.2 Trade Costs in a Model of Supply and Demand

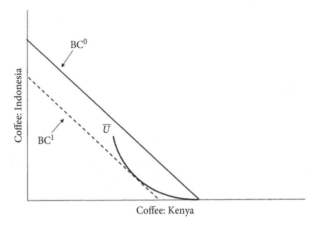

Figure 2.3 Gains from Variety: The Case of Coffee

market. If this wedge shrinks, total consumption of imports will would rise as the price to the consumer falls, leading to greater economic integration. The producer also gains due to higher sales revenue. In this simple model, rising trade can also occur due to shifts in supply and demand (due to, say, productivity advance, entry of a larger number of producers, or population growth). The shift out of the supply curve from S^0 to S' is an example. Economists distinguish these rises due to shifts in demand and supply from falling trade costs/greater integration.[4]

This model is limited because it focuses only on products that are always available at some price. It is entirely plausible, however, that having access to goods that were not previously available can also raise consumer welfare. Figure 2.3 illustrates a simplified version of these welfare gains. In effect, because consumers "love variety," the minimum expenditure necessary to obtain a given level of welfare, $\bar{U}$, has fallen from BC^0 to BC^1 when new goods (coffee from Indonesia) become available.

What are examples of new goods that became available in the past? From the 1500s, many "New World" goods hit the global marketplace. In Asia, sweet potatoes New World crops not only increased agricultural productivity but very likely provided much-desired variety to the diets of peasants and elites alike. Similarly, Europe capitalized on New World crops, including the potato, but also began consuming items such as sugar, tea, coffee, and

[4] See O'Rourke and Williamson (2002).

cocoa. One estimate suggests that for the average European, "new" goods such as tea and sugar were equivalent to a 10% rise in real incomes.[5] Because transportation improvements provided better trade connections with many other parts of the world, this is likely an underestimate of the true gains. The ability to purchase agricultural goods from different sources with different qualities and to rely on them in times of local shortages helped lower consumption volatility, also benefitting consumers who were understandably averse to sharp changes in consumption.

Economic historian Jan de Vries called these changes in the 17th century an "industrious revolution." De Vries argued that the increase in variety available to consumers in Northwestern Europe led to higher real incomes but that consumers had to work harder to achieve these gains. In fact, de Vries claims that labor began working an extra 100 days or more in this period in order to generate the income necessary to purchase the newly available luxury items. Workers sacrificed "saint Monday," and numerous religious holidays were removed from the calendar. The industrious revolution is an example where greater market access led to higher market-based production and specialization and ultimately to higher personal incomes.

The European conquest of the Americas, and the expansion of markets, also may have had another effect on long- run economic growth in Europe. The Williams thesis, intensely debated by economic historians over the years, alleges that the Industrial Revolution, which began in the 18th century, could not have occurred without New World slavery. The exploitation of African slave labor on Caribbean plantations, and the greater availability of low-cost raw materials from the American colonies, raised merchant profits. British merchants plowed profits into investment in new machinery and developed new technologies leading to rising labor productivity (output per worker).

Early rebuttals of this thesis argued that profits from colonial sugar were too small to explain the large amount of investment underpinning the British Industrial Revolution. Estimates from the literature suggest that these profits could have accounted for at most 10% of British investment in the period. This figure requires that nearly all profits be successfully redirected toward industrial outcomes, which is dubious. Moreover, neither

---

[5] See Hersh and Voth (2022).

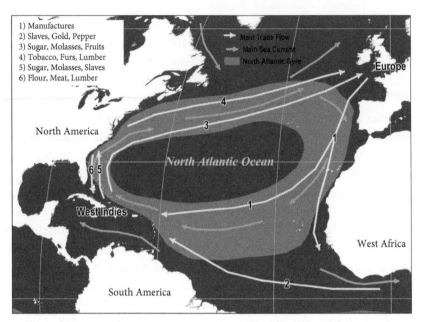

1) Manufactures
2) Slaves, Gold, Pepper
3) Sugar, Molasses, Fruits
4) Tobacco, Furs, Lumber
5) Sugar, Molasses, Slaves
6) Flour, Meat, Lumber

Figure 2.4 North Atlantic "Triangle Trade," 18th Century.
Source: Rodrigue (2020)

number is particularly large, leading the "neo-classical" school to dismiss the Williams view.

On the other hand, New World and global markets did boost European (and especially British) trade and incomes. New research emphasizes that the New World also provided a larger market for European producers of manufacturers. Indeed, in the 18th century, the American colonies purchased the lion's share of the growth in British manufactured exports. Following the dictum of Adam Smith: the size of the market determines the division of labor. Productivity might have advanced due to greater market size, which in turn allowed for increased specialization.

The well-known "triangle trade" associated with the 18th century was part of this process. The triangle trade, illustrated in Figure 2.4, involved the nefarious African Atlantic slave trade, colonial exploitation of sugar and tobacco plantations, and commerce between regions bordering the Atlantic economy. In a typical trade, Europeans would exchange manufactures such as gunpowder, guns, and textiles with the west African slave centers for human cargo. Local traders offered slaves in quantities that depended on the relative cost of capturing unfortunate souls compared to the prices of

European manufactures. Nearly twelve million Africans were transported to the Americas to work on sugar plantations, tobacco farms, and cotton farms.[6] The intensity varied from locality-to-locality.

The local slave economy in the Caribbean, Brazil and South America, and the southern United States produced previously rare commodities on the back of heavily exploited slave labor in exchange for European manufactures and timber from the northeastern United States and the maritime provinces. Rum from the Caribbean was also shipped to the British colonies in the northwest Atlantic and onwards to Europe. Returns accrued directly to the plantation owners and indirectly (and minimally) to slaves in the form of clothing, food, alcohol, and other small consumables. Living standards soared for plantation owners on the back of such exploitation, such that Haiti, now the poorest place in the Western Hemisphere, claimed, in 1800, the title of the richest in terms of total output per free person.

Meanwhile, in western Africa the slave trade diminished long-term development prospects. Brutal conflict, kidnapping, and political re-consolidation focused resources more on exploitation of the already scarce population endowment rather than investment in productive capital or in land. Economic historian Nathan Nunn has shown that the localities in Africa that most heavily exported slaves in the 1700s are today relatively poorer than areas less affected by the historical Atlantic slave trade.

For Europe, integration with the New World may not have been as decisive as the Williams conjecture posits. It is unlikely that economic growth in Europe and Europe's relatively high living standards were decisively driven by the slave trade. The European settlement of the Americas in the 17th and 18th centuries certainly provided a larger market for European manufactures, which ultimately stimulated investment in developing new products and more efficient production processes. The "triangle trade," and the new Atlantic economy, likely contributed, in part, to sustaining the divergence in living standards between northwestern Europe and the rest of the world that appeared from the 16th century.

Scholars now refer to this European economic "fast break" as the "Great Divergence." Increased specialization in manufactured goods and cheaper raw materials undoubtedly marginally enhanced capital accumulation in the 18th century and income levels for Europeans. However, this is not the

---

[6] Perhaps as many as six million more Africans were taken in the Saharan, Red Sea, and Indian Ocean routes.

same as arguing that the slave trade was responsible for the Great Divergence and the Industrial Revolution. Both England and Portugal were heavily involved in the Atlantic slave trade in the 18th century. Their economic paths diverged, however, in this period. The Industrial Revolution can be almost fully explained without reference to the African slave trade.

For instance, institutional divergence was a principal driver of modern economic growth, according to recent research. These changes occurred at this decisive point in time, leading to both a Great Divergence favoring Europe over China and a "Little Divergence" favoring northwestern Europe over southern Europe. Spain, Portugal, and Italy fell behind England and the Netherlands at this point. One reason for this is that English merchants held significant sway over the fiscal policies of the King. The Glorious Revolution of 1688 limited the ability of the English monarch to saddle the population with unsustainable debt and to impose arbitrary taxes. Both of these, debt and taxation, were a form of expropriation of private capital. Such theft leads to lower investment in profitable commercial and industrial activity. Once the king was constrained after 1688, investment could flourish and so-called bourgeois values and culture could take root. Portugal, Spain, and other nations where monarchs ruled without such constraints were unable to incentivize such investment. The Little Divergence would persist until the 20th century, with countries in northwestern Europe being more heavily engaged in globalization and witnessing stronger economic growth than their southern neighbors did.

3

The Great Specialization

1820–1914

Between 1820 and 1914, cross-border movements of goods grew significantly faster than total production. Out of every dollar of spending, an ever-increasing share was accounted for by commodities and services provided by citizens of foreign countries. Figure 3.1 shows the evolution of global exports relative to global production in these years. Behind this great rise in international economic "integration" was a striking fall in the *cost* of trading.

What impact did lower trade costs have? Globalization induced significant changes in the productive activities of virtually every single locality within reach of global transportation networks. Globalization hastened the demise of handicraft/industrial activity on the Indian subcontinent over the course of the 19th century. The American, Argentinian, Canadian, and Ukrainian plains were transformed into global bread baskets. Northwestern Europe accelerated its process of urbanization and industrialization giving rise to German industrial leadership, Danish mechanization in farm products (butter and pork), and a process of convergence in living standards in poor European countries to the leader, Great Britain. This process, dubbed by Kevin O'Rourke and Ronald Findlay the "Great Specialization," has roots in the early and mid-19th century.

What Drove the 19th-Century Trade Boom?

The cost of international trade declined significantly in the 19th century, causing international trade to grow faster than total production. An accounting exercise illustrates how much trade costs mattered in the late 19th century (Figure 3.2). In the 1870s, declines in trade costs explain the majority of the growth of trade (73% to be precise). Growth in income explains the remainder. From the 1890s until World War I, the importance of income growth rises. Up to 50% of the rise in global trade between 1890 and 1900,

One from the Many. Christopher M. Meissner, Oxford University Press. © Oxford University Press 2024.
DOI: 10.1093/oso/9780199924462.003.0003

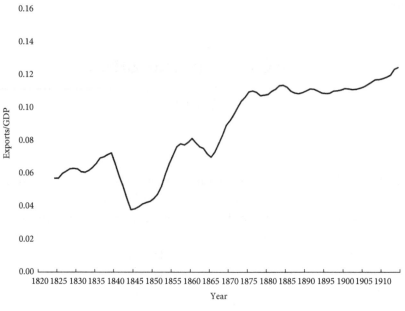

Figure 3.1 Ratio of World Exports to World GDP, 1800–1914 (five-year moving average)

Source: Author's calculations based on data from Federico and Tena-Junguito (2019)

and 63% between 1900 and 1910, is accounted for by economic growth. The declines in the barriers to international trade explain the remainder. Integration rose throughout the 1820–1913 period but decelerated by the 1880s. The next section discusses in more detail the decline in trade costs.

Time–Space Convergence and the Drivers of Integration

Many different forces allowed for greater integration and reduced barriers to international trade in global commodity markets prior to World War I: improved transportation links, more timely information due to the telegraph, lower tariffs, greater stability in exchange rates, and global financial integration were paramount forces driving trade costs lower. These changes are crucial for explaining the rise of a global market in commodities, consumer goods, and capital equipment (railways, telecommunications, etc.) in the second half of the 19th century.

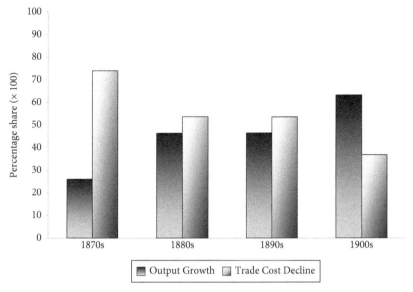

Figure 3.2 Decomposition of Growth in World Trade: Output versus Trade Costs, 1870–1910

Source: Author's calculations based on data from Jacks, Meissner, and Novy (2008)

Fundamental to increasing integration was the massive decrease in the cost of shipping goods and the impressive increase in maritime shipping speeds. The oceangoing steamship was a central force driving this maritime revolution. Increasingly efficient steamengines came to dominate between the 1820s and the 1870s. Steel hulls improved shipping capacity and screw propellers made steam ships move faster. Steamships progressively became more cost-effective and reliable than sailing vessels on many, but not all, routes. Starting with the shortest routes, often navigable river ways and short sea routes, the steamship eventually dominated long-haul trade like that between Great Britain and New Zealand or pre–Panama Canal trade between New York to the east coast of China.

In addition, steamships also required smaller crews to work them than sail ships, lowering the costs of shipping. Shipping tonnage, that is the size and capacity of cargo ships, also grew dramatically. Between 1830 and 1850 alone, average capacity quadrupled increasing at an average pace of 8% per year. Figure 3.3 demonstrates the dramatic fall in maritime freight between 1800 and the 1870s. The cost to ship a ton of coal, according to a British index

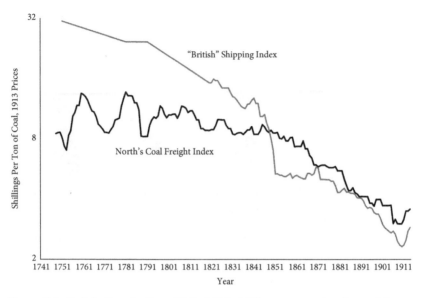

Figure 3.3 Freight Rate Indices, 1741–1913, shillings per ton-km for coal, log scale, ten-year moving averages

Source: Author's calculations based on data from O'Rourke and Williamson (2002), p. 35, Figure 7, by permission from Oxford University Press and the European Historical Economics Society and the Journal of Economic History and the Economic History Association

of freights, declined at an average rate of 0.8% per year, achieving a value in the 1870s almost half of what it was circa 1800.

Nevertheless, sailing ships retained a considerable presence until late in the 19th century, especially on longer routes. As late as 1870, only 1/5 of British shipping tonnage was steam driven. Even before the steamship, Maury's pilot charts introduced in the 1850s helped sailing ships maintain an advantage by tracking regularities in maritime weather patterns. By effectively crowd-sourcing the collection of maritime data via ship logs, Maury was able to collect and analyze an impressive data set just as many data scientists would do today. While using big data to increase efficiency is common now, Maury was truly a pioneer. His analysis of these data showed when and where it was best to sail. Through his research, Maury contributed to massive efficiency improvements in global sailing. Sailing vessels decreased their port-to-port sailing times by 30% to 40% on average. Shipping time between Australia and England fell from 126 to 63 days by 1853. Another event, the opening of the Suez Canal in 1869, dramatically cut the distance between European and Asian ports. The effective distance between London and Bombay (Mumbai) fell by 47%. The repercussions were self-evidently massive.

Organizational and handling improvements including better port facilities also made for lower shipping times. Tramp ships plied the commercial ports of the world in search of freight and were big users of the new telegraph technology. With the telegraph, the crew of tramp ships could correspond and keep up with the latest information on world markets when in port. Now, virtually instantaneously, ship captains and commodity merchants could discover the location of the greatest demand for their services. On the supply-side, they could quickly communicate the availability of shipping capacity to commodity suppliers.

Prior to the telegraph, communication was slow, and supply and demand conditions might have easily changed by the time a ship arrived in port, easily making the voyage un-profitable. These uncertainties and risks presented a significant barrier to entry in the commodity-trading industry. The telegraph helped minimize these uncertainties, boosting the supply of shipping capacity and the number of merchants willing to engage in trade. Competition in commodity trading increased and consumers benefited from lower prices and greater supply.

The railroad gave even more impetus to long-distance trade. Railway mileage mushroomed between 1820 and 1914,connecting ocean ports to hinterlands and establishing faster and more secure transportation services for both commodities and passengers. By the mid-1850s, a continuous railroad connection between the American Midwest/Chicago and the Atlantic port of New York was established. In 1869 the "golden spike" was laid connecting the east and west coasts of the United States with a railroad. Railroads in certain parts of Latin America and Asia also surged. Farmers in India, once dependent on slow and unreliable road or water transport, connected with global and domestic markets due to the railroad. Mileage on the Indian subcontinent rose from zero in 1853 to roughly 60,000 kilometers in 1913. Railway construction was highly uneven within Asia, however. China operated only about 8,800 kilometers in 1913. In Brazil and Argentina, railway lines connected inland coffee growers, cattle ranchers, and wheat farmers to European and North American markets. In 1913, Brazil benefited from about 24,000 kilometers of track and Argentina operated over 33,000 kilometers.

The telegraph also dramatically improved market integration. Nearly instantaneous communications technology like the telegraph and later the telephone allowed market participants to gauge market conditions in real time. Better signals about demand and supply enhanced market efficiency allowing the right amount of goods at the right time to come to market. Timely information diminished costly stockpiling that occurred when market conditions could change. Prior to the telegraph, producers could not immediately act upon the news. The lack of information about market conditions often led to shipment of items- in anticipation of high demand only to find out another significant shock had occurred or that competitors had already arrived on the scene. Timely information lowered the risk of engaging in long-distance trade.

Experimental telegraph lines were pioneered in Great Britain and the United States in the 1830s and 1840s. By the 1880s, the world was wired! London and New York were connected by telegraph in 1866 thanks to innovations in insulating and laying deep-sea cables. From July 27, 1866, communication time between London and the United States dropped from 10 to 12 days (i.e., the time it took to traverse the north Atlantic by ship) to less than one hour. London and Melbourne were connected by telegraph in 1871. Britain was connected to India via Aden (Yemen) in 1870. Most of the world was on the global network by the end of the 1870s. The diffusion of the telegraph undoubtedly contributed to the global trade boom of the 19th century by improving information and reducing uncertainty about market opportunities.

Policy Changes as Drivers of Integration

Trade policy also changed radically from the mid-19th century, spurring integration and specialization. Prior to the 19th century, a host of government-imposed tariffs, surcharges, and prohibitions limited the ability of consumers to purchase foreign goods. These policies generated many inefficiencies including raising prices of imports and reducing the variety of products available. This changed radically after the second quarter of the 19th century. Great Britain took the lead, standing unflinchingly for "free trade" until World War I. Other countries in Europe followed the lead by lowering tariffs to historical lows by the latter half of the 19th century.

This process of "trade liberalization" began in the 1840s. Acting unilaterally in 1846, Great Britain slashed tariffs on foreign agricultural commodities by repealing its long-standing "corn laws." Robert Peel, prime minister and leader of the Conservative Party, led the parliament to approve an unprecedented liberalization of British grain markets. On May 15, 1846, 327 members of Parliament voted for repeal while 229 voted against. Peel ostensibly represented the interests of the wealthy agricultural elite that voted him into office and which would ultimately be financially hurt by such a move. However, a decisive split in the party emerged, allowing passage. Recent research suggests that many members of the Conservative Party represented landholders who had progressively "diversified" themselves away from land rents and agriculture by taking long positions in modern economic sectors.[1]

Repeal of the Corn Laws was expected to lower grain prices, hurting the economic prospects of the least efficient and least diversified of British farmers and landowners. Head-to-head competition with more efficient and lower-cost farmers in North America and beyond would likely lead to much lower profitability and even to foreclosure or removal of land from production. It turns out that significant fractions of the agricultural elite had insured themselves against repeal. Many of the landed gentry had diversified investment portfolios that included stocks and shares in industrial endeavors. Smaller, less diversified, landowners were driven to financial ruin. At the same time, wage workers in manufacturing, whose consumption basket heavily tilted toward food, gained as the cost of living was expected to fall. Real wages for workers would go up despite the expected decline in nominal wages in manufacturing as the supply of workers in manufacturing relative to agricultural workers increased. Industrialists and owners of firms also gained since nominal wages, a key component of their costs, were directly tied to food prices. Lower food prices implied higher profits, leading Great Britain to specialize in industrial and manufacturing pursuits.

Britain's repeal of its Corn Laws and the elimination of most of its other tariffs by the 1850s led it to become the world's leading supporter of the idea of "Free Trade." This regime change turned the intellectual tide against the old mercantilist practice of protecting domestic producers and aiming for persistent trade surplus at all costs. On the European continent, the Zollverein emerged as a customs union between members of the German Confederation. This trade agreement lowered internal barriers to trade among what would eventually become the German Empire and also worked

---

[1] See Schonhardt-Bailey (1991).

to secure trade agreements with neighboring trade partners. In the decades following repeal, tariffs in the richest European nations fell from about 28% (1846) to 8% (1870). Worldwide, the average tariff fell from about 49% in 1846 to roughly 21% in 1870.[2]

The Cobden–Chevalier trade treaty of 1860 between France and Great Britain was another watershed in world trade history, playing a large role in sparking the decline in tariffs. This treaty was an example of a preferential trade agreement (PTA) and represented a bilateral (i.e., two-country) approach to negotiating tariffs as opposed to a globally coordinated multilateral approach. The treaty mandated lower tariffs and abolished import prohibitions in the French case. As part of the Cobden–Chevalier agreement, Britain agreed to lower its tariffs on light wines, which pleased the wine growers located near Bordeaux. Lower French duties on various woolen manufacturers helped boost British exports.

The Cobden–Chevalier Treaty established a precedent for assigning the "unconditional" Most-Favored Nation (MFN) status to a treaty partner. Because of this clause, there was a quick rush to sign more treaties. Between 1860 and the early 1870s, nations negotiated a series of bilateral treaties with over half of the country-pairs in Europe granting (unconditional) MFN status (Figure 3.4). MFN status led to a spate of follow-on treaties because a country like France automatically had to extend its lowest tariffs with Britain to third countries who also had an MFN treaty with France as well. Countries had every incentive to sign a treaty with France and with all other signatories. Being outside of the network would divert trade to those inside the network. Due to these treaties, average tariffs, especially on manufactured goods, fell significantly, and international trade in the goods that witnessed reduced tariffs increased significantly.

Not all trade deals were negotiated among equals. Imperial conquest and colonization forced tariffs down in much of Africa, India, and other parts of East Asia (Figure 3.5). When outright colonization and control were infeasible, Western powers were often still able to force tariff concessions. In 1853 US Commodore Perry and his US Navy warships approached the long-isolated nation of Japan. Until the arrival of Commodore Perry, Japan lived under a self-imposed policy of "autarky" and self-reliance. Wayward citizens of Japan could be executed for going beyond the realm. Commercial trade and direct contact with all other nations were strictly limited and controlled. Although the government allowed a small handful of foreign products from

---

[2] See Tena-Junguito, Lampe, and Tâmega-Fernandes (2012).

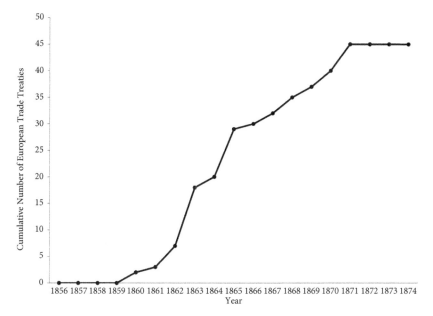

Figure 3.4 Cumulative Number of Trade Treaties in Europe with an MFN
Clause, 1856–1874

Source: Author's calculations based on Accominotti and Flandreau (2008), Appendix 2. Note: There
are fourteen countries in the sample and ninety-one country pairs or possible treaties

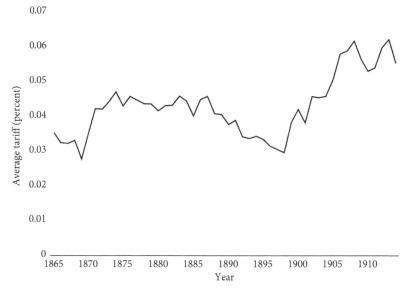

Figure 3.5 Average Tariff Rate for Four Asian Economies (China, Japan,
Indonesia, Thailand), 1865–1914

Source: Author's calculations based on data from Federico and Tena-Junguito (2019)

China and elsewhere to arrive through a small treaty port near Nagasaki, the Japanese remained almost entirely self-sufficient and closed off.

Not surprisingly, the country represented a vast profit opportunity for Western producers who could provide new goods at low prices thanks to their use of industrial technology. Indeed, the mutual gains from trade are scarcely better exhibited than in the case of Japan. Japanese producers of silk, green tea, and other traditional products also stood to gain from trade with a larger market. Evidently, the government suppressed this possibility prior to the 1850s, however.

Commodore Perry's mission was, in large part, aimed at prying open Japanese markets for American producers. In this, he was entirely successful. Although commerce with the rest of the world was highly regulated with a system of special "treaty ports" prior to 1850, Japan largely eliminated tariffs and other prohibitions in the late 19th century. In the decades following Perry's visit, Japan was transformed politically and economically. Once self-reliant on goods such as woolen yarn, fuel, and grain, Japan began to import these commodities in vast quantities. Prices in Japan for these goods fell enormously, thereby raising the purchasing power of Japanese households. Similarly, Japan refocused its economy heavily on exporting silk goods, raw silk, and green tea. By the 1870s, the prices of these products in which Japan had a comparative advantage rose to new heights. Wages in sectors in which Japan had a comparative advantage climbed while the factors of production in relatively inefficient industries and sectors fell.

In China, Western powers also forced an opening up. Following the Opium Wars in the 1860s, Western nations secured the right to trade with China via a number of special Treaty Ports. Meanwhile, the Chinese government, which had been weakened due to these wars and significant internal civil strife, sought revenue from the deal. Treaty Ports negotiations allowed Western commodities to enter the country at preferential tariff rates. Westerners also received a sort of legal immunity remaining subject to foreign law rather than the indigenous justice system. A commercial ecosystem grew up around the Treaty Ports. Foreign merchants selling on consignment for foreign producers, or on their own account, interacted and contracted with local "compradors," or buyers, to sell into the local market. Competent compradors were capable of knowing the ins and outs of the varied monetary systems of China, the legal and cultural norms, and market preferences. Compradors arranged trade credit for local merchants and even adjudicated disputes. The city of Shanghai grew from obscurity in this period into a major urban area. By the 1920s it was one of the largest and fastest-growing conurbations in the world achieving nearly one million inhabitants. In this period, Shanghai became a premier cosmopolitan city, the vestiges of which remain today in the architecture and culture of the French and "international" settlement neighborhoods. By World War I, the number of foreign-born (i.e., not Chinese) residents in Shanghai reached up to 21,000.

The advent of the Treaty Port system, ultimately comprising more than two dozen cities and ports, had the potential of opening up a market of more than two hundred million consumers who, although much poorer on average than the average consumer of Northwestern Europe, were eager to purchase cheaply priced textiles (e.g., nankeens) and other manufactured products and raw materials like fuel and cooking oil. Chinese consumers increased their imports of British goods ninefold between 1830 and 1860. Trade with Europe and the United States continued to grow strongly in the decades before World War I. Consumers gained not only by having access to low-priced foreign goods that were close substitutes for local products but also by having access to a greater variety of goods.

Exchange rate stability also helped generate deeper integration. From about 1880, trade flourished under the umbrella of the "classical gold standard." By the late 1870s, France, Germany, Scandinavia, Holland, Britain Belgium, Switzerland, and the United States, among many others, were all full-fledged members of the gold standard club. Each member promised the following: (1) the domestic monetary unit would be defined in a fixed amount of gold; (2) the government would, upon demand, pay out this fixed amount of gold in exchange for local currency also often dispatching other liabilities (e.g., taxes, debt payments) with gold; (3) governments would not place any limit on international gold movements and shipments. Each domestic currency might have had a different name, but all of them were defined in fixed amounts of gold. This implied that the rate of exchange between any two currencies would be very stable. While the exchange rate could diverge from the legal parity momentarily, the commitment to the parity by member countries kept exchange rates tightly fixed in the longer run.

Monetary reforms in the 1870s went further than simply fixing exchange rates. There was also a tendency to standardize and make currencies more uniform. Countries did this by making local currencies near multiples of each other, with about 25 Belgian and French francs worth one British pound sterling; 20 German marks equaled roughly one pound sterling; 4.86 US dollars were needed to buy one British pound; and there were roughly 5.2 French francs per dollar.

The broad-based diffusion of the gold standard traces back to the International Monetary Conference of 1867, convened in Paris by Napoleon III, emperor of France. Representatives from more than a dozen and a half countries attended this meeting. The meeting was intended to solicit nations' interest in a world monetary union. Failing this, a consensus was sought on whether gold or silver, or a combination of the two, would back all countries' currencies. Prior to this, the world was split into blocs of nations using exclusively gold (Britain, Portugal, Australasia), silver (China, India Russia, Germany, Eastern Europe, and Northern Europe), and the "bimetallic" countries backing their currencies with silver and gold at a fixed exchange rate (France, the United States, etc.). The conference failed to obtain firm commitments from any nation to switch from the status quo. Great Britain's representatives affirmed their commitment to the traditional British system of coinage and that no binding decision for Great Britain would emerge from the conference. Nevertheless, the worldwide switch to gold (Figure 3.6) was foreshadowed by the votes of many countries' delegates in favor of the gold system.

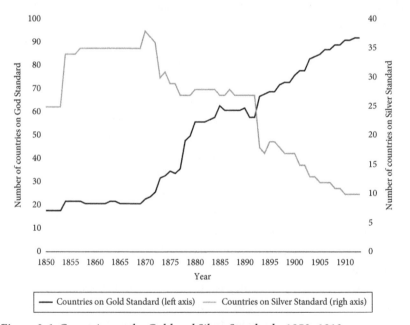

Figure 3.6 Countries on the Gold and Silver Standards, 1850–1913
Source: Author's calculations based on data underlying Meissner (2001)

In the wake of the Franco-Prussian war, of 1870–1871, the newly unified nation of Germany led by Otto von Bismarck was the first major country to embark on the switch to gold. The German decision dragged the French, as well as most other European nations, and even the US, onto gold. By 1900, nearly all economies with the notable exception of China had obtained significant exchange rate stability by adhering to the gold standard. Pegging to gold allowed market participants to avoid the financial costs of "hedging,-" or insuring exchange rate changes. This stability limited the uncertainty (and risk) about the returns to trade relationships that could arise from large exchange rate swings and major policy divergences. This served to encourage deeper trading relationships.

The global financial network also expanded in this period. London claimed the title of the world's premier financial center. The extensive financial ecosystem based in London financed the bulk of global trade. The primary means of financing trade was the "bill of exchange." This credit instrument was issued by London banks, which specialized in verifying the creditworthiness of trading companies and foreign banks. In addition, the legal environment and the Bank of England helped create a large and liquid secondary market for bills of exchange. Banks could readily sell these IOUs on the open market, making it easier to generate cash and liquidity when necessary. The Bank of England also stood ready to buy these credit instruments, especially when endorsed or "accepted," by leading banks with sterling reputations.

By the 1860s, a number of banks headquartered in London and elsewhere in the British Empire opened international branches and subsidiaries and deepened global linkages. These banks specialized in generating better credit information, managing the accounts of businesses with global affairs, and arranging trade finance Banks, with British roots, such as the Chartered Bank of India, Australia, and China, the Oriental Bank, the Standard Bank (of South Africa), and Hong Kong Shanghai Banking Company (HSBC), possessed global networks that catalyzed trade. Other economic leaders like Germany, France, Japan, and Belgium also established banks with significant global networks. The German Deutsche Ueberseeische Bank/Banco Aleman Transatlantico (affiliated with Deutsche Bank), the French Banque de Paris et de Pays Bas (BNP), the Yokohama Specie Bank, and the Banque Sino-Belge are several companies that spanned the globe at this point. While only about two dozen banks operated internationally in the 1850s, by 1910, about two hundred banks had multi-country offices. At the same time, most major banks in every country maintained "correspondent" connections with banks in the major countries. It is no understatement to say that international banks were to international trade what reagents are to chemical reactions.

Creating a Global Trade Network

The 19th-century network of world trade was far from a world where every nation traded with every other nation. In this period, small, isolated, or poor countries rarely traded directly with one another. A less developed country like Brazil traded little to nothing with other economies like India, South Africa, and even China. Instead, Brazil concentrated its exports and imports on several main markets. Britain, Germany, the United States, and Argentina accounted for 70% of Brazil's exports and nearly 45% of its imports in the late 19th century.

Great Britain, however, was at the heart of the international system, trading either directly or indirectly with almost every other nation. Due to its sheer size and high income, the United States was important for global trade but still largely focused on its domestic economy. The share of trade in US GDP was usually below 10%. After 1870, Germany became a rising industrial rival to Great Britain. Germany built up an international marketing and financial apparatus, opening direct relationships with trade partners and expanding the range of goods exported to those with which it already traded. The German advance was the envy and scourge of the incumbent British exporters from the 1880s onward. Observers of the day, especially diplomatic envoys and consuls, portrayed British exporters as inflexible while characterizing German exporters as providing superior service. Diplomatic reports observed that British exporters and merchants shunned small orders, refused to adopt the metric system, provided limited trade credit, and failed to speak local languages. German exporters allegedly did quite the opposite on all these fronts, offering generous credit lines, adapting to local conditions, and satisfying large and small orders.

The Gravity Model of International Trade

What explains the international division of labor and trade patterns of the 19th century? The trade theories discussed below are mostly concerned with the composition of a country's exports, global patterns of specialization, and the overall impact of trade on welfare. Before we move forward, however, it is worthwhile to discuss new empirical approaches to understanding "who trades with whom." With minimal assumptions about the preferences of consumers and the simple observation that engaging in international trade is more costly than domestic trade, we can arrive at a very good understanding of the geography of international trade.

This approach is called the "gravity" model of trade. The gravity model is familiar to many from the basic laws of physics. As high school students learn, Isaac Newton theorized that the gravitational attraction between two objects depends positively on the size of the two objects and inversely on the distance between them. An analogous relationship holds for international trade, and this has been recognized by economists since the late 19th century.

First, gravity says that the magnitude of trade depends on the economic size of the trade partners. The larger the combined GDP of any two countries, holding constant the costs of trade, the more two countries would be expected to trade with each other. This logic implies that small countries export a larger share of their output than bigger countries. This follows because "domestic exports" also obey the logic of gravity and the rest of the world is much larger for a small country than for a big country. Figure 3.7 shows the share of exports in total output (GDP) for four nations between 1870 and 1910. This measure of "openness" to trade is rising for all countries but is highest for Denmark, a relatively small country.

Second, we must examine the effect of distance. The British trade share was high despite its large economy since it was relatively close to a number of important markets. Japan's trade share remained low because of its geographical isolation from the world's largest markets. London, Le Havre, Hamburg, and New York City lie 19,000 kilometers away from Japan's main ports. Gravity asserts that after holding size constant, nearby nations would be expected to trade more than two similarly-sized-but-distant nations. Distance increases the costs of transporting goods, but these direct costs are a small share of the economic costs associated with trade.

More generally, the economic model of gravity focusses on the inverse relation between trade and trade cost. These "frictions" are not directly analogous to distance-driven gravitation in the physical world. Trade costs, as discussed before, include information, the costs of credit, market familiarity, risk induced by adverse movements in exchange rates, the legal environment which stipulates what happens in the case a party to the exchange does not

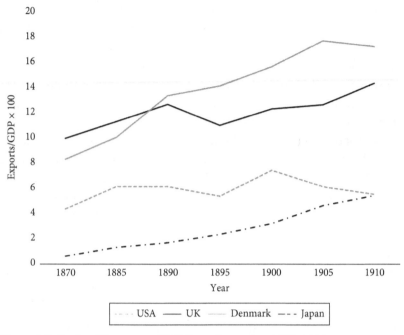

Figure 3.7 Ratio of Exports to GDP, Four Countries, 1870–1910
Source: Author's calculations based on data from Federico and Tena-Junguito (2019)

carry through with previous commitments, and so on. Economic gravity is one of the most successful empirical relationships in all of economics. Figure 3.8 shows that in a sample of twenty-seven countries between 1870 and 1914 bilateral trade is inversely related to bilateral distance.

Of course, for many of the nations of Europe, it made sense to trade heavily with other nations in Europe due to gravity. Interestingly, Great Britain traded more with countries and regions outside of Europe than with partners in Europe mainly due to its Empire connections. Without such strong connections, the principal trade partners for most European nations were mainly other European nations. By trading with near neighbors, they economized on transportation costs. They also shared common legal foundations and languages. The most economically advanced nations of Europe also kept exchange rate fluctuations to a minimum. Although trade costs and the size of two economies are extremely helpful in predicting how much two countries will trade with each other both in the past and today, this relationship does not tell us much about what products countries will trade with each other.

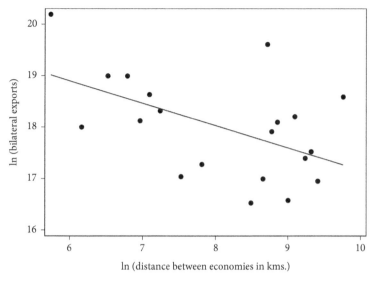

Figure 3.8 Bilateral Trade versus Bilateral Distance, Binned Scatter Plot, Twenty-Seven Countries, 1870–1914

Source: Author's calculations based on data from Jacks, Meissner, and Novy (2008)

What Nations Traded: Patterns of Specialization Prior to 1914

There are three main paradigms in economics to explain what types of products countries export and import. The "Ricardian" model of trade (named after David Ricardo) relies on technological differences to explain patterns of export specialization. The Hecksher–Ohlin model (named after two Swedish economists working in the early 20th century) holds that nations have different allocations of resources and factors of production (e.g., capital and labor). Nations trade the goods that use intensively the factor(s) that are locally relatively abundant. Finally, there is "New Trade Theory," originated by Paul Krugman and others in the 1970s. This theory argues that consumers love variety, and variety can be identified with the place of origin. International trade allows for multiple varieties of the same good. With free trade, Dutch consumers now have access not only to the locally produced, inimitable Dutch-style bikes, but residents can now easily purchase mountain bikes designed in California and racing cycles from France and Italy.

The Ricardian Model: Productivity and Know-How as Drivers of Trade

Modern interpretations of British economist David Ricardo posit that nations have differing abilities and know-how in the production of goods. These differences give rise immediately to comparative advantage. Comparative advantage means that nations specialize in goods that they can produce with relatively smaller amounts of resources or with the lowest "opportunity cost." A decrease in trade costs increases specialization and makes consumers better off since trade partners can offer the goods in which they have a comparative advantage at lower prices than domestic producers. Productive resources are now shifted to the industry in which the home country has a comparative advantage. Foreign consumers now purchase these goods in exchange for their exports, raising prices on both countries' exports and the real incomes of both countries. Real incomes rise for all counties. The observable implication is that the "terms of trade," defined as the ratio of export prices to import prices, improve when trade barriers fall.

Moving back to the example of Japan in the mid to late 19th century, Daniel Bernhofen and John Brown found clear evidence of such outcomes.[3] Nations in East Asia like Japan had great experience in silk manufacture due to significant experience in sericulture and local climate. Prior to Perry's ultimatum, Japan had very little local manufacturing in cotton thread, fabric, and clothing. Within a decade, however, Bernhofen and Brown showed that prices for silk producers (exports) rose while the prices of cotton products (imports) fell. The gains from trade, as measured and summarized in the terms of trade, were large and are estimated to have grown almost threefold in the six years following 1858. Moreover, the value of opening up to international trade for Japan has been calculated to be on the order of 8% of 1853 GDP. Between the late 1850s and the 1870s, Japanese imports per capita grew a hundredfold. Japan's experience after the 1850s was unique. Few other major economies were subjected to such a dramatic fall in trade barriers. Japan's growth in trade and the magnitude of the terms of trade boom are specific but illustrative. As trade costs also declined for other countries, due to more efficient, long-distance shipping, new railroad connections, and so on their term trade also rose.

[3] See Bernhofen and Brown (2004).

The Heckscher–Ohlin Model: Factor
Endowment Driven Trade

Why did Argentina, Canada, and the United States export agricultural products while Britain exported manufactured goods? Swedish economists Bertil Ohlin and Eli Heckscher contributed an explanation for these patterns. They interpreted 19th-century trade, and comparative advantage, as driven by differences in "factor endowments." Economies in the Americas, Australasia, and Africa had abundant land and mineral resources, while Japan, China, India, and Western Europe had high population density (i.e., a high labor-to-land ratio). The Heckscher–Ohlin theory postulates that differences in relative factor endowments created opportunities for gains from international trade.

The logic behind this result is that nations should specialize—become net exporters—in products in which they have a comparative advantage. If a nation has a good climate and open land for wheat farming, not growing wheat is a bad economic choice since such a nation *gives up* more wheat than a densely settled country with little available arable land. The opportunity cost of not focusing on wheat farming is high. Similarly, for the densely settled country with a poor climate for wheat, self-sufficiency in food production, when trade is possible with the other nation, would not make economic sense. Why not forgo an unproductive agricultural orientation and focus on labor-intensive production?

This logic goes a long way toward explaining trade flows, production patterns, and the international division of labor in the 19th century. Indeed, for a country like Argentina, it made sense to trade wheat and meat products for European manufactures since by 1900 it had amassed a territory of over 1.3 million square miles with only three inhabitants per square mile. Britain's population density was nearly 166 times higher at 500 people per square mile.[4] The relative scarcity of land in Great Britain raised the cost of food production while the abundance of people lowered the relative price of labor (i.e., wages), giving Britain a "comparative advantage" in labor-intensive manufacturing such as textiles. As trade barriers fell from the mid-19th century, nations with disparate climates, soil qualities, mineral endowments, levels of education, and availability of savings and capital now had a major

[4] Population density at the time (people per square mile) was roughly 21 in the United States, 1.41 in Canada, 159 in India, 292 in China, and 285 in Japan.

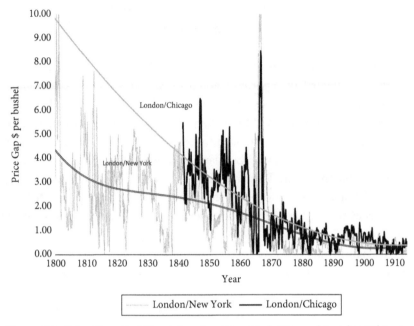

Figure 3.9 Price Gaps for Wheat, London/New York City and London/Chicago, 1800–1914

Source: Author's calculations from data underlying Jacks (2006)

reason to trade. As predicted by the Heckscher–Ohlin model, this led to significant specialization along the lines of comparative advantage at the country level. Some economists have gone so far as to call this period of globalization the "Great Specialization."

Heckscher–Ohlin theory has several implications. First, as trade costs fall, prices of tradeable products should converge. The data confirm that the price of wheat in British Markets fell between 1800 and 1914 toward the price in the world's largest exporter, the United States (Figure 3.9). Second, nations produce more than they consume in goods which use the factor of production they are well endowed with. Figure 3.10 shows that countries with the largest land endowments relative to their population tended to have higher shares of exports in "primary" or non-manufactured products. The next, and perhaps most surprising, theorem is the Stolper Samuelson, which predicts "factor price equalization" and "income convergence." Assume there are two main inputs, labor and land. When trade costs fall,

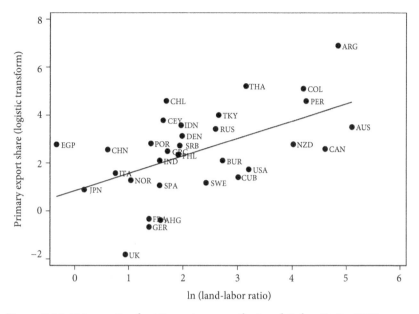

Figure 3.10 Primary Product Exports versus the Land-Labor Ratio, 1890
Source: Author's calculations from data underlying Clemens and Williamson (2004a). Notes: The y-axis is measured as the logistic transform of the share of exports in primary products

wages in labor-abundant nations rise relative to the returns to land-owning. In contrast, wages fall in labor-scarce regions relative to the returns from land and capital. Rising demand for the relatively abundant factor and falling demand for the least abundant factor occurs precisely due to greater specialization in the good that uses most intensively the abundant factor of production.

Economic historians Kevin O'Rourke and Jeff Williamson argued strongly that the first great era of globalization led to *convergence* in incomes—at least among the leading nations in Europe and the Americas that traded most heavily. Since factor price equalization is not a prediction of the Ricardian model, from first principles, it appears that the factor-endowment trade theory is a good theory, at least for these specific cases.

The argument runs as follows. Labor was relatively scarce and land was abundant in the Americas throughout the 19th century-, while labor was abundant in Europe and land was scarce. Trade costs fell dramatically in the mid-19th century, increasing international trade. These

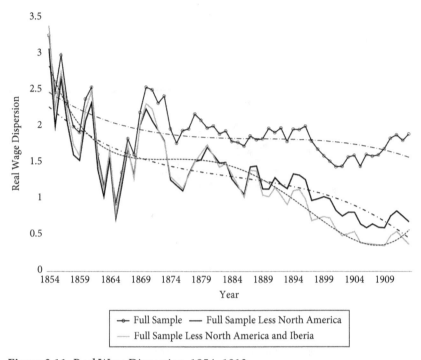

Figure 3.11 Real Wage Dispersion, 1854–1913
Source: Author's calculations based on Williamson (1996), p. 278, Figure 1

changes drove specialization along the lines of comparative advantage and pushed up demand for labor in Europe, thereby raising wages relative to the rents accruing to landowners. In the Americas, the opposite happened. Demand for labor fell, pushing wages down. Land rents, related to the returns on land-owning from farming and ranching, moved upward. Since Gross Domestic Product (GDP) is the sum of payments to all factors of production, the effect of this factor price equalization was for GDP per capita to converge, but not necessarily equalize. If the trend was for divergence, O'Rourke and Williamson's approach predicts lower divergence than would otherwise have occurred. Figure 3.11 illustrates the decline in real wage dispersion for a sample of countries in Europe and the Americas between 1854 and 1913 which is strongly consistent with the idea that increased integration was a force for factor price convergence. It is important to understand here that convergence was part of a broader process and that other economic forces may have worked to offset some of the pressure toward convergence.

"New" Trade Theory: Economic Geography and Intra-Industry Trade

Economic convergence is predicted by Heckscher–Ohlin trade theory and is a strong prediction of neo-classical growth theory just the same.[5] The data only partially support these convergence theories. The real wage gap in favor of the United States relative to Great Britain should have fallen by at least 50% according to the Heckscher–Ohlin model of trade in the late 19th century. Instead, the wage gap closed by only 5% between 1870 and 1910.[6] In fact, there is also significant evidence of income divergence in the 19th century, even among tightly integrated economies. Most of Asia, Africa, and Latin America failed to follow the same growth path as Western Europe after the mid-18th century. The gap between per capita incomes in Britain and India was about 32% in 1700 (in favor of Great Britain). By 1900 this gap had widened to 395%, a nearly fivefold gap. An unskilled worker in Britain earned two to three times more than his counterpart in China in the early 1700s, but that gap increased to roughly ten times by 1900. Why did Asia, Africa, and much of Latin America fail to take full advantage of the global economy? Another, newer theory of international trade can help us understand these observations.

"New Trade Theory" suggests that increasing returns to scale matter for trade. In this theory, firms face a fixed cost of production. These "increasing returns to scale" imply a level of market power that economists call monopolistic competition. The monopolistic part of the term is that firms from different countries sell products that are unique but which have imperfect substitutes (think Nissans, Volkswagens, Hyundais, and Fords or Nikes, Adidas, Asics, and Reeboks). Competition is shorthand for the idea that firms compete away all economic profits through "free entry." Instead of having two economies compete head-to-head in producing a "homogeneous" product, nations (or the firms therein) specialize in a particular brand. Again, think of cheddar cheese (Irish, Vermont, or Canadian) or coffee (Peet's, Starbucks, Illy, Nespresso, Douwe Egberts, Café Bustelo). Economists call this "intra-industry" trade.

[5] Neo-classical growth theory, often associated with Robert Solow's model of economic growth, suggests that poorer countries catch-up and converge to richer countries when countries have comparable demographics, saving patterns, technologies, and institutional arrangements.
[6] See Crafts and Venables (2003), 340.

Consumers are assumed to love variety, so nations have an incentive to trade even in seemingly nearly identical products. In the 19th century, Japan, China, Italy, and France produced silk textiles all differentiated by their country of origin. Belgium, France, Germany, Great Britain, India, and the United States produced cotton and wool fabrics and clothing. This pattern of specialization was dubbed intra-industry trade since when trade occurred they would not be trading resource-intensive commodities for labor-intensive manufactures but instead industrial or manufactured products for other manufactured products.

In fact, within Europe, significant "two-way" trade within industries like textiles (even within silk and cotton textiles and fabrics) was very important at the time (Table 3.1). For France, the share of trade in similar products circa 1870 was nearly 30%—about the same as it was in the 1970s. For the twelve countries making up the EU in 1992, the share of total exports classified as "intra-industry" was one-third in 1913. Intra-industry trade increased to

Table 3.1 Share of Trade with Principal Regions, 1860, 1910, 1996.

Exports (% of total) Destination						
Source		Europe	North America	South America	Asia	Africa	Other
1860	UK	46.7	25.5	11.5	12.8	2.5	1.0
	Europe	67.5	9.1	7.7	10.0	3.2	2.5
1910	UK	35.2	11.6	12.6	24.5	7.4	8.6
	Europe	67.9	7.6	4.2	9.8	4.8	2.4
1996	UK	59.7	13.3	1.8	11.2	2.6	11.4
	Europe	76.2	7.2	2.1	10.7	2.5	1.3
Imports (% of total) Source						
Importer		Europe	North America	South America	Asia	Africa	Other
1860	UK	31.0	26.7	10.1	23.2	4.5	4.5
	Europe	61.0	14.3	7.8	12.1	3.2	1.7
1910	UK	45.1	23.8	9.1	10.3	4.8	6.9
	Europe	60.0	14.0	8.2	10.0	4.5	3.4
1996	UK	57.2	14.0	1.9	16.9	1.9	8.1
	Europe	70.7	8.5	2.9	10.5	2.7	4.7

Source: Baldwin and Martin (1999).

50% in 1992. In 1910 2/3 of exports and imports for European economies (besides the United Kingdom) were to other European nations—nations with very similar factor endowments. For the United Kingdom, 2/3 of exports and over half of all imports were from non-European trade partners. These observations leave the impression that "new trade theory" may be highly relevant for the first wave of globalization.

New trade theory also helps us understand economic polarization and divergence. Extensions to this theory lead to interesting predictions about the location or "geography" of economic activity, specifically manufacturing activity. In this theory, economies of scale, barriers to trade generate a desire of firms to be close to large markets and to each other. This is called "agglomeration." The theory gives rise to the dynamic "inverse U" pattern of economic location which is illustrated schematically in Figure 3.12. When trade barriers are high, economic activity is dispersed, and there are low levels of specialization. Foreign competitors cannot enter local markets because of the significant trade barriers and hence the local cost and price advantage of domestic supply. When trade barriers fall, however, local producers will be exposed to the chill winds of foreign competition and market share may

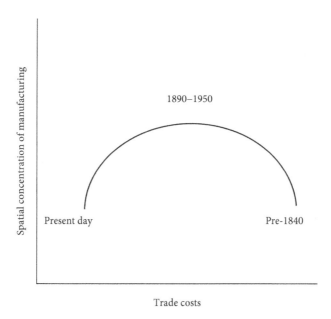

Figure 3.12 Economic Geography and Trade Costs: The "Inverse U" Relationship

decrease. If the process goes far enough, and trade costs are in an interme-diate range, entire industries may relocate to where the largest demands are. This is called the "home-market effect." If being close to key industrial inputs, such as unskilled or skilled labor, natural resources, or manufactured inputs, matters, then even more extreme localization of production (agglomeration) can occur due to the cost advantages of proximity. Since industrial activity was historically associated with higher productivity, this explanation for ec-onomic geography also predicts economic divergence as a result of global-ization. This is the opposite of the Heckscher–Ohlin model which predicts convergence!

Evidence presented by Nick Crafts and Anthony Venables in Figure 3.13 shows that the United States and western Europe accounted for over 2/3 of global industrial output by 1880, while the share of these places in 1750 was a minuscule 1/5. Contrast this experience with the process of de-industrialization that occurred in the Ottoman Empire, India, and China in the same period. All these places had significant indigenous industrial

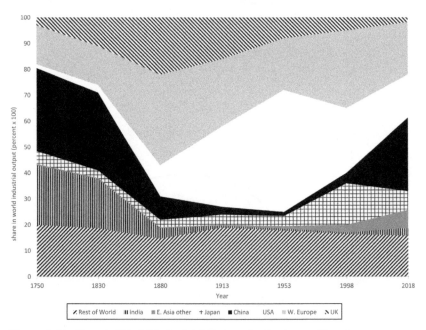

Figure 3.13 Share in World Industrial Output, by Region or Country, 1750–2018

Source: 1750–1998: Crafts and Venables (2003) © by the National Bureau of Economic Research; 2008: author's calculations based on United Nations Industrial Development Organization (2021) and Richter (2020)

activity in the early 19th century. By the early 20th century, much of the manufacturing activity had disappeared. Prior to 1800, India was a net exporter of calico cloth and historically dominated in spinning cotton thread. China was also historically self-sufficient in terms of manufactures. By the beginning of the 20th century, local industries had been decimated. In India, David Clingingsmith and Jeffrey Williamson note that high British productivity and falling transportation costs worked to favor British cotton exports to India, ultimately contributing to the decline of India's hand-craft industry.[7] While this explanation seems to explain some of the data, it is still unclear how much open-economy forces mattered relative to long run local trends such as political instability arising from Mughal decline and British imperialism, and a lack of policy autonomy that worked to drain India of national wealth.

Evidence on real wages from the United States and Britain also shows some support for this theory. Wages in manufacturing in the United States had long been higher than British wages due to the relative scarcity of American labor and high levels of productivity. At the same time, the United States became increasingly industrial up to 1910 accounting for an ever-larger share of global manufacturing output. A large wage gap persisted despite the enormous influx of immigrants. As mentioned, the US–British wage gap declined only by about 5%, while the Heckscher–Ohlin model predicted a fall of more than over 50%.

One simple explanation for the divergence paradox, if one still wants to argue for the Heckscher–Ohlin theory of trade, is that globalization and trade were not the only processes at work in the 19th century. Local factors also mattered a great deal for explaining economic growth during the first period of globalization. Modern growth theory suggests that physical capital accumulation, human capital, organizational know-how, innovation and technological spillovers in increasing returns to scale industries, and other specialized local technologies that boost the total output of all factors of production are important for explaining cross-national gaps in income.

In an influential study of productive efficiency in the late 19th-century cotton textile industry, economic historian Greg Clark suggested that workers in Europe and North America were much more effective at their jobs than workers in India or China.[8] North American weavers attended

---

[7] See Clingingsmith and Williamson (2008).
[8] See Clark (1987).

six machines (e.g., looms) while Indian, Chinese, or Japanese operatives attended only one. Firms in India paid their workers sixteen times less than workers in the United States and ten times less than in England by the simple logic that workers are paid according to their marginal (revenue) product. And yet, the British maintained their industrial dominance for many years in the face of immense "low-wage" competition.

What causes differences in the level of efficiency and the amount of investment in human and physical capital? At the firm level, workers are more efficient when organizational and managerial techniques motivate workers and incentivize them to work hard while on shift. Japanese textile firms located in China in the late 19th century reportedly managed their Chinese factory workers better than British-owned textile firms in the same city as the Japanese had greater awareness of local culture.

Human capital and learning-by-doing are also important. Investment by workers and firms in human capital and physical capital depends on the expected rate of return to such investment. Demand for schooling or skills is high when a skilled workforce to operate and maintain a complex production system is in demand. The supply of schooling on the other hand depends on political economy. Peter Lindert finds countries that gave the franchise to wider segments of the population, and many countries did just that in western Europe and North America between 1850 and 1913, had higher levels of educational attainment.[9]

Stanley Engerman and Ken Sokoloff demonstrated that in Latin America, where economic inequality was always high, vested interests worked to defend their privilege and status by oppressing democratic movements and blocking access to education.[10] Their argument suggested that a nation's efficiency and productivity were tied to its factor endowments which in turn drove patterns of specialization and economic returns.

In terms of the demand for physical capital, demand is high when skilled, efficient, and compliant workers and natural resources make capital productive. A stable and well-enforced system of property rights and a functional and impartial judiciary system make investors feel confident that capital deepening, land improvements, or mining operations, all of which involve significant up-front costs, will not be taxed away, confiscated by arbitrary state action, or destroyed by thieves and competitors.

[9] See Lindert (2004).
[10] See Sokoloff and Engerman (2000).

Summary

Economic historians agree that the first great wave of globalization witnessed dramatic declines in trade costs. New technologies and new approaches to economic policy had a dramatic impact on living standards around the entire world. The changes were transformative and substantive. Globalization was accompanied by strong economic growth in some countries, but other countries lagged. Even within the countries that experienced strong economic growth, there were various interest groups that gained less or even suffered economic losses from liberalization. As we will see, how local political systems reacted to these distributional issues was crucial in explaining the ongoing trajectory of globalization.

4

International Investment, 1820–1914

Global capital markets flourished in the late 19th century. Never had so much foreign investment taken place in human history. Great Britain was the world's largest foreign lender at the time, but France, Germany, Belgium, and the Netherlands also accumulated large net foreign asset positions. The outflow of capital from Great Britain was so significant that a major national debate centered around whether too much capital was going abroad, starving British entrepreneurs of funding. Was the free movement of capital at the time advantageous for borrowers and lenders, or was it something best avoided?

International capital markets lay dormant or were heavily disrupted between 1914 and the 1970s. However, an earlier golden era of integration existed in the late 19th century. Global capital markets were as integrated in 1910 as they were at the end of the 20th century, according to the standard measure of integration in international capital markets—the ratio of the value of foreign assets to world GDP. Several other measures of capital market integration are available. "Prices"—or their inverse, bond yields—converged strongly over time. On the "quantity" or value side, large outflows from the major net creditors worked to eliminate "home bias" in investors' portfolios. Investors in these years, mainly from Europe but increasingly from the United States and other leading countries, could easily find a way to lend their money to cash-strapped governments, startup cash-hungry railway concerns, or fledgling enterprises on six continents. They did so by purchasing bonds, "debentures," or equity assets directly from international investment banks or indirectly on the large and liquid financial markets in the main global capital markets of the time: London, Paris, Berlin, Brussels, and Amsterdam. New York did not emerge strongly until after World War I.

But how exactly did these global investors allocate their money? Risk and return drive investment decisions and most investors prefer to earn high returns and to minimize risk. On the real side of the economy, economic theory suggests the *marginal product of capital*—that is the gain in output from an additional unit of investment—is high in places where capital is

One from the Many. Christopher M. Meissner, Oxford University Press. © Oxford University Press 2024.
DOI: 10.1093/oso/9780199924462.003.0004

scarce relative to the other factors of production. Since the less developed countries are likely to be the places that need more capital and have lower labor productivity, they should have received the largest share of foreign investment in the period.

Was this true in practice? For reference, we can ask the same question of the late 20th century, a period of strong integration. Here, the data from the 1980s and 1990s surprised Nobel Prize winner and professor Robert Lucas because this was not the case. The poorest, least productive countries received only a small share of foreign capital in the 1980s and 1990s. Could the same "paradox" have been true in the heyday of 19th-century globalization?

During the 19th century, investors were more interested in less developed countries than their late-20th-century counterparts were. But were international capital markets more efficient in the 19th century? Did such investments promote growth and development in the emerging markets of the time? This chapter provides some background to these important questions.

The Sources of Global Capital Flows

The main borrowers of foreign capital in the 19th century were the up-and-coming economies of the period. These included countries of recent European settlement like the United States, Canada, Australia, Argentina, and Brazil. The next largest set of borrowers included Southern and Eastern European nations, including Russia. These were followed by poorer nations like India, the Ottoman Empire, Egypt, and other smaller Latin American nations. Foreign investment averaged about 20% of gross capital formation and reached up to 50% for borrowers like Australia, Canada, and Argentina.

The lion's share of foreign investment originated from the British economy where the sophisticated financial system channeled the nation's significant savings to foreign investment opportunities. France, Germany, Belgium, the Netherlands, and, increasingly, the United States also participated in lending to the rest of the world. Estimates of British foreign assets are 189 million pounds in 1850 (35% of British GDP), 1 billion pounds in 1875 (100% of GDP), and close to 4 billion pounds by 1914 (175% of GDP). Between 1870 and 1914, gross annual British capital outflows averaged 6% of GDP. Interest and returns on foreign investments hovered around 5% of GDP in the 1870s and shot up to 10% in the year before World War I. Roughly 1/3 of the entire British investment portfolio was invested in foreign assets prior to World War 1. Within the foreign portfolio, the British Empire loomed large. Roughly 40% of British foreign investment went to the British Empire.

Cross-border capital flows were often *intermediated* by financial institutions with international connections, such as the merchant banks of London. These included the Baring brothers and the Rothschilds or J. S. Morgan. The Rothschilds also had establishments on the European continent, where other firms like Deutsche Bank, Paribas, Credit Lyonnais, and Societe Generale (one with French origins and one with Belgian origins) operated. *Intermediation* is defined as the act of channeling savings to entrepreneurs, firms, and governments who pledge to repay such loans at a future date with interest. Intermediation relied on improvements in international communications like the telegraph and later the telephone, colonial affiliations, financial stability, and most of all, the ability of the financial sector to judge adequately the risks and returns of potential investments. Intermediation was a multi-stage process. In London, merchant banks would arrange the sale of foreign bonds to interested investors. These investors were often British investment banks, insurance companies, and investment trusts. Shares and bonds were often traded on the London Stock Exchange. Stock brokers transacted with London Stock Exchange market makers known as "jobbers."

As regards information gathering, institutions like the Credit Lyonnais in France established an intensive and impressive research department.[1] Analysts systematically gathered market intelligence (i.e., data) and assessed in real-time the creditworthiness of foreign governments and businesses. Staff crunched the numbers gauging repayment by analyzing the ratio of debt-to-tariff revenue, interest-payments-to-tariff revenue, and export growth. These inputs helped banks like Credit Lyonnais decide where to direct loanable funds and the prices and quantities that could be sold on the market.

Other international banks and intermediaries in Great Britain and elsewhere also relied on their managers' reputations for reliably choosing high-yield, low-risk investments for their clients' portfolios. Institutional investors (and smaller private investors) on the secondary market monitored the financial press of the time to make better decisions on portfolio allocation. The *Times of London*, *The Economist*, and other semi-regular publications

---

[1] See Flandreau (2003).

like *Fenn on the Funds* or the *Investor's Monthly Manual* (a supplement of *The Economist*) supplied market quotes, data, and commentary for sophisticated global investors.

Measuring Capital Market Integration

In theory, investors' expected rate of return on a financial investment should equal the marginal product of capital. Returns on investments, after accounting for risk and other transaction costs, should be equalized across markets, regions, and countries. Were it not the case, an investor could gain financially by taking some small amount of money where rates of return were low and investing that money where rates of return were higher. Market competition and "arbitrage" would eventually equalize returns.

What drives integration in capital markets in practice? Differences exist between rates of return for the same reasons that price differentials on commodities remain. Additionally, there are many formal and informal barriers and costs to finding high-yielding investments. There are also costs to finding an intermediary to transfer your savings from one market to another. Often capital market "arbitrage" requires exchange of one currency for another, so foreign exchange transaction costs also lead to differences in rates of return. Additional costs arise when the markets for assets are "illiquid," meaning it is relatively difficult to find a buyer or a seller in a certain amount of time. Time is money, so waiting time for a transaction counts too. "Middle-men" called market makers or dealers actively help "clear" the market, balancing demand and supply through time. But, since they have to hold large stocks and risk their own money or capital, if a stock or bond fails to pay on time (i.e., default) they often charge a premium to cover their risks.

The London Stock Exchange, the world's premier financial market at the time, allowed trading on the vast majority of global bond issues by foreign companies and sovereign governments. Although the market was reliably liquid, entry into "jobbing" was restricted and liability was unlimited. These costs were passed on to investors, so that borrowers had to offer higher returns to compensate for the costs of anti-competitive market-making. The impact of all these costs was also to increase return differentials between markets. Additionally, these "frictions" reduced the overall amount of international lending relative to a hypothetical world with zero capital market frictions.

Another factor is risk. Investors may require a higher rate of return to compensate for bearing the risk of investment. These risks include the risk of default or not getting repaid as per the original contract. Civil disturbances, negligent governments, duplicitous entrepreneurs, and volatile economic and natural environments raised risk and therefore the required rate of return in financial markets. In sum, numerous transaction costs and "frictions" exist in capital markets, which keep prices from totally converging. The size of the differences in rates of return can help us understand how integrated a capital market is.

As mentioned, yields on comparable assets generally converged over the course of the late 19th century. As it happens, there were many different kinds of assets available for investment at this time, and it is critical to compare like with like. One of the most popular asset classes was long-term sovereign bonds, which carried periodic coupon payments equivalent to the promised interest rate on the face value of the bond. From the mid-19th century, long-term borrowing costs for seventeen economies fell, and the dispersion in these rates also declined (Figure 4.1). The average interest rate in this chart was 6% in 1870 and highly variable, but by 1913 it stood at 4.3% with a remarkably smaller dispersion.

By 1910, countries like Russia and Portugal could borrow on international capital markets at just about one percentage point above the "risk-free" reference bond issued by Britain. Several decades earlier, in 1870, the difference in these interest rates was on the order of two to two-and-a-half percentage points,respectively. These figures emphasize the increase in integration, but substantial gaps remained. The larger part of these gaps can be explained with country-specific risks that investors would have to bear if they were to invest in such countries.

Similar convergence occurred across a range of other assets besides long-term government bonds. Short-term interest rates—usually 30-, 60-, 90-, or 120-day maturities—converged, moved in synch, and reverted quickly to low values in London, New York, Berlin, and Paris (Figure 4.2). By the 1880s, the British pound sterling could be purchased in New York for payment in 30, 60, or 90 days at a guaranteed exchange rate (hence exchange rate risks were covered) via sterling "drafts."[2] These forward sterling drafts carried an implicit interest rate for investment in sterling. This enables economists to compare short-term interest rates in New York versus London. Research

[2] A draft is similar to a check. It can be cashed at the bank that issued it at some point in the future.

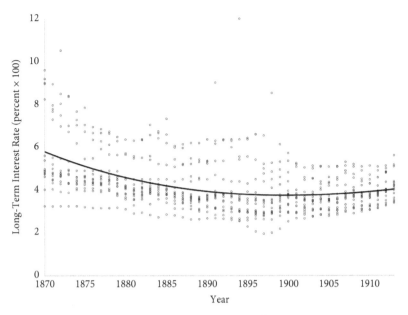

Figure 4.1 Long-Term Interest Rates, Sovereign Debt, Seventeen Countries, 1870–1913

Source: Author's calculations based on data in Jordà, Schularick, and Taylor (2021) and Jordà, Schularick, and Taylor (2017)

shows that these interest rates equalized throughout the period 1880–1913, suggesting that leading international capital markets were strongly and tightly integrated.

Investors also invested their money efficiently. Efficiency is defined roughly as achieving a given rate of return with minimal risk. A wide variety of securities was marketed in London, the world's leading capital market. Government debt from almost every sovereign and British colonial entity was available for investment. If such an asset was not traded in London, then an investor could simply purchase it in Paris, Amsterdam, Berlin, or Brussels. While London specialized in lending to the New World and the British Empire, the Paris Bourse tilted toward Eastern Europe and French colonial endeavors (mainly in Africa). Likewise, while a range of securities was available in Berlin, south-eastern Europe, and northern European securities were more preponderant. All these markets listed assets from railroads, public-private utilities like harbors and water treatment systems, and of course private companies in endeavors as diverse as mining, banking and finance, and textiles.

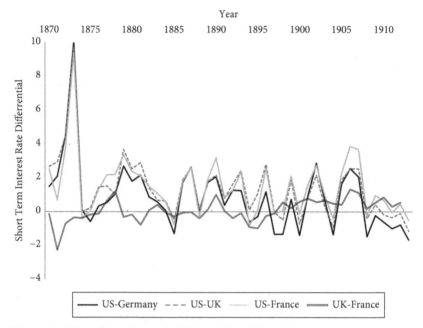

Figure 4.2 Short-Term Interest Differentials, 1870–2013
Source: Author's calculations based on data in Jordà, Schularick, and Taylor (2021) and Jordà, Schularick, and Taylor (2017)

The wide range of securities available led to geographically and sectorally diversified portfolios. Figure 4.3 shows portfolio allocations for several major British investment trusts around 1900. The largest sectors were railways and government bonds, though utilities and industrial interests were increasing strongly after 1900. The main recipients after the United Kingdom were North America and Latin America. Indeed, in 1900, British investors put only 20% of their portfolio in the United Kingdom, with the remaining 80% invested abroad. Overall, there is strong evidence based on simple measures of rates of return that international capital markets in the 19th century worked to reduce capital scarcity in the regions of the world where development was most promising but where capital remained hard to come by.

The Lucas Paradox: The Mystery of the "Missing Capital"

Rates of return might have been converging over time, but not all countries received equal amounts of capital. In fact, British capital flows favored

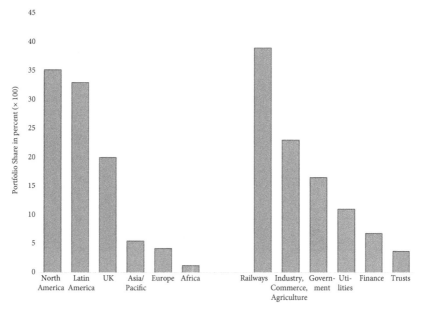

Figure 4.3 Portfolio Shares by Region and Sector for British Investment Trusts, 1900

Source: Author's calculations based on Sotiropoulos, Rutterford, and Keber (2020), pp. 800 and 802

countries with bright prospects for economic growth. Places with higher levels of GDP per capita tended to receive slightly more capital than middle-income regions. Figure 4.4 shows how the richer and wealthier quintiles of countries obtained similar shares of British capital inflows to the poorest nations at the time. It should be noted, however, that this skew is not as far from theoretical predictions as it was in the late 20th century. What explains the difference?

In the late 20th century, Nobel Prize-winning macro-economist Robert Lucas highlighted a global "paradox." The "Lucas Paradox" argued that capital tended to shy away from LDCs. This is akin to having too many people on one side of the see-saw at the playground. The see-saw is stuck without proper balance. Similarly, capital flows tended to perpetuate income gaps. What explains why no one wanted to move to the other side of the metaphorical see-saw? Were investors unaware of the profitable investment opportunities in the poorer regions? Did the governments and entrepreneurs of these LDCs have a reputation for defaulting on their obligations, thus limiting lending? Was there a sound economic rationale for these lending patterns?

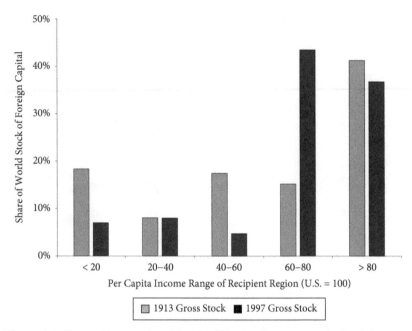

Figure 4.4 Share of International Stock of Foreign Investments by Recipient Income, 1913 versus 1997

Source: 1913: author's calculations based on GDP data underlying Clemens and Williamson (2004a) and foreign investment data in Stone (1999); 1997: GDP data are from Bolt et al. (2018) and foreign investment data are from Milesi-Ferretti (2001)

Investment is a forward-looking activity. People invest where growth prospects are *expected* to be best. At the macro-economic level, countries with a rapidly expanding labor force and with large and accessible natural resources or cheap, abundant, arable land provided strong and dependable returns. British capital "chased" the European emigrants to their destinations since upon arrival these migrants would be incorporated quickly into the labor force providing labor to farm the land, harvest resources, and work in the factories. Capital also favored areas with open, arable land and abundant natural resources like Canada (land to grow wheat, precious metals, and timber), the United States (cotton, wheat, and later petroleum and other minerals), Australia (sheep for wool), New Zealand (sheep for wool and meat, dairy cows), Argentina (land for wheat, land for grazing cattle), Chile (copper), and Peru (guano, heavy on nitrates and a good fertilizer). After controlling for the size of a country, growth potential, as measured in the indicators above, accounted for much of the variation in capital flows in the

19th century. These capital flows served the goal of growth by augmenting the level of investment to a degree that such flows in recent decades have not done.[3]

Borrowers had different "ability and willingness" to repay. The amount and quality of information about a borrower's prospects to repay typically mattered. Repayment was more likely if funds were committed to "productive" purposes. Information about a borrower's ability and willingness to pay is limited in capital markets because borrowers prefer to strategically exaggerate their ability to repay and to hide their weaknesses. Lenders anticipate this "adverse selection" and gather as much information as possible about borrowers. Even when investors exercised adequate due diligence, many resource-exporting countries were subject to shocks. Harvest failures, supply shocks, political turmoil, and wars often impeded repayment. It's no surprise that Portugal (1891), Brazil (1898), and Spain (1882 and 1899) all defaulted in the midst of political revolutions and turmoil. Today, credit scores and sovereign debt ratings signal a borrower's likelihood of repayment, but no such formal mechanism existed in the 19th century. Instead, lenders, as mentioned above, looked at available statistics, including the ratio of debt interest payments to exports or population, the ratio of government revenue to debt interest payments, and repayment history.

Other factors drove borrowing costs down too. Economic historians Michael Bordo and Hugh Rockoff suggested that the gold standard offered a "good housekeeping seal of approval" to investors.[4] Lenders preferred stable prices and exchange rates. They perceived countries adhering to the gold standard, the same monetary system as Britain, France, and Germany, as less risky. This tipped investment toward countries on the gold standard. The gold standard shifted the supply of loanable funds available to gold-standard countries "to the right" and thus lowered the interest rate at which they could borrow.

Bordo and Rockoff's seal of approval worked as per an asymmetric information signaling model from basic microeconomic theory. Countries opting for the gold standard took a costly action (or set of actions) that was infeasible, or at least prohibitively costly, for less financially capable countries. When a negative shock occurred, gold standard countries promised to

---

[3] See Clemens and Williamson (2004a).
[4] See Bordo and Rockoff (1996).

react by implementing potentially painful economic policies (see Chapter 5 for why this is the case), showing that they would sacrifice the economy for the goal of exchange rate stability. In this way, capital markets tended to favor investment in the countries that opted for and adhered to the gold standard on a consistent basis.

Sticking with the gold standard was crucial for another reason. Most foreign debt was payable in the investors' currency, usually the gold-backed British pound sterling. Debt payable in a currency with a floating exchange rate created uncertain returns for investors. In the event of a depreciation against sterling, debt could quickly become unpayable. This raised borrowing costs, so borrowers and investors preferred gold-clause debt. Only a few countries that were large enough or financially developed enough could borrow in their own currency, like Austria-Hungary, Belgium, France, Great Britain, Germany, and Russia. Of these, only France, Germany, and Great Britain borrowed exclusively in their own currency.

Imperial relations also counted for a lot and lowered borrowing costs. The British government incentivized the holding of colonial stocks and bonds, thereby increasing the demand for these assets. The Colonial Stock Act of 1900 conferred the same "trustee" status on colonial bonds that British government bonds enjoyed. The colonial powers also gave a final seal of approval to colonial budgets. Investors also knew that colonial entities would be reticent to default on debt when the British crown had the ability to impose sanctions on local colonial agents and governments. But more than that, economic historians Niall Ferguson and Moritz Schularick argue that the British Empire, especially in the so-called settler economies, boasted relatively un-corrupt governments, sound public finances, and stable money.[5] In short, investments in the British Empire were low-risk. As a result, these areas tended to borrow more cheaply than comparable regions and received more capital as well.

Impact of Capital Flows

Modern economic theory suggests free international capital flows allow for efficient allocation of scarce capital. What do we know about the overall benefits? Economists and observers have long attempted to gauge the impact

---

[5] See Ferguson and Schularick (2006).

of 19th-century capital flows. We have seen how capital flowed across borders prior to 1914 to take advantage of profitable opportunities. It seems like investors preferred to invest a substantial share of their portfolios abroad. What was the likely impact on these countries that participated in the first global capital market?

What if the impact of capital outflows from Great Britain (and other major sources of foreign capital) was negative? Contemporary observers and even economic historians of the late 20th century debated this issue. In fact, a protectionist/mercantilist view of capital flows flourished in Great Britain. Adherents of this view claimed the outflow of loanable funds from Great Britain diminished British economic growth. Outflows starved British entrepreneurs and companies of capital as the City of London profited from investments in far-flung and distant lands.

Economic historians reached a different conclusion. The idea that Britain was underfunded is specious. The empirical evidence for such underfunding was likely spurious. For such an argument to be true, it must have been the case that the return on capital was higher in Great Britain than in foreign countries and that investors persistently neglected such opportunities. To the contrary, risk-adjusted returns were higher in government and railway bonds in the British dominions and other rapidly developing regions when compared to those in Britain. Evidently, financial markets in the first wave of globalization took a dim view of the prospects for British economic growth in the late 19th century in comparison to the settler economies in which they were investing.

Interestingly, foreign investment and British economic "decline" may have been two sides of the same coin. However, the reason is not because Britain was starved of capital. Instead, it's possible that too much capital flowed into Great Britain! During this period, Great Britain also experienced significant capital inflows. An unknown, but not insignificant, number of non-residents invested in Britain. They also left a significant amount of cash on deposit at London City banks. The official reserves of many other countries were invested in British government debt. The pound sterling was the "safe asset" of the period, much like the US dollar has been since World War II. In turn, Great Britain acted as the world's banker. Banks, Trusts, and Assurance companies based in the City of London took in short-term funds from the rest of the world (as well as from domestic investors and depositors) and then reinvested these funds in foreign economies about which they had superior information regarding economic prospects. The impact of both the recycling of funds and the global demand for sterling reserves, was arguably to *slow* British economic growth. Foreign demand shifted up for British assets, thus pushing equilibrium interest rates on British assets down. By reducing British interest rates, this also led to a (real) appreciation of the British currency eating away at the competitiveness of British manufacturing. The process is very similar to the so-called Dutch disease that afflicts many resource exporters.

Kevin O'Rourke and Jeffrey Williamson investigated the impact of capital flows on receiving countries in a neo-classical economic model. Capital inflows raised the capital-labor ratio and hence raised wages by increasing the marginal product of labor. The authors estimate the rise in the amount of capital available per worker to assess the rise in the productive capacity of an economy. Then, with the help of some assumptions about the aggregate production function, the change in output per worker can be estimated. Denmark and Norway received a large boost to their capital stock between 1870 and 1910 such that real wages were over 8% higher in 1910 than they would have been otherwise. In new world countries, like Canada and the United States, capital "chased" the stream of immigrants. These flows limited the decline in wages in the receiving countries, reducing observed wage convergence. Assessing what might have happened without capital flows is complicated because of the complementarity of the immigrant and capital flows. Capital exporters, such as the United Kingdom, France, Germany, or Belgium, had lower wages due to capital outflows. For Great Britain, this decline due to capital exports is estimated by O'Rourke and Williamson to be on the order of 20%. Figure 4.5 shows a direct positive relationship between improvement in the capital stock due to inflows and real wages in a small set of countries.

O'Rourke and Williamson go on to think even more broadly about the global economy and capital flows. The question is, did capital lead to income convergence or divergence? The Heckscher–Ohlin model of trade with international flows of factors has to be reevaluated when there are more than two factors of production. Such analysis is usually carried out in the so-called specific factors models of international trade. Here, land, labor, and capital are the factors, and land is specific to producing agricultural output, while capital is used only in manufacturing. In such a world, factor flows can be substitutes or complements for international trade. Adding capital makes analysis trickier. Economists have long held that capital "chased" labor to the new world in the 19th century. In most cases, however, the capital was applied

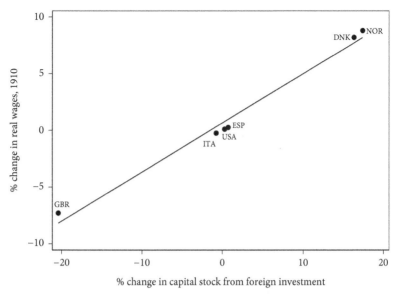

Figure 4.5 Impact of Cumulative Capital Inflows, 1870–1910, on Domestic Capital Stock and Real Wages

Source: Author's calculations based on data underlying O'Rourke and Williamson (1999), Table 12.3

to infrastructure or to supplement government revenue (see Figure 4.3). In this instance, capital flows probably enhanced the ability of new world commodity exporters to export (thus complementing trade). Such capital inflows also probably raised the wages of workers in these countries or at least sustained them at high levels.

Capital inflows raised the level of incomes in receiving countries by making workers more productive, but they probably did not raise long-run growth rates. There is little doubt that international capital helped build the modern infrastructure of the western offshoots, and other emerging markets of the time, but it is unlikely that such infrastructure would never have been built in the absence of these flows. Instead, global capital probably accelerated such construction of productive capacity by providing a pool of funds at a lower cost than by using only domestically available capital. It could even be argued that delaying some infrastructure investment would have led to lower obsolescence and better quality of such equipment due to advances in product quality over time.

Not all capital was prudently invested in the types of capital that would make workers more productive, however. Albert Fishlow distinguished *development borrowing* and *revenue borrowing*.[6] The former involved construction of useful infrastructure such as ports, railways, sewage systems, and roads. Incentives were aligned properly such that governments, to the extent they were involved, would dedicate streams of future revenue to repayment. Private development followed relatively sound and transparent accounting and was supervised by foreign businessmen with connections to the financial industry. Some railways and other projects certainly did fail due to economic shocks, injudicious choices and poor engineering, nefarious self-dealing, and kleptocratic authorities. One famous incident involved the Central Railway line in Peru. Peru had borrowed more than 12 million pounds to aid construction of a railway network in 1872. By 1876, with its main export of "guano" in decline, Peru was forced to default on its loans. The Central Railway line remained unfinished, leaving British investors with little to show for their efforts.[7]

More broadly, revenue finance seems to be associated with generally weak economic and political institutions. Such borrowing plugged a gap in government finances when governments could not generate sufficient tax revenues. Mark Dincecco has recently shown that limited constraints on the executive and fiscal centralization enhanced revenue streams, implying that the need to borrow on international markets might have decreased.[8] The opposite held in places as diverse as late-19th-century Brazil (after 1888), Peru, Spain, the Ottoman Empire, Egypt, and Portugal. In these places, borrowing increased on the back of little collateral and even less enthusiasm (and ability) to repay. Of course, capital markets did attempt to assess these risks beforehand. Credit Lyonnais analysts performed rudimentary analysis of debt sustainability but with a limited amount of data. Not every risk could be known and hence priced into the loans in such an environment. Apparently, no one forecasted the fall in the price of guano in Peru, nor the harvest shock that would hit Argentina in 1889. When countries were too reliant on one crop or commodity for revenue to repay, debt default was often the outcome. Such countries had little to show for all the borrowing they did compared to the fast-growing, and more balanced, economies of Canada, Australia, New Zealand, and the United States.

Summing up, it appears that capital flowed more and more freely from the mid-19th century. The high rates of return on foreign investments were

[6] See Fishlow (1995).
[7] See Miller (1976).
[8] See Dincecco (2009).

attractive, especially as information about markets improved and monetary stability reigned. Capital promoted economic development in the receiving countries the most when it raised the rate of investment in productive infrastructure. When capital was not directed to productive ends it usually created financial instability. In fact, capital inflows had more malignant effects that are often associated with financial crises and instability in the balance of payments. We now turn to an examination of this instability in the international financial system.

5

Inter-Dependence and Instability in the Classical Gold-Standard Era

Was the classical gold-standard era, between 1880 and 1913, an era of macroeconomic stability? Economists portray this period as a mythical golden age. Stable money and finance, low inflation, and strong economic growth prevailed. Orthodox monetary and fiscal policy triumphed. Macroeconomic stability reigned.

The classical gold standard provided the monetary foundation for the first global economy. The classical gold standard effectively fixed exchange rates between countries. Fixed exchange rates lowered the cost of international transactions, which promoted integration. Consequently, the gold standard also raised international commodity price and interest rate correlations. Prices converged. Trade expanded. Unprecedented market integration followed. The gold standard also swiftly eliminated trade "imbalances." Real and nominal exchange rate stability was the hallmark of the era. Since integration raised welfare and currency crashes are best avoided, what was not to like about the classical gold standard?

In principle, the gold standard offered no free lunch. First, it significantly increased macroeconomic "inter-dependence." The economic fate of nations (i.e., the welfare of local producers and residents) was no longer determined by local factors. Because of this, the gold standard clearly had "distributional" effects. Global market forces now determined commodity prices and interest rates.

With globalization and lower trade costs, prices came to be set at the "world" level. Greater international competition helped improve consumer welfare. However, local farmers previously relied on high prices to compensate them for harvest failure or natural disasters. Now the world price (expressed in domestic currency) for wheat, among other products, was set by global market conditions instead of local conditions. Global shocks could not be absorbed by the exchange rate.

One from the Many. Christopher M. Meissner, Oxford University Press. © Oxford University Press 2024.
DOI: 10.1093/oso/9780199924462.003.0005

Similarly, in financial markets, global market conditions strongly influenced local interest rates and borrowing costs. Local financial conditions now depended on distant events. Borrowers received analogous benefits to those of food consumers since they could now tap bottomless global capital markets at lower, competitive interest rates. However, local financial markets were now forced to adapt to shocks in the global capital market.

The sanguine view emphasizes stability and efficiency, but this view provides a limited and distorted view of global economic history. While leading nations potentially benefited from the gold standard regime, less developed economies were less likely to do so. The former had accumulated experience with sophisticated financial markets, boasted larger economies, and achieved reasonable political responsiveness to economic and financial shocks. These countries managed the downside risks of globalization relatively better. They followed the "rules of the game" seemingly effortlessly. Financial markets provided stabilizing support. Leading countries lent each other a helping hand when required. Less financially and economically developed economies experienced higher instability and worse macroeconomic performance. Similarly, within countries, the gold standard benefited some interest groups while harming others. In the United States, as in other less-developed and less financially central nations, the gold standard was perennially contentious. Farmers and other exporters viewed the gold standard as a restrictive regime imposed by a financial elite who were negligent of their welfare.

The Case for the Golden Age of Stability

A gold standard is a "commodity money" standard. Used across the world for millennia, commodity money systems largely disappeared by the late 20th century. Since the 1970s, nearly all countries operate fiat money systems, meaning there is no physical commodity backing their currencies. However, some countries opt to back their money with other currencies like the dollar. This is known as a fixed exchange rate system. The gold standard carries lessons even today since many countries still rely on fixed exchange rates. Cryptocurrencies like Bitcoin also bear resemblance to the gold standard since tokens must be "mined" like gold. Stablecoins are similar in spirit to the gold standard since they are supposed to be convertible into various assets or currencies at a fixed price.

Commodity money systems in the 19th century were mainly based on gold and silver. Gold or silver coins served directly as money, but paper currency *convertible* into gold or silver was also prevalent. Paper money weighs less and is easier to transport than metal coins. Precious metals are also valuable and in scarce supply. Did scarcity confer a special monetary status on gold? No.

Gold served as money because everyone believed that everyone else valued gold. Sea shells, elk horns, rocks, and even cigarettes could have performed the same function. A commodity money standard relied on scarcity to prevent an excess supply of money. Gold or silver money allegedly disciplined governments and banks from creating too much money since they could not immediately create gold or silver. This helped avoid ruinous inflation and financial uncertainty.

Low inflation and price stability were not assured, however. Consider that the gold standard (or a commodity money standard more generally) can only work if the government continually adheres to the official mint price (e.g., $20.67 per Troy ounce of gold in the United States from 1879 until 1933). The stroke of a pen could easily change the mint price or eliminate convertibility. Devaluing the currency relative to gold violated the unwritten rules of a commodity money system. But for centuries, princes, kings, and others who controlled the levers of financial policy had been breaking those promises. When expenses were unusually high, during wars, for instance, royal mints were ordered to "clip" coins. The mint then passed underweight coins off as full-bodied coins, thereby pocketing the difference. The gold reserve could thereby go that much further in helping a government meet urgent expenses. When that strategy failed, governments simply printed money or IOUs. Contemporaries called this a "forced currency."

A proper gold (or commodity) standard requires a free market for gold. International flows of gold and gold ownership must be unrestricted. Precious metals' flows between markets were essential to pay for trade imbalances over the long run. For example, from the 16th century through the 19th century, European nations ran persistent trade deficits with Asia/China. Europeans exchanged a portion of silver extracted from American mines for Asian luxury commodities like silk, tea, and spices. The drain of precious metals proved to be a long-run structural feature of the global economy associated with the Great Divergence.[1] Later, in the 19th century,

---

[1] See Pomeranz (2000). Also see Flynn and Giraldez (1995) on precious metal flows and the global economy.

The Economist regularly reported gold shipments between countries prior to World War I. The financial press closely monitored the gold reserves of leading nations because gold reserves were a crucial indicator of a currency's health status.

Inherently, a gold standard is no more stable than a fiat money regime since gold convertibility can always be suspended at will. Stability, therefore, depends on the ability to *credibly commit*. When commitment was credible, the gold standard worked successfully in the late 19th century. "Credible" means it makes sense to take an action when the time comes to take the promised action. A non-credible commitment is like a "bluff." When a bluff is called, a different action than that which was promised is taken.

To understand the gold standard, it helps to consider it as a "rule." Credibility depended on the rule being generally advantageous to those making monetary policy decisions. For instance, the British government decided that changing the mint price of a pound sterling in the late 19th century would lead to worse outcomes than constant adherence to the historical mint price. What are those bad outcomes?

Markets would punish those who violated the commitment. Borrowing costs would rise. The financial system would shrink. British power would be curtailed. By changing the mint price of gold, or the gold parity, investors would lose trust in the stability of a currency like the pound. They would be less likely to lend money to Great Britain and they would rely less on the London banking system. The world-class banking system in the City of London relied on the trust of a large foreign clientele as well as domestic savers. Britain's reputation for credible commitment to convertibility at the historical mint price promoted the fortunes of the financial industry. Strong economic growth depended in part on this financial system.

Britain's financial system and economy relied on the stability of the currency, sound public finances, and adherence to the rule of law. Large investments and wealth would not be expropriated by a surprise burst of inflation. Economic historians Douglass North and Barry Weingast argued that the Glorious Revolution of 1688 gave rise to sound public finances and enhanced credible commitment.[2] This persisted and contributed to British economic dominance. Without these sound finances, the economic and military power and the global influence of Great Britain would have been

---

[2] See North and Weingast (1989).

severely curtailed. By the 1870s, leaders argued that the gold standard was the regime of choice for "advanced" nations.

Most countries made the gold standard their monetary regime from the 1870s onward. Previously, the world was split between gold standard countries, "bimetallic" countries using silver and gold, and a group using silver only. Global coordination and cooperation were responsible for the changes after 1870. Instead, the transition took place spontaneously.

Could the world have adopted one monetary system? In fact, in 1867, a French-led initiative attempted to create this global monetary union. Global cooperation failed to deliver a universal gold-based system in the 1860s, despite high-level diplomatic efforts at the International Monetary Conference of 1867 held in Paris. Representatives of twenty nations attended this meeting to discuss these matters. The key question for delegates was whether the system should be gold, silver, or bimetallic. The British delegate, representing the single most important country for trade and finance in the world, was asked which system Britain preferred. He replied, "The English nation is in a position much more independent upon this question than most continental nations." Delegates from less influential nations supported a system based on the system of their trade partners. Since most countries had extensive trade ties with Britain, and the British were steadfast in their commitment to gold, the conference delegates agreed to a gold-based system.

The agreement was non-binding, and the project never moved forward. A global monetary union never emerged. Despite this, most countries hurriedly began the switch to a gold system from the early 1870s. The move would not be due to centralized decisions. Instead, a decentralized "scramble for gold" occurred. Ironically, the classical gold standard that emerged did resemble a monetary union in some respects. Indeed, the tradeoff countries faced when opting for gold were not too dissimilar from those facing a country contemplating joining a monetary union.[3]

Why was adherence to the gold standard akin to joining a monetary union? Both types of regimes eliminate the exchange rate as a shock absorber and imply a loss of the ability to stabilize the economy with monetary policy. Fixed exchange rates (or monetary unions) reduce transaction costs in trade and finance. This brings benefits. Also, according to theory, economic

---

[3] The central ideas were developed in the "optimum currency area" (OCA) literature. See James Meade (1957), Robert Mundell (1961), Ronald McKinnon (1963), and Peter Kenen (1969).

adjustment to (demand and supply) shocks under a common currency is less costly with high labor and capital market integration. Also, when shocks are highly correlated across countries, a monetary union is less costly. Without high integration or correlated shocks, adjustment under a monetary union is prolonged and more costly. In such a case, a common monetary system imposes relatively more short-run economic pain in terms of inflation or unemployment.

The "scramble for gold" began in 1872 after the newly unified German Reich opted for a gold standard in 1871. Germany's chancellor, Otto von Bismarck, declared that a great country like Germany should follow other leading nations like Great Britain and adopt a gold standard. Germany had also recently defeated France in the Franco-Prussian war. Contrary to earlier historical work, recent research has shown that the war reparations paid by France to Germany were not the decisive factor. Trade relations mattered more. Since German trade with Great Britain was strong, and growing rapidly, linking up to the British monetary system seemed to make economic sense.

A host of other countries quickly followed the German lead in the 1870s. The gold standard came to dominate in Western Europe and eventually throughout the world. The gold standard "went viral" (Figure 3.6) because of network externalities. The more countries using the gold standard, the greater the benefits of gold for all other countries. Once large economies like Germany and Britain were both on gold, smaller economies saw an increased economic gain from a gold system.

As the gold-based system gained prominence, the demand for silver plummeted, and the demand for gold skyrocketed. This caused the exchange rates of silver countries to depreciate over the long run and to fluctuate wildly in the short run vis-à-vis gold-based countries. This exchange rate volatility reduced trade and capital market integration. This intensified the scramble for gold. Staying on silver, when the major countries were on gold, exposed countries to harmful levels of economic uncertainty. The incentive to stay on a silver system was strongly diminished.

Some economists argued that a silver system could boost exports. However, the secular (nominal) depreciation of silver countries was not necessarily advantageous. The theory of purchasing power parity (PPP) predicts higher inflation in silver standard countries and deflation in gold countries. These movements would act quickly to offset any competitive gains from nominal depreciations. This is exactly what occurred. Over the period

1870–1895, the average inflation rate for India, a silver standard country was 0.7%. Great Britain experienced an average decline in prices of 1.1% per year in the same period.

France provides an interesting case study in regime choice. France was the leading bimetallic country since the 1820s.[4] Both silver and gold backed the French franc. Gresham's Law perpetually threatened the durability of France's bi-metallic system. Gresham's Law states that "bad money drives out good money." "Bad" money is a precious metal that is losing value relative to the other precious metal. Gresham's Law is a result of arbitrage that takes advantage of the difference between the official silver/gold mint parity and the market price of gold in terms of silver. In the early 1870s, silver was the "bad" money and gold was "good" since demand for gold was increasing and the demand for silver was falling. Gresham's Law threatened to drain France of gold and leave it with only silver. Becoming a de facto silver country would expose the French economy to intolerable levels of uncertainty, reduced trade, and inflation. French policymakers were troubled by such prospects.

In the short term, France could only escape from Gresham's Law by eliminating convertibility of its currency and limiting coinage of silver at the mint. In the long run, France ultimately opted out of bimetallism and moved to gold in 1878. The policy decisions between 1873 and 1878, in the context of tricky international relations, make the story of France's eventual abandonment of bimetallism even more interesting.

In the 1870s, French silver and gold reserves as a share of the world total remained significant. This gave French leaders some confidence after 1872 that bimetallism could be maintained despite Germany's switch. France's official mint value for silver versus gold was historically set at 15.5 to 1. Its credible commitment to this price and its enormous reserves helped maintain this ratio on global markets for the fifty years prior to 1872.

So why did the value of silver begin to fall against gold in the 1870s? Demand and supply mattered. In this case, it was French demand for precious metals that mattered. Marc Flandreau argued that it was precisely in 1873 when the French began limiting silver inflows, that bi-metallism met its demise. France disallowed silver inflows in order to strategically stymie German sales of silver and purchases of gold in their transition to the gold standard. The French preferred not to facilitate Germany's transition to gold

---

[4] See Flandreau (1996).

since it had recently humiliated the nation in the Franco-Prussian war of 1870. By the mid-1870s, the global monetary situation had spun out of control. France would ultimately drive itself off bimetallism by inducing others to "scramble" for gold.

Why did countries make a run for gold? The world expected a fall in the value of silver because French demand for silver was now strictly limited. France had signaled a potential de-monetization of silver, and that it might not be the buyer-of-last-resort for silver on world markets forever. Bimetallic and silver countries either had to move quickly to gold or suffer the inflationary consequences of silver's depreciation. A scramble for gold ensued whereby nations attempted to leapfrog each other and sell silver for gold at the highest price possible before silver fell further in value. Once it was clear that a nation's economically significant trading partners were headed to gold, it was economically and financially sensible to choose a gold standard.

By 1878, most of France's major trading partners had moved to gold, which had at least two implications. First, it would be too difficult to maintain a solid gold reserve in the long run as the value of silver relative to gold fell in world markets and Gresham's Law began to drain France of gold. Second, it made sense to coordinate with a nation's principal trading partners, which by now were mostly on gold.

Which nations adopted gold when? Great Britain was a gold country throughout the 19th century, as were Canada, Australia, and New Zealand. Germany adopted in 1872 and the Netherlands did so in 1875. The Scandinavian countries were solid members of the gold club from 1874. France was a faithful adherent from 1878, as was Belgium. The United States adopted a de facto gold standard in 1879. From 1880 onward, the gold standard provided remarkable exchange rate stability for these leading nations. Figure 5.1 shows how stable exchange rates were in Germany, France, and Great Britain.

Less stability prevailed in other regions. A group of countries often referred to as the "periphery" entered and exited the gold standard and had a hard time credibly committing to the gold standard. Countries that came off and on the gold standard included Argentina, Brazil, and Chile in South America and Greece, Italy, and Portugal in Europe. Countries that delayed their adoption of the gold standard and backed their currencies with silver (Japan, India, and China, for example) experienced inflation and depreciation of their exchange rates against gold countries.

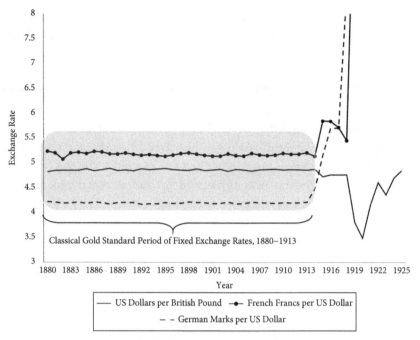

Figure 5.1 Exchange-Rate Stability in the Classical Gold Standard

Source: Author's calculations based on data in Jordà, Schularick, and Taylor (2021) and Jordà, Schularick, and Taylor (2017)

Stability and Macroeconomic Outcomes

Did the gold standard provide stability? How did it impact macroeconomic outcomes? The gold standard succeeded in the most economically advanced and financially developed countries. Leading countries in
Western Europe had very few severe financial crises in the period. Great
Britain experienced no serious banking crisis between 1880 and 1914.
Currency crises in northwestern Europe were rare. No country in the region suspended convertibility of the currency into gold in the period.
Exchange rates between the leading countries in this region were "locked
in," moving at most a small fraction of a percentage point from the declared
mint parities. Prices remained stable over the long run. Economic volatility was low, and economic growth was strong and persistent. Commodity
price movements were highly correlated, while interest rates converged
and moved in lockstep. Trade, capital flows, and international migration
flourished.

In addition, imbalances in current accounts and in balances of payments often adjusted smoothly and quickly. When imbalances did persist, they did not necessarily lead to instability. Sizeable current account deficits emerged in many countries that borrowed from abroad.[5] Argentina, Australia, and Canada were large capital importers and their deficits persisted for years if not decades. Figure 5.2 shows the evolution of current accounts for the major borrowers and lenders of the time and compared to other periods after 1870. In the first wave of globalization, current account deficits on the order of 5% of GDP in absolute value were not uncommon. As can be seen, the average global deficit is high and persistent compared to other periods, but most comparable to the patterns seen in the second wave of globalization after 1973. The capital that flowed into the borrowing nations often came as outflows from Great Britain, France, and Germany. Though these outflows were somewhat cyclical by nature, they remained generally strong throughout the period. Compared to the period of the Great Depression, which we will investigate in Chapter 9, this was indeed a period of significant stability and "smooth adjustment" of the current account. How did it work?

How the Gold Standard Operated

David Hume first described what has come to be known as the *price-specie flow mechanism* model. This model explains how the gold standard nearly *automatically* kept countries out of long-run balance of payments trouble. "Trouble" is defined as a current account deficit that is unsustainable because it generates an accumulation of debt so large that it will with great likelihood become unpayable. In other words, the gold standard, allegedly, acted like a rubber band or a spring, tending to push countries back to surplus at some point.

To see how it works, assume a trade deficit arises in a country. In this case, gold specie (i.e., money) would flow away from the deficit country to the surplus country in order to pay for the trade deficit. The decline in the monetary base in the deficit country pushes down on this country's price level. In the surplus country, prices begin to rise. As foreign goods became relatively

---

[5] To recall, the current account (CA) equals national savings (S) minus aggregate investment (I). The implication is that deficit countries tend to be increasing their net indebtedness to the rest of the world while surplus countries are increasing their net lending to the rest of the world.

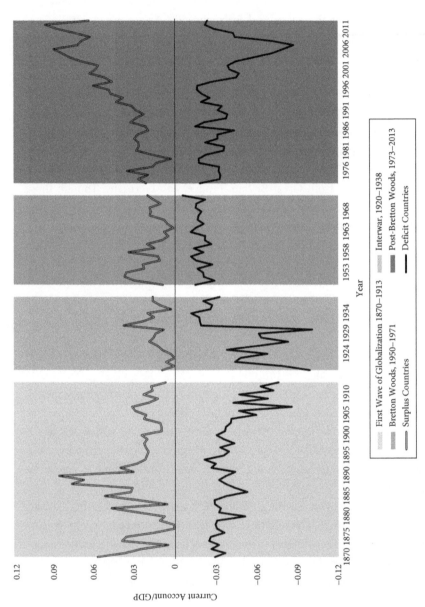

Figure 5.2 Average Current Account/GDP Surplus and Deficit Countries, 1870–2013

Source: Author's calculations based on data in Jordà, Schularick, and Taylor (2021) and Jordà, Schularick, and Taylor (2017)

more expensive, imports decline and the trade balance improves for the deficit country. Imbalances adjust assuming gold flows freely across borders. But this was not always true. Gold flows were mostly too small to equilibrate the observed imbalances of the period.

Subsequent research emphasized international capital flows. International borrowing and lending can serve to equilibrate the trade deficit. The standard accounting identity for the balance of payments shows how. Simplifying only a little, the sum of the current account and net capital inflows must equal the change in gold (or foreign exchange) reserves.[6] Assuming reserves are not changing, this implies that one way a trade deficit can be financed is by borrowing from abroad.

Simple theories of adjustment in the balance of payments are not readily vindicated by the historical record. Persistent trade deficits imply persistent borrowing. Since debt cannot be accumulated forever, some adjustment should have taken place. And yet, countries like Canada and Australia ran trade deficits for many consecutive decades. Why did current accounts not revert toward surplus more quickly? Generally, economists would predict that changes in relative prices would eventually occur. A lender or creditor like Great Britain should have sustained increases in relative prices. Borrowing nations would see relative deflation and gain competitiveness. But, these correlations are not particularly evident in many cases in the late- 19th-century data.

This is somewhat disturbing since arbitrage in financial markets, and in goods markets, should rule out even momentary deficits if relative prices matter. Imbalances rely on international price differences and/or differential returns on assets. Neither of these relative prices should be out of line for too long, according to the logic of market integration. Thus, in theory, smooth adjustment in the 19th century had to rely on extreme price flexibility and highly efficient financial markets. But, again, reality was seemingly different.

A deeper explanation for sustained, but benign, imbalances, focuses on credibility. To understand credibility, let us focus again on the implicit and unwritten "rules of the game" of the gold standard. The focus is on central banks such as the Bank of England, the Bank of France (Banque de France), and the Reichsbank. Central banks, like the Bank of England, should have

---

[6] The current account consists largely of the sum of exports and imports of goods and services. This is the trade balance. The remainder, mostly small in this period, is accounted for by (net) migrant remittances, (net) repatriated profits and investment income, and (net) unilateral transfers. In some instances, remittances were significant, according to Esteves and Khoudour-Castéras (2009). Net capital inflows equals the difference between capital inflows (new borrowing from abroad/new foreign liabilities) and capital outflows (new lending to foreign residents/new foreign assets).

played by the rules of the gold standard game in order to make the gold standard work effectively. What were those rules?

The first rule relates to monetary policy. Maintaining the gold standard required central banks to move interest rates appropriately in response to the trade balance. A trade deficit necessitated raising interest rates and contractionary monetary policy.[7] Raising domestic interest rates drew in capital and gold and tempered the trade deficit by creating a deflationary tendency. Higher interest rates are associated with more expensive credit, lower aggregate demand, and lower prices. This policy change could in principle correct a deficit. A surplus country should have done the opposite and lower policy rates. The consequence of this rule was that nations forfeited their autonomy over monetary policy in order to maintain gold convertibility.

But central banks in the major countries rarely obeyed this rule. Arthur Bloomfield studied the issue and noticed that before World War I, central banks often acted in a manner *opposite* to that required. Contrary to the prescribed orthodoxy, central banks in major countries typically did not move interest rates in the appropriate direction that the trade imbalance would "require." For instance, as gold leaked out of a country, interest rates did not rise immediately. This empirical anomaly led to further research on how the classical gold standard actually worked.

The answer was credibility. According to economists Michael Bordo and Ronald MacDonald, the classical gold standard functioned as a "target zone." Market expectations of policy actions that would be taken in the *long run* were shaped by the credibility of the commitment to the gold standard (or lack of it). When the going got tough, most countries would inevitably get going, raising interest rates to protect gold reserves.

How did a country achieve credibility in practice? When a nation had credibility, financial markets believed that the nation would eventually raise interest rates when it became absolutely necessary to do so. In a target zone, an exchange rate fluctuates within proscribed limits (in the gold standard period this was plus or minus fractions of a percentage of the official par value exchange rates referred to as the gold points). Within these bounds, policymakers achieve monetary autonomy (i.e., they do not have to play by the "rules"). When the exchange rate is getting near the boundaries, expectations matter. Capital markets expect an eventual policy change that will

---

[7] The rule is symmetric, so a surplus requires lower interest rates. Whether surplus or deficit countries make such changes, and in what relative proportion, is a long-standing debate about which type of country (surplus or deficit) must bear the "burden of adjustment."

maintain the peg and which will be consistent with the rules of the game even if contemporaneously the rules are being "violated." In this case, markets bet that a depreciating exchange rate will eventually appreciate. Instead of selling a currency short, markets will go long on the currency. This increase in demand for the once-depreciating currency acts to appreciate the exchange rate back toward parity. A trade deficit can be "covered" in the short run with capital inflows instead of losses in gold. These capital inflows may consist of short-term loans instead of long-term development loans.

Cooperation was another way to survive. Cooperation had similar results to what modern economists call *reserve pooling*. In the 19th century, this type of cooperation took place on a largely ad hoc basis. At times, currencies threatened to break through the gold point boundary. Gold would be drained, and convertibility of a currency could be threatened. This would result in a currency crisis or a sharp and sudden change in the exchange rate. At times of incipient currency crises, some central banks asked for golden lifelines from foreign central banks. Loans of gold from countries not under speculative attack to countries facing pressure on gold reserves helped in numerous instances. In the Baring crisis of 1890, the Bank of England borrowed £3 million from the Bank of France and contracted for another £1.5 million from the Bank of Russia. In 1898, the German Reichsbank sought and received assistance from England and France. In 1907, the Bank of England again turned to the Bank of France and the Reichsbank. Numerous other instances of cooperation occurred throughout the 19th century, as Barry Eichengreen has emphasized.

Interest rate movements, short-term capital flows, and cooperation were not always sufficient. When all else failed, governments and central banks could take matters into their own hands by physically limiting gold flows. So-called gold devices, an early example of "capital controls" or "exchange controls," were sometimes employed by the Bank of England and even more so at the Bank of France and the Reichsbank. When necessary, these central banks restricted gold outflows in order to protect the convertibility of the currency. When adverse speculation on a currency faded, such controls could be relaxed, and the currency could be level at its par value again.

In an influential and insightful paper, Michael Bordo and Finn Kydland described the gold standard as a "contingent rule," pointing out that temporary abandonment of policies compatible with a hard peg in the face of visible turmoil like a war or major economic shock was indeed possible.[8]

---

[8] See Bordo and Kydland (1995).

Expectations of resumption of convertibility would work to reinforce stability. If an exchange rate was depreciating, authorities would be expected to take disinflationary measures in the near future. Market speculation on this led to stabilization. But it is important to realize that this explanation's foundation is the ultimate expectation that central banks and governments will eventually act to correct disequilibria and maintain price stability and that it is in their interest to do so. This was an expectation that was radically altered after World War I. As we shall see, this loss of credibility contributed to the severity of the Great Depression.

The target zone/contingent rule parable, with credibility and cooperation as the cornerstones, helps explain the stability of the classical gold standard in the leading countries. This parable also explains the failure of the gold standard to be synonymous with stability in the "periphery" prior to 1914 and then later for all countries in the inter-war period. There is a key similarity between the "periphery" pre-1913 and what happened to many countries in the inter-war period. In both instances, nations lacked credibility or could not rely on cooperation.

The Rules of the Game: Balance of Payments and Stability

Evidence of the great stability and deep interdependence enjoyed by economically advanced countries during the classical gold-standard period abounds. Some economists refer to the "core" countries in this context, including Great Britain, France, Germany, Belgium, Netherlands, Denmark, Sweden, and Switzerland. Between 1880 and 1913, exchange rates in the core rarely deviated by more than one-half of a percentage point from their legal gold parities ($4.86/1£ in the United States–Great Britain case). Such deviations from parity as arose were quickly eliminated. The average deviation from parity was essentially zero.

In these core countries, adjustment of current accounts back to balance rarely posed a problem due to price flexibility, credibility, and cooperation. Central banks raised interest rates when and if necessary. Markets expected this would happen, and the commitment to do so was credible. Major financial crises occurred, but again, most of the core countries managed them well enough. Between 1880 and 1914, none of the core countries lost convertibility of their currency into gold. In sum, these nations experienced great stability under the classical gold standard. This stability was coupled with persistent economic growth, flourishing trade, strong investment, and low price variability. Trade integration worked to promote productivity growth, to increase competition, and to raise welfare of consumers by keeping the cost of living low and the variety of goods high. Investment made workers more productive and drove the second industrial revolution. Low price variability allowed for actors to make reliable expectations about the future.

But not all countries had such luck, nor were they as credible. The so-called periphery faced greater instability. Many nations, including Russia, Italy, Greece, Spain, Argentina, Chile, Brazil, Mexico, Japan, and even the United States, faced much greater exposure to instability. These countries faced economically harmful exchange rate variability and currency crashes. Banking crises and government debt defaults were more prevalent here than in the core.

These countries lacked the financial depth and political will to sacrifice monetary policy and economic growth for exchange rate stability. Therefore, they generally lacked credibility. While they did attempt to join the gold standard and navigate the choppy waters of the international financial system, shocks would eventually put these countries to the test. The United States eventually graduated to be part of the core by roughly 1900. In the 1880s and 1890s, however, the United States remained a borderline case where adherence to the gold standard was highly contested in domestic politics and frequently doubted by international capital markets, especially in the 1890s.

Financial under-development was a persistent problem. Periphery countries usually had small and illiquid money markets where arbitrage was difficult to carry out. Raising interest rates to remunerate skeptical investors was infeasible. Finding competitive quotes for sellers at the right moment was challenging. Such a country had to keep its banking system from extending too much credit, enact a fiscal policy that did not lead to over-borrowing, and ensure sufficient gold was on hand in the financial system. None of these were easily achieved in environments featuring political instability, low constraints on the executive branch of government, and generally weak institutional frameworks.

So-called sudden stops were a common problem. They often unfolded like this. Capital flowed to a country promoting railroad construction or experiencing a real estate and population boom. These international capital flows often "stopped" precipitously (hence the name *sudden stop*) due to international financial shocks that changed risk appetites or due to a local economic shock like a harvest failure, revolution, war, or banking panic.

The balance of payments identity explains immediately why a sudden stop is often followed by a sharp rise in the trade surplus. Without capital inflows, a trade deficit cannot be financed. Exports must rise and imports must fall. Reserves could also be used to pay for imports or accumulated interest on debt, but only for so long. Speculation about the exchange rate could quickly drain a nation of reserves. To boost exports, the exchange rate must depreciate or severe deflation must occur. Economic recession occurs as building and investment cease. Financial markets expect borrowers will be unable to repay hard currency loans as the exchange rate falls or as the economy crumbles. Interest rates and the risk premium required to satisfy skeptical investors rise.

Eventually, the currency would be devalued. The goal would be to promote recovery and repayment of debt with exports. There were side effects of this strategy. The banking and financial system could grind to a halt due to slower economic growth. Repaying foreign debt payable in hard currency or gold raised the specter of public and private debt default. Eventually the entire financial system could implode. Argentina (1890), Brazil (1890–1891), Greece (1885), and Portugal (1891) are several examples of this dynamic, but Chile (1887), Italy (1893), and Spain (1882) experienced similar outcomes.

Canada, Australia, and the United States had slightly different experiences. These were among the countries without a central bank but reasonably developed financial markets. All of them continuously maintained the gold standard between 1880 and 1914 despite financial turbulence. Public finances were also relatively strong from the 1850s. Canada and Australia relied on capital inflows to promote development. Australia had a weak and unregulated banking system, whereas the US banking system was fragmented and prone to local shocks transmitted nationally through domestic money market arrangements.

In the early 1890s, Australia had a major real estate and credit boom, financed by British lending, turn into bust. The banking system collapsed. Australia suffered very slow economic growth in the 1890s. The United States had perennial banking panics (1873, 1882, 1893, 1907), and currency speculation blighted the nation in the early 1890s. A protracted national debate about abandoning the gold standard had come to a head. Later, a banking crisis emerged in 1907, and the US Treasury called upon JP Morgan to rescue the financial system with loans and guarantees. US banks exercised the right to temporarily suspend the convertibility of bank deposits into gold throughout the period. The United States managed to grow its economy despite the financial headwinds.

Canada possessed a stable banking system, in marked contrast to that of its neighbor to the south—the United States. Canada's system was modeled on the 18th-century Scottish banking system which was a system characterized by financial stability. The Canadian banking system survived moments of stress by virtue of cooperation with London banks, which extended emergency credit lines, and by enacting temporary measures to forestall incipient liquidity crises. The high level of market power (there were less than a dozen Canadian banks while in the United States there were over ten thousand) and the diversification benefits of extensive branch networks also helped foster stability.

The Reality and Record of Financial Stability and Instability

As argued above, there was a large credibility gap between the core and periphery in this period. Core countries achieved significant stability. Exchange rates remained stable, and financial crises were rare. Poor, small, and financially underdeveloped countries frequently suffered large shocks. Printing excessive amounts of paper money, depreciation, and volatility were not uncommon. Financial ruin stalked the periphery. The following sections explore the historical record of capital flows, financial stability, and exchange rate regimes between 1800 and 1914.

Capital Flows as a Cause of Financial Instability

Global capital flows were the hallmark of the first wave of globalization. Global financial crises also featured prominently. The first of five such crises between 1820 and 1913 started in the mid-1820s. The first wave of capital went to Latin America in the 1820s shortly after independence. New governments borrowed to consolidate their new regimes and to build infrastructure. These new nations lacked a reliable tax base and fiscal system, so they were forced to borrow. Initial optimism among lenders from Europe led to outright dismay within years. Political instability and unfavorable global market conditions led to the inability or unwillingness to repay by the mid-1820s. A number of new Latin American nations defaulted on their debts in this decade.

Before the bubble crashed, Gregor MacGregor, a Scottish-born fraudster, duped under-informed British savers into investing in a non-existent Central American nation of untold potential called Poyais. This fraud sent further shock waves through the markets when it was disclosed. The supply of foreign capital for investment quickly dried up. The defaults and depredations shattered the returns accruing to British investors, leading to large losses.

The next crisis would occur in the late 1830s and early 1840s. International capital flows resumed in the early 1830s. This time, they aimed to help develop the infrastructure of the United States as well as poorer countries within Europe. Foreign capital helped build canals and assisted the westward settlement of the emerging nation. State debts doubled between 1835 and 1842, with half of the debt being held in Britain. States and state-sponsored banks borrowed to build the canals and other "internal improvements."

Between 1841 and 1843, nine US states, including Michigan, Pennsylvania, and Maryland, defaulted on their foreign-held debts. Mississippi and Florida refused to pay significant portions of outstanding debt, ultimately repudiating their obligations. Governor A. G. McNutt of Mississippi, who three years earlier had sponsored the issue of five million dollars in bonds, vetoed a proposal by the legislature to repay, striking an unrepentant, anti-Semitic, and anti-foreign note in his veto message.

The debt default demonstrates the "agency problem." Local and state governments issued bonds payable with receipts from land sales and bank profits. Over-investment ensued. Governments, the agents of foreign investors entrusted to invest prudently, could not be held accountable. When revenues failed to materialize due to a sudden economic downturn, the system crashed. Debt went unpaid. The defaults led the states in question to be "blacklisted" on London stock markets until the mid-20th century. To avoid future problems, many states passed balanced-budget amendments that still exist today.

Yet another global financial meltdown started in 1873. By the late 1860s and early 1870s, foreign investment was booming again. Improvements in communication due to the telegraph and shorter shipping times helped European investors to improve their information about borrowers. Places as diverse as Egypt and the Ottoman Empire, India, New Zealand, Brazil, Mexico, the United States, and Canada all benefited from a new wave of enthusiasm for foreign lending. Railway lines and other heavy infrastructure received a large share of European capital.

Once again, the boom-bust cycle of international lending emerged. The boom in Austria-Hungary called the *Gründerzeit* ended in the *Gründerkrach* financial panic of 1873. This may have kicked off an international crisis of epic proportions. About fourteen countries defaulted in 1876, including Egypt, Turkey, and Mexico. The former two economies had borrowed to bolster the revenue of their governments and to build palaces instead of investing in infrastructure. In addition, the decline in the price of cotton after the end of the American Civil War decreased available resources for repayment. The global economic slowdown of the 1870s made it virtually impossible to repay their debts.

Although it may have been more virtuous ex ante, building infrastructure was not sufficient to avoid crisis. The United States had furiously been extending its railway network in the 1860s, completing the transcontinental railway in 1869. The United States endured a severe banking and financial crisis in 1873. This crisis was associated with a notorious corruption scandal associated with construction of the transcontinental railway and other branch lines. The crisis implicated the highest echelons of government, including several prominent congressmen.

Some countries avoided crisis and are illustrative. Despite borrowing on international markets, non-defaulters included Brazil, Canada, New Zealand, and India. Brazil benefitted from its political system. Large landowners held Brazilian bonds and had veto power over the emperor's plans for taxing and spending. In Canada and New Zealand, strong economic growth based on exports of necessary commodities to Britain limited capacity of the government to borrow, and close relationships with London banks who could be incentivized to rollover loans in the short term kept these countries from defaulting. India had the backing of the British Empire too.

The next global financial crisis began in the early 1890s. The late 1880s witnessed yet another round of enthusiasm for overseas lending. By the early 1890s, two significant emerging economies, Argentina and Australia, suffered major banking crises with long-lasting economic effects. While Australia's government did not default on its sovereign debt, Argentina's did. Argentina's currency also dropped precipitously, but Australia's held stable. The ultimate impact of this global crisis was a staggering economic depression in Argentina and Australia. In Australia, many financial institutions failed, and GDP dropped by up to 20% from its peak in 1889. Both countries took a decade to recover from the shock. Other nations with pre-existing financial weaknesses, from Brazil to Germany, witnessed banking panics, output losses, and currency instability. The two crises morphed into a global financial pandemic, the first global crisis since the 1870s.

Argentina's crisis originated in the 1880s when the government enacted a significant banking reform. The government obliged banks to limit their loans (or note issues, as they were called at the time) 100% with government bonds. This policy was mutually beneficial for the financial sector as well as the government since the government could expand its cash flow on the back of direct bank advances while the banks could now issue more loans backed by government issues. Intense land speculation, railway construction, and infrastructure building accompanied this "fiesta financiera." The government added an incentive to lend into the real estate boom by guaranteeing mortgage loans. Foreign banks from London to Berlin brought to market new loans for Argentina's federal and municipal governments, even holding some Argentinean assets on their own accounts.

In 1890, the Buenos Aires Water and Drainage Company failed to repay its obligations, sparking a major international financial crisis. Baring Brothers, established in 1762, was a notable and respected member of the London merchant banking community. The bank was deemed insolvent due to the Argentine defaults. This situation was kept quiet, momentarily, while the Bank of England arranged for a "lifeboat" injection of capital to save the failing bank and to prevent contagion. Rumor soon spread throughout the City of London that a major banking house was likely to fail, sparking a run for liquidity.

The financial contagion was global. Neighboring countries' borrowing costs skyrocketed. European creditors pulled their funds out of Argentina and limited new borrowing. International investors assumed that if one Latin American country was failing, then others must have similar problems. In addition to purely informational spillovers, financial collapse in Europe threatened an economic downturn, lower import demand, and lower revenue for Argentina's neighbors with key trading partners in Europe. International financial flows dried up, postponing development plans for many countries outside of Europe.

Italy also experienced a major crisis in 1893. Italy joined the gold standard in 1884. A massive credit boom ensued. The government deficit rose to 5% of GDP. Rome experienced a land boom. Loosely regulated banks competed to issue mortgages of dubious quality. Why not? After all, the Pope himself had lobbied the government to insure the liabilities of the Banca Romana.

A series of negative shocks hit the country starting in 1887, when a trade war with France erupted. Capital from France ceased to flow to Italy, putting pressure on the gold reserve. Interest rates in global capital markets continued to rise due to events in Argentina and London. By 1893, the Banca Romana had gone bankrupt, an inquiry finding massive fraud and a hopeless balance sheet. In the same year, the country exited the gold standard and the prime minister, Giolitti, was forced from office.

The global economy would endure yet another major global crisis in 1907. This was the last major crisis before World War I. After 1900, the international financial system roared back to life. The geographic spread of capital flows was unlimited, with countries receiving a share of the funds in proportion first to their size then in relation to their growth prospects, and available information. Some economic historians believe that the spark that set this crisis off was the 1906 San Francisco earthquake and the devastating fire that ensued. Insurance companies in London took heavy losses, creating higher global interest rates and a demand for liquidity.[9] The Bank of England raised the discount rate from 3.5% to 7% in late 1906.

As monetary conditions tightened, financial crises soon erupted in Canada, France, Germany, Sweden, Denmark, Chile, Japan, and the United States, among others. In the United States, the economic and financial fallout was so severe that the nation resolved to end the cycle of boom-bust-panic that had regularly occurred since the Civil War. Congress would ultimately approve the creation of a new central bank for the United States. The Federal Reserve, a modern central bank, was founded in 1914. The Fed's mission was to make the currency more "elastic" and to promote the international usage of the US dollar.

The outbreak of World War I in the summer of 1914 disrupted international financial markets, a shock from which these markets never fully recovered. By late August 1914, nearly all nations had suspended gold shipments and the gold standard. Capital flows were scarce, and the world prepared for war.

Summary

The rise of global integration between the 1820s and 1914 was unprecedented. Technological and economic changes helped to bring nations closer

---

[9] See Odell and Weidenmier (2004).

together than ever before. The resulting increase in global economic competition undoubtedly forged a more efficient allocation of resources, leading to greater prosperity for most who participated actively in the global economy.

On the other hand, integration brought greater inter-dependence and inter-connection. Capital flows combined with the fixed exchange rates of the gold standard created new constraints for nations. Some nations were able to cope with these constraints and managed to stay afloat. Other countries, often those in the periphery, tried in vain to participate in the global economy and to follow the leading nations. Soon these nations found out that they often lacked the credibility that was requisite to maintaining stability. Recurrent financial crises and endemic economic instability was a natural result. At worst, these crises delayed development for many countries; at best, they were associated with extreme volatility and economic challenges.

Were the benefits of integration less than the costs of increased inter-dependence? It is unlikely to be the case, though no one has attempted to quantify the issue. Many nations willingly participated in the first wave of globalization, so that it is likely the aggregate net benefits for the diverse interest groups involved were positive. Even if US farmers voiced concerns about being beholden to world price patterns, others in the economy amassed huge fortunes, while many others found their material lives had dramatically improved. Even if a country like Argentina or Canada lived at the whim of British interest rates, the increase in productive capital that international markets afforded may have been worthwhile. Untold numbers of European and Asian immigrants made better lives for themselves and their families in the global economy. The economies that sent them to these new frontiers benefitted from higher wages and inflows of remittances too. This is not to deny that a vocal minority of nativist workers in the receiving countries, especially in the United States, felt the heat of intensified competition and a perceived a dilution of their social and cultural dominance.

There is one prominent exception to this idea that the aggregate benefits obviously outweighed the costs. European colonies were forced to open up by imperialistic aims. Many of these places were involuntarily brought into the global economy. Whether these economies benefitted in the long run or not remains a matter of great debate. Whatever the case may be, it cannot be denied that the global economy impinged on nearly every aspect of daily life for almost everyone on the planet in this period. The global economy had emerged in an irreversible and inexorable process.

6

The Great Migrations

Many places around the world still exhibit the ethnic, cultural, and linguistic legacy of the great migrations of the 19th century today. These movements of people were undoubtedly the largest and most sustained long-distance population movements in history. By and large, the majority of these movements were voluntary. Migration was a natural consequence of the technological and policy changes which also shaped the explosion in international trade in the period. Demographic trends also mattered.

In the 19th century, only minimal formal barriers to resettlement and cross-border movement existed. Passports were not in use and visa requirements had yet to appear. Immigration from certain areas was strongly encouraged by many local governments, especially in the "southern cone" of Latin America (i.e., Argentina, Brazil, Chile, and Uruguay), Canada, and Australasia (Australia and New Zealand). Immense declines in transportation costs ignited this explosion of migration, but a range of other forces discussed below also pushed migration higher. Immigration had a number of important consequences for trade, capital flows, and the global business cycle.

A historically unprecedented share of the world's population moved across long distances between 1850 and 1914. Today, cities such as London, Paris, Singapore, Sydney, Toronto, Los Angeles, and New York have high fractions of the population who are foreign-born. However, the foreign-born as a percentage of the total population in the major receiving nations has never been higher than in the last decades of the 19th century and the first decade of the 20th century. In the United States in 1910, roughly 14.5% of the population was foreign-born. In Argentina, the ratio was still higher at 30%. Singapore, part of the British-controlled "Straits Settlements," had an incredibly high rate of immigration of 993 people for every 1,000 residents.

Significant international movements occurred between Europe and the Americas between 1800 and 1914. Roughly forty-five million people moved east-to-west from Europe to the Americas in these years. By the 1850s, the inflow of Europeans into the Americas finally exceeded that of the coerced

One from the Many. Christopher M. Meissner, Oxford University Press. © Oxford University Press 2024.
DOI: 10.1093/oso/9780199924462.003.0006

Africans who had been enslaved. In Asia, it is estimated that more than fifteen million people left their place of birth in India and China for places like Burma, Malaysia, and Thailand with a small fraction embarking for the Americas. Between 1881 and 1910, the number of immigrants moving to the principal Southeast Asian receiving areas totaled nearly 3.6 million—equaling about 60% of those arriving in the United States during the period. The highly integrated international labor markets of the period led not only to cultural change but to economic transformation affecting job opportunities and wages, the skill composition of the labor force, the pattern of international trade and capital flows, and even the business cycle and balance-of-payments adjustment.

Wage Gaps—The Driving Force for Migration

At the time, the incentive to migrate was dominated by wage differences. Workers who could earn more abroad than at home had an incentive to move from the low-wage labor market to the high-wage labor market. Of course, economic, physical, social, and psychic costs of moving were not insignificant. Still, in statistical study after statistical study, the wage gap is a significant determinant of the magnitude of migration between any two countries.

Wage gaps existed, in part, because of differences in factor endowments—primarily the amount of labor relative to the land area of a local market. Where the population-to-land ratio was low, as it was in almost all the Americas, real wages were high. Land, food, and other important raw materials, including housing material, fuel, and wool or cotton, being relatively inexpensive in such places allowed workers to enjoy a high standard of living. In China, India, or Japan, as in many parts of Europe, relatively high population density put downward pressure on real wages and the cost of a basic standard of living was relatively high. The vast majority of the population lived at a subsistence level. Besides factor endowments, productivity advantages due to technological differences in industry or agriculture as well as institutional differences in labor markets also played a role in driving differences in the marginal product of labor (i.e., wages).

All else equal, workers are likely to improve their standard of living by moving from high-density/low-wage regions to low-density/high-wage regions. In the 19th century, workers in the Atlantic economy moved *en masse* out of Europe and into the Americas (Figure 6.1). For Ireland (net)

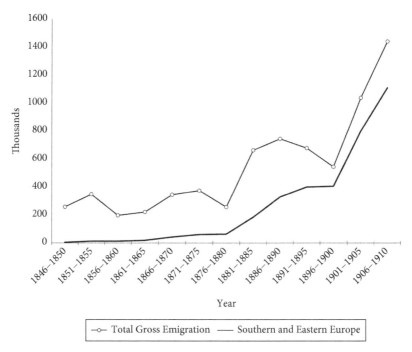

Figure 6.1 Gross Inter-Continental Emigration from Europe, 1846–1910
Source: Chiswick and Hatton (2004) © Copyright by the National Bureau of Economic Research

emigration between 1850 and 1913 represented 44% of the population in 1913. The same calculation yields a ratio of 38% for Italy between 1870 and 1913, 24% for Norway, and 14% for Sweden. Meanwhile, France "lost" less than 1% of its 1913 population to emigration.

In India, people moved to less-densely-settled plantation economies both in Asia and even to the West Indies. Both regions provided greater economic opportunities and wages were potentially higher. A significant number of Chinese crossed the Pacific Ocean, landing in California, beginning with the gold rush of 1848 until their free entry into the United States was halted in 1882 with the Chinese Exclusion Act.

Who Went Where and When?

One of the main receiving countries in the 19th century was the United States. Immigrants early in the century arrived from Northwestern Europe,

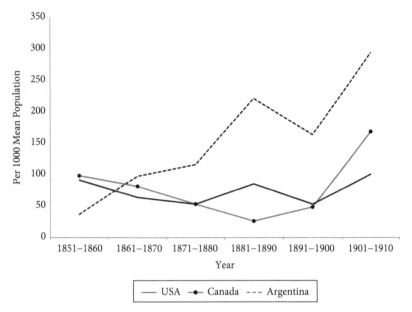

Figure 6.2 Total Immigration, Rates per 1,000 (mean) Population, USA, Argentina, and Canada, 1851–1910

Source: Author's calculations. Immigration data from Willcox (1929), population data underlying Clemens and Williamson (2004a)

including Great Britain and Ireland. By the 1870s, immigration from Germany and Scandinavia dominated. From the 1880s, people came largely from Southern and Eastern Europe: Italy; the Habsburg Empire; Ukraine/Russia, and so forth.

Out of all countries and colonies in Latin America, the southern cone received the largest number of European immigrants prior to 1914. In Brazil, immigration from Portugal and Italy dominated, although a significant number of Germans and Eastern Europeans also arrived. Italians and Spaniards made up the bulk of inflows to Argentina. Chile's immigrants had backgrounds mainly in Southern Europe, but a sizeable German population also took root in Chile. Figure 6.2 shows that the immigration rates as a share of the resident population for Argentina were twice as high as those seen in Canada and the United States. Figure 6.3 illustrates that in the United States, the foreign-born share of the population was never below 10% between 1850 and 1914, hovering around 14% from the 1860s until the eve of World War I.

Within Europe, movement within and across international boundaries also occurred. After the Irish famine of the late 1840s, tens of thousands of

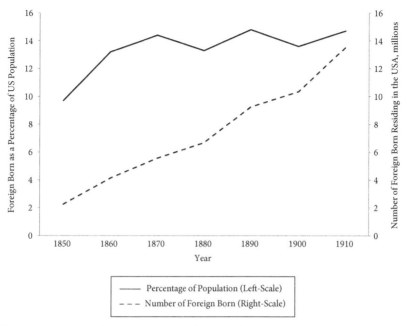

Figure 6.3 Foreign Born Residing in the United States and Foreign-Born as a Share of the Population, 1850–1910
Source: Gibson and Lennon (1999)

ethnic Irish resettled in England. By 1851, it was reported that nearly half of Liverpool's population consisted of Irish immigrants. More generally, rural residents of many countries, especially those of Eastern and Southern Europe tended to flock to the rising industrial centers and cities within Europe like Paris, the Rhine valley, Southern England, and the Low Countries. Jobs in these places might have paid higher wages, but they did not necessarily provide better living conditions. There were extreme environmental problems associated with modern industrial and urban life. Air quality was atrocious and water treatment was minimal, leading to significantly lower life expectancies and high morbidity for urban residents. In order to attract workers, real wages had to offset or compensate workers for these urban dis-amenities.

In Asia, a large number of laborers departed from India, gravitating toward areas of large plantation agriculture across South and Southeast Asia. These workers were referred to as "coolies" and were attracted by steady-wage employment on palm groves, on rubber and sugar plantations, and in tin mining. A small fraction of movement out of India was by shopkeepers and small entrepreneurs. Indian emigrants were sometimes brought on contract to the Caribbean, where they also participated in agricultural and plantation activity. Guyana, Trinidad, and Dutch Guyana (Suriname) took 4/5 of the roughly five hundred thousand Indian migrants to the Americas.

East Asian emigration was also significant. It is estimated that more than twenty million Chinese left their homes in mainland China during the period, largely ending up in Southeast Asia. A number of Chinese emigrants sailed for the United States beginning with the gold rush of 1848. The total number of Chinese immigrants in the United States just prior to the Chinese Exclusion Act of 1882 was between 100,000 and 150,000, accounting for up to 1 in 10 people in California. Early on, some Chinese came to mine gold, earning San Francisco the nickname "Old Gold Mountain" in Chinese. Chinese immigrants also participated in building the rapidly expanding railway infrastructure, including the trans-continental railway (Figure 6.4), while others found success in local agriculture. A number of Chinese also

ACROSS THE CONTINENT.

Figure 6.4 The Transcontinental Railway: Chinese Workers in California's Sierra Nevada

Source: Online Archive of California and Bancroft Library

Notes: Joseph Becker, "Across the continent, the snow sheds on the Central Pacific Railroad, in the Sierra Nevada Mountains"

went to Latin America. Cuba and Peru received the most with perhaps around 250,000 arrivals between 1847 and 1900.

In Africa, fewer people moved out to other continents, probably in part due to low land-labor ratios, but also due to outright racism and other barriers in the potential receiving countries. While the transatlantic slave trade had been abolished by the early 1800s, human cargo still crossed the Atlantic mainly to Brazil until the 1880s. In addition, the Indian Ocean/ Middle East slave trade continued, carrying up to 5–10 million people out of Africa in this period.

Africa also received some immigrants. A small number of descendants of slaves and freed slaves (up to 20,000) from the United States and the Caribbean embarked upon an experiment in nation-building in Liberia beginning in the 1820s. South Africa (and its predecessor colonial outposts like the Transvaal, Orange Free State, etc.) and southeastern Africa received some European immigration and new settlement. In 1911, 255,000 people, or 20% of the population, were foreign-born and of European origins, with a much smaller share from South Asia (British India) and Southeast Asia (Malaysia).

Meanwhile, a small number of Europeans worked the helms of the colonial apparatus, but the total number of European-born people residing in Africa (excluding South Africa) never exceeded a small fraction of the population. The population of Australasia (i.e., Australia and New Zealand) grew quickly due to immigration from the United Kingdom and later from Italy. The percentage of foreign-born was 22% in 1901. The global labor market was concentrated in the Atlantic-facing economies, with another locus of activity in South and Southeast Asia.

What Moves You?

The costs of migration were extraordinarily high at the beginning of the 19th century, but they fell dramatically prior to 1914. Many of the same forces that affected the transportation costs of commodities affected the movement of people. The pattern of migration between Europe and the Americas demonstrates that the costs of moving were not the same for any given country, nor were they constant across time. Moreover, even holding costs constant, the economic conditions at home also mattered for migration decisions.

Probably the single biggest contributor to the massive rise in migration was the fall in transportation costs across the 19th century. By making it more affordable to travel long distances, intercontinental migration received a strong boost. The increasing availability of affordable railway connections as well as declines in the costs of maritime navigation helped turn potential migrants into actual migrants.

European emigrants had several stages in their journey to American shores. First, they had to move from the interior of their country to arrive at a port with direct or indirect connections to North or South America. Obviously, the development of the railway, canals, and better roads facilitated this type of movement. Once arrived at a port city, European immigrants boarded ships bound directly for the Americas. Often passengers from Eastern Europe passed through a hub port such as Southampton, Hamburg, Genoa, or Le Havre first, where the largest passenger liners of the day could take them to the Americas in less than two weeks. Most migrants traveled "third-class," enjoying only minimal frills during their voyage. The Cunard lines, White Star (notorious for deploying the Titanic), HAPAG, and NDL dominated the passenger lines between North America and northwestern Europe.[1] These companies together carried about 50% of all immigrants to the United States between 1881 and 1913.[2] Their extensive advertising campaigns and frequent rate wars, not unlike airline fare battles today, capitalized on a latent desire to move out of Europe.

Shipping costs were not the only important constraint on migration, of course. A number of other forces determined the level of migration. Unless they had concrete information about their destination, few migrants could imagine traveling more than 5,000 kilometers in the hope of securing higher wages. To obtain better information, migrants relied on established "first-movers" who could act as a contact and source of information in the destination. First-movers could be family members, acquaintances from the local village, or even professionals who specialized in matching immigrants with employers. Chinese immigrants in California often relied on the assistance of benevolent co-fraternities (*huiguan*). A number of companies combined in the 1880s to form the Chinese Six Companies or the Chinese Consolidated Benevolent Association (CCBA). Contemporary anti-immigration

---

[1] HAPAG is the acronym for Hamburg-Amerikanische Packetfahrt-Aktien-Gesellschaft while NDL stands for Norddeutsche Lloyd. The two companies merged in 1970 to become HAPAG-Lloyd.
[2] See Keeling (1999).

extremists accused these organizations of human trafficking, but it is more plausible to view them as helpful in insuring against the risks of a long-distance move to unfamiliar territory.

Finance for transcontinental moves, necessary for many, was often sourced from household savings, other family members, or possibly even professional agents. Every financial transaction depends on either trust (i.e., information that you are a reasonable risk) or else it relies on a system that can eliminate fraud and make sure creditors will be repaid. Evidently, securing financing for a move was often challenging at a time of low financial development. Without sufficient information about the risks involved, and/or familiarity with the locality, migration would have to be self-financed and hence delayed.

Regardless of transportation costs, demographic forces altered the propensity to migrate as well. Where the population was young and male and had fewer employment opportunities at home, migration would be higher. The demographic transition underway in much of Europe generated an abnormally large excess of births over deaths as infant mortality rates fell. Fertility rates did not immediately fall, leading to large pools of potential migration in many countries. France, experiencing an early demographic transition, had overcome such forces earlier and consequently sent fewer emigrants than other nations in Europe. Oppositely, Spain failed to initiate its demographic transition in this period, which limited emigration from an otherwise less developed, low-wage economy. In the short run, harvest conditions and other shocks like civil unrest might also determine the likelihood of migration. Ireland and India suffered great famines resulting from poor harvests. These were associated with out-migration. From time to time, anti-Semitic pogroms flared up in Eastern Europe, forcing some families to exercise their "exit option" and move abroad.

Figure 6.5 presents one possible framework for thinking about the rate of out-migration from a typical European country in the 19th century. At the beginning of the timeline, risk, information, and credit constraints bind and keep people at home. After this, a few pioneers may leave the locality, because of their adventuresome spirit, better information due to connection to networks beyond the village, or their better financial position. Once established, these pioneers may contact family and friends back home, providing valuable information and possibly financing if the move had been advantageous. This "chain migration," dependent on the structure of the social and family network, accelerates the process of out-migration. Peak emigration

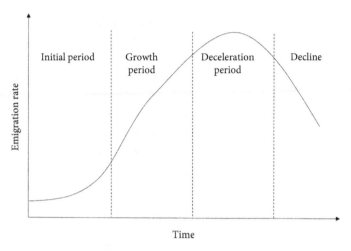

Figure 6.5 Diffusion Model of Emigration
Source: Author's adaptation based on Åkerman (1976), p. 25, Figure 2.2

coincides with the area labeled "deceleration" where the level of the labor supply of the sending area has dwindled. Job opportunities and wages at home are sufficiently high to reduce the economic advantage of leaving. Many of those that remain are elderly, too young to move, or too attached to leave. Migration flows eventually decline as the process continues.

Large wage gaps persisted between localities in the 19th century. Figure 6.5 speaks to the question posed by one economic historian which is not "why did people move?" but instead "what explains why so few people left?" Indeed, looking at wage differences, the economic gains seem to be very large. However, the slow initial outflow is some evidence that the set of costs and barriers to migration are numerous. In the same way that commodity price gaps often measure the costs of international trade, wage gaps are an indicator of the economic barriers to movement of people. Besides legal limits to immigration, the barriers to the movement of people include demographic and social conditions, capital market "frictions," transportation costs, and also popular sentiment in the receiving countries.

The "Birds of Passage"

While the long-run trend was for convergence of wages between countries, the short-run also holds interesting evidence for the effects of migration.

As the 19th century progressed, information and transport barriers fell sufficiently to support a large amount of back-and-forth migration. By 1914, a significant share, possibly as many as 25% to 30% of immigrants to North and South America had made at least one return trip to their native country.

Some of these returnees may have been attuned to the business cycle. In fact, net migration followed the international business cycle closely, being highly "pro-cyclical." While economists have long recognized that inflows of foreign workers to the United States rose and fell with the international business cycle, new data has shown that outflows—which were significant in magnitude—were actually highly correlated with the business cycle too. In this regard, a rise in *net* immigration corresponded to business cycle upturns while recessions and financial crises brought a lower net flow of people across borders.

The implications of this for wage dynamics in the business cycle are important. First, immigration helped wages become less "pro-cyclical." For example, during an economic upturn, labor supply grew faster than it would have under a no-immigration policy. So, while aggregate labor demand expanded outward during the boom, aggregate labor supply also shifted outward. The effect was that wage growth was smaller than it would have been without immigration. If this is true, economic expansions could persist longer since wage pressures did not drag down profitability. Oppositely, in the downturns, higher emigration provided a safety valve for labor markets. By reducing labor supply at the same time that labor demand was falling, wages would not decline as much as in a no-out-migration scenario.

What is more, the theory of international adjustment suggests that spatially integrated labor markets can make for smoother adjustment in the balance of payments. Assume this time that a country has a negative shock to the demand for its output, and so it begins to run a trade deficit. The result is downward pressure on the aggregate demand for labor. If nominal wages cannot fall quickly, there is a strong possibility for a rise in unemployment. If workers return to their home countries, as the number of job opportunities declines, then the probability of finding employment increases for those who remain. Consequently, the rise in unemployment after a negative shock is smaller than it might be without migration. In economies where labor is highly mobile, the economy can return to full employment more quickly following a negative shock. Figure 6.6 emphasizes the cyclical variations in US immigration. There can be little doubt that the countries in the Atlantic

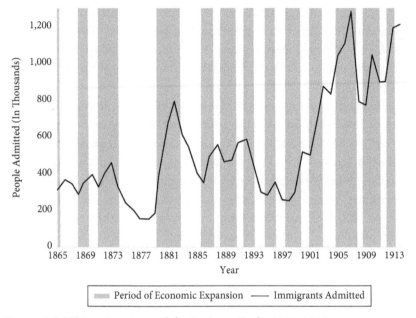

Figure 6.6 US Immigration and the Business Cycle, 1865–1913

Source: Immigration: United States Bureau of the Census, Historical Statistics of the United States (1960) series C88; Business cycle dates: Burns and Mitchell (1947)

economy were better able to adjust to shocks due to this flexibility in international labor markets.

Migrant remittances (cash payments by emigrants to their home countries) were another important force in stabilizing local economies after economic shocks. Anyone who has visited communities where the foreign-born tend to reside might have seen storefronts and advertisements for wire-transfer companies or passed by banks with international connections specializing in such transfers. This financial infrastructure meets the demand of immigrants who regularly send significant portions of their paychecks back to their home country. Western Union, a global leader in international wire transfers today, started business in 1871 in the United States. In the late 19th century, some estimates suggest that immigrants sent home, on average, the equivalent of between 1% and 3% of their home countries' incomes.[3] In the years before World War I, in Italy, remittances made up about 6% of GDP.[4]

---

[3] See Esteves and Khoudour-Castéras (2009).
[4] See A'Hearn and Venables (2011).

Remittances also flowed in toward countries in periods of financial stress in the 19th century, further helping to stabilize an economy. A nation experiencing lower capital inflows usually has to cut consumption dramatically and induce other countries to buy its exports—greater exports often also necessitate a large exchange rate depreciation. But remittances helped to limit the severity of financial crises in the 19th century by maintaining current incomes and consumption. Remittances, therefore, also helped countries to stay on the gold standard since the alternative adjustment mechanism would be to devalue, cut import consumption, and raise exports. International patterns of migration sometimes helped stave off brutal "sudden stops" of capital inflows, extreme turnarounds in the current account, and the disruptive financial crises that tend to accompany such events.

Summary

International labor markets grew much more tightly integrated after 1850. Transportation improvements, growing global demand for commodities requiring labor to be reallocated nearer their source, and demographic changes drove this process. By the eve of World War I, the share of foreign-born in the main receiving countries in the Americas averaged 25% or more. Native wages grew more slowly when immigrants competed directly with natives, but sending countries' wages rose significantly. This process contributed substantially to the observed convergence in living standards in the Atlantic economy in the period. Migration patterns in the Atlantic economy also had a major impact on the business cycle and economic volatility. Less is known about the convergence process in Asia, due to insufficient data, but migration almost surely contributed to convergence in this region too. Immigration tended to provoke a backlash from native workers, especially in the United States. As happens so often today, native workers perceived that they could raise their wages by limiting immigration. Anti-immigration policies emerged strongly between the world wars, as we will see in the next chapter.

7

The Beginning of the End

Backlash to the First Wave of Globalization

The first wave of globalization significantly expanded the intensity of international trade, foreign investment, and migration. As we have seen, there were many drivers of this complex process of global integration. Lower trade and transportation costs certainly boosted integration in all three areas that we have studied. What was the ultimate impact of rising integration? Economists generally believe that integration has the power to improve welfare and increase efficiency. There are other potential (side) effects of globalization, and not all of them are positive.

It is generally understood that trade and integration may benefit some sectors or factors in an economy more than others. Displacement, competition, and change are never easy. These negative consequences can alter the political landscape and can generate un-even gains from integration. Trade disrupts uncompetitive industries and sectors—workers can lose their jobs. Global capital flows may increase financial instability, which can lead to economic misery. Immigration stiffens competition in the labor market. In this chapter, we explore some of the "distributional" issues in globalization by examining the gains to not only the economies overall but also different sectors or interests in an economy. Ultimately, these distributional issues led to fewer political and economic disruptions wherever and whenever economic policy was attuned to the potential for discord and acted effectively to compensate those groups which might have suffered from globalization.

Convergence or Divergence in Economic Outcomes

As discussed in Chapter 3, the Heckscher–Ohlin model of trade predicts that globalization should drive income convergence. Still, the very same model predicts that lower trade costs will raise the returns to land in a

One from the Many. Christopher M. Meissner, Oxford University Press. © Oxford University Press 2024.
DOI: 10.1093/oso/9780199924462.003.0007

land-abundant nation, boosting the incomes of land-owners. Wages in these economies will grow more slowly (or decline) relative to land rents. Oppositely, in labor-abundant countries, wages will be driven upward relative to land rents. Demand for labor rises since these countries will specialize in labor-intensive products. The bottom line is that, although trade raises aggregate welfare and income, some factors will gain from integration while other factors will gain less or even lose.

Even so, in the first wave of globalization, convergence between countries was not guaranteed. Figure 7.1 shows that global income inequality between nations increased during the first wave of globalization. François Bourguignon and Christian Morrisson constructed this figure using data on GDP per person and income shares by income decile for thirty-three countries or groups of countries covering nearly the entirety of the global economy. While Western Europe and the United States experienced strong and persistent economic growth, other regions in Asia and Africa fell behind, and inequality between countries increased. Chapter 3 discussed the logic of agglomeration, which can drive divergence.

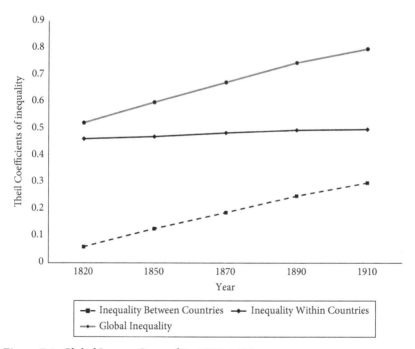

Figure 7.1 Global Income Inequality, 1820–1910

Source: Author's calculations based on data in Bourguignon and Morrisson (2002)

Another explanation for divergence besides agglomeration is the process of European colonization of Africa, Asia, and the Americas, which characterized the period between 1500 and the mid-20th century. Still, colonization alone cannot explain divergence, since some colonies and former colonies like the United States, Canada, or New Zealand did quite well in terms of economic growth. What distinguished the colonies of British India, West Africa, and the Caribbean, which did not grow strongly in this period, from places like Canada, Australia, and New Zealand, which had high and fast-rising incomes? The former places have been referred to as "extractive" colonies, while the latter are called "settler" colonies.

Two types of colonies with very different paths of institutional development emerged. "Settler" colonies possessed European colonists who stayed in residence and built strong-property rights. The institutional framework, the foundation for economic growth, resembled those enjoyed in their origin countries (i.e., Great Britain). In these places, colonists planned to live indefinitely and to build a local economy that would be a "going concern." "Extractive" colonies were institutionally different. Colonists failed to establish strong property rights systems in places like West and Central Africa. These areas, and others around the world with similar environments, were rich in natural resources and/or suitable for production of valuable commodities like palm oil, sugar, cacao, and so on, but they were also rife with tropical diseases such as typhoid, dengue fever, cholera, and malaria. The mortality of European settlers due to these deadly diseases was high. The risky disease environment limited Europeans' interest in outright settlement, which had negative consequences for the institutional environment.

Instead of molding these colonies into the image of the homeland, where the state was considered a "going concern," these colonies became "extractive" enterprises. According to the harsh calculus of the European colonial administrations, investment in the institutional infrastructure that would sustain modern economic growth and industrialization was not worthwhile. The results were weak property rights, encouraging expropriation, limited accountability and constraints on the executive branch of government, and autocratic instead of democratic political processes. According to economists Daron Acemoglu, Simon Johnson, and James Robinson, there is a long-run "persistence" of weak "property rights" and institutions in these areas. Institutional development is slow to change, persistent, or even path dependent. As a result, there is a negative correlation between income

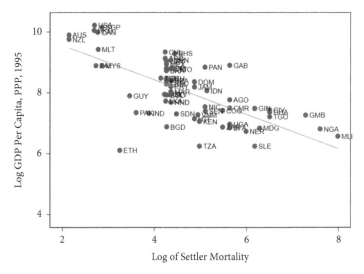

Figure 7.2 GDP per capita in 1995 and "Settler Mortality"

Source: Author's calculations based on Acemoglu, Johnson, and Robinson (2001), Figure 1 and Table A.2

per person even today and "settler mortality" in the centuries prior to 1950 (Figure 7.2).

The trans-Atlantic, African slave trade that was active until the mid-19th century also mattered. Between 1500 and 1900, nearly twelve million Africans were enslaved and sent to work on American commodity plantations (sugar, rice, and cotton). Since its earliest days in the 17th century, the forced labor of slaves allowed European consumers and producers to benefit from lower commodity prices than if free laborers had been employed. European capital was also used to fund the international slave/commodity trade between Africa, the Americas, and Europe, connecting global banking interests with Caribbean plantation owners. What was the long run impact on the European and African economies?

Research by economic historian Nathan Nunn shows how the atrocity of global human trafficking may have helped contribute to persistent divergence between Africa and the rest of the World (Figure 7.3).[1] Areas that lost the largest proportions of their native populations in Africa to the slave trade between the 17th and the 19th century are significantly poorer and less productive than regions (in Africa) that lost fewer souls to the slave trade.

---

[1] See Nunn (2008).

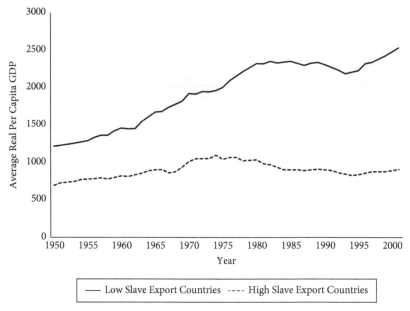

Figure 7.3 GDP per capita 1950–2001 in African Countries and the 19th-Century Atlantic Slave Trade
Source: Nunn (2008)

Larger slave exports occurred where greater ethnic strife was prevalent. On the other hand, rugged geography often protected areas from the slave trade. Those unlucky enough to have been residing in low-lying coastal areas more accessible to European slavers and the local slave traders suffered over the long term because the slave trade itself eroded the social capital (i.e., trust, relationships between people, cultural norms) that is a foundation for economic growth.

Gareth Austin subjects these theses to extensive critical examination.[2] According to Austin, both arguments promote a "reversal of fortune" argument that relies on sketchy data on pre-colonial population density and ethnic identity. It is also questionable, on historical grounds, whether the trans-Atlantic slave trade created aggressive small bands or mini-states that terrorized local populations and led to sustained under-development.

Austin discusses the heterogeneity of colonial experience in Africa in the 19th and early 20th centuries. The experiences of Congo, Soudan, South

[2] See Austin (2008).

Africa, and Uganda illustrate the point. The people of Congo indeed suffered from terrible atrocities and resource extraction. In the "peasant" colony of French Soudan (Mali), similar exploitation of natural resources was unseen. In places like Ghana and Uganda, rural agriculture was led by African "capitalists." Evidence also suggests that even in so-called extractive colonies, European colonizers aimed for longevity of rule. Moreover, European systems of property rights were introduced in Africa in some cases (e.g., in Lagos). In addition, it is not clear that colonies and early states subject to slavery and European exploitation aimed to maximize extraction and banditry. Colonizers and European slave traders exercised less control than postulated, while indigenous rulers had greater agency and ability to avoid excesses than these influential theses argue. In sum, there is ongoing and intense debate about the net impact of colonialism and the European-managed trans-Atlantic slave trade on Africa.

Backlash: Taking Shelter from the Global Economic Storm

The preceding section provided some examples where interaction with the global economy was not clearly a "positive sum" game, or when the global economy was ostensibly unable to generate a bigger global economic "pie." Policymakers have historically been aware of the potential downsides of engagement with the global economy. Politicians and early thinkers from Colbert and List, all the way to Alexander Hamilton, have advocated high tariffs to "protect" and "nurture" the "infant" industries of the less industrialized economies. Tariffs protect local industry from foreign (more advanced) competition. Local producers receive an economic incentive and fill the gap between the restricted foreign supply and domestic demand. The infant industry argument is valid when a period of learning-by-doing is required to become productive and price-competitive with industrial leaders. Ideally, governments remove these tariffs after local industry becomes sufficiently productive.

Politics mattered for trade policy in this period. Politicians, seeking political support, or firmly believing in the gains from protectionism, often espoused the idea of infant industry protection in the 19th century. Interest groups, representing particular industries and sectors, actively (and sometimes successfully) lobbied governments in many cases for higher tariffs. This was especially true when trade costs fell and international competition intensified after the 1860s. In certain cases, coalitions formed, allowing tariffs and protectionism to become a political winner.

In Britain, free trade dominated for most of the 19th century, despite protectionists' best efforts. Activists and advocates of tariffs tried to blame silver-standard countries for "unfair" competition, arguing for tariffs as compensation. Between 1875 and 1900, silver depreciated against gold. Silver-standard countries (mainly in Asia at that point) witnessed persistent exchange rate depreciation against gold-standard countries. By 1900, silver had fallen 60% in value relative to gold. British textile industrialists argued that they faced increased competition from India, driven by this persistent depreciation. By the late 19th century, a loud minority clamored for "fair trade" or tariffs to compensate for the unfair advantage gained by silver-country exporters. Joseph Chamberlain led the campaign for higher tariffs.

Tariffs ultimately remained very low in Great Britain, but elsewhere, a "backlash" to globalization materialized. Tariffs went up quickly after 1870 in many countries (Figure 7.4). Inefficient European grain farmers were under severe pressure in the period. Wheat exported from the United States, Canada, and Argentina threatened the livelihoods of these farmers since New

Figure 7.4 Average Tariff Rate, Twenty-Seven Countries, 1865–1913

Source: Author's calculations based on data underlying Clemens and Williamson (2004a)

World wheat was significantly less costly and of higher quality. Italian pasta makers preferred Canadian durum wheat since it made better pasta, but local Italian farmers naturally felt the pinch. Canadian wheat was a very good substitute for Italian wheat, leaving the local sector with a smaller market share as the Canadian prairies supplied more and more to global markets.

In the postbellum United States, protectionist interests, often those of Northern industrialists, benefitted from high tariffs averaging 50% on a wide range of manufactured goods. In the woolen textile industry, the high average tariff was equivalent to a 300% tax on imports. The woolen tariff was structured in part to protect the woolen manufacturers and in part to offset the high tariffs on imported inputs like raw wool and wool yarn. Hiding behind these tariff barriers seemingly did little to spur productivity growth or increase competitiveness. US exports of woolen textiles never totaled more than a trivial amount of total production.

The tinplate industry also wangled a massive 70% tariff in 1891 after passage of the McKinley Tariff. Current scholarship shows that the tariff was indeed effective at tilting demand toward domestic producers.[3] Still, the iron ore and coal of Pennsylvania, crucial inputs to tinplate, eventually made these tariffs redundant. These abundant supplies helped US producers to lower their costs. The domestic tin plate industry would have come to dominate imports without the tariff, due to the availability of these new, cheaper sources of raw materials.

A similar story emerges from the North American steel rail industry. Early on, in the 1860s, British producers out-competed American producers and captured a large share of the American market. From the 1870s onward, the rail industry benefitted from tariffs above 40% in *ad valorem* equivalent terms. The high tariff itself was probably not crucial to the ultimate outcome since the rail industry ultimately learned to produce more efficiently and also had access to increasingly cheap raw materials like iron ore and coal. Overall, US welfare was apparently not much higher or lower due to the tariff than it might have been without tariffs.[4] There are two clear implications. One is that the tariffs redistributed welfare from consumers and users of rails to the producers. Second, other factors besides tariffs must have been more crucial to industrial success and economic growth than trade policy.

---

[3] See Irwin (2017).
[4] See Head (1994).

Looking at the bigger picture, economic growth in the United States arguably suffered due to high tariffs on capital goods imported from Great Britain, Germany, and other European economies. Tariffs reduced investment in manufacturing, causing long-run growth to be lower. Income per person was 10%–12% lower than it might have been under free trade.[5] On the other hand, in the United States, economic growth was nothing short of persistent, strong, and stable between 1865 and 1913. The United States experienced high economic growth *despite* high tariffs, not because of them. Because the United States had a large and expanding internal market, abundant natural resources, and reasonable levels of competition, the United States was able to shake off the economic drag from its high tariffs.

Several countries in Europe raised tariffs beginning in the 1880s. This "backlash" to globalization led to a considerable slowdown in the growth of international trade for certain countries. In Germany, the "grain invasion"—inexpensive wheat coming from the New World and the plains of Eastern Europe—created a lobby group for agricultural protectionism. Germany's leader, Bismarck, obliged these requests in the 1880s, at the same time raising tariffs on other industrial products.

Other nations in Europe raised tariffs too. In 1892, the French government approved the Méline Tariff benefitting domestic wheat farmers and even some manufacturing industries. The Méline Tariff stifled New World grain imports and European, manufactured imports. While most countries continued to increase their share of trade in GDP, this ratio stagnated between the 1890s and 1914 in France due in part to the new tariffs.

Did countries suffer from higher tariffs? Economic historian Paul Bairoch studied this outbreak of protectionism. He argued that economic growth was not notably lower in these nations than it was in the low-tariff, free trade group of nations like Great Britain, Belgium, and the Netherlands.[6]

In Latin America and other parts of North America, tariffs also remained high. In Canada and Argentina, high duties on selected goods provided much-needed revenue for governments. Canada placed high tariffs on finished products but allowed crucial inputs to be imported at low tariff rates. One of the stated objectives of the "National Policy" was to incentivize industrialization by shielding Canadian manufacturers from American (and foreign) competition. Argentina imposed high tariffs on manufactured

---

[5] See DeLong (1998).
[6] See Bairoch (1972).

consumer goods, sugar, wine, and tobacco but refrained from high tariffs on iron, steel, chemicals, and cotton yarn.

Some recent research by economic historians Kris Inwood and Ian Keay suggests that tariffs spurred investment and entry of new firms in the domestic iron and steel industry in Canada.[7] Still, decreasing unit labor costs and rising domestic demand stemming from high rates of immigration (also incentivized in the National Policy) played a strong complementary role. In Argentina, high tariffs protected nascent, but un-competitive domestic manufacturers. It may be incorrect to argue that Canada and Argentina used tariffs to generate domestic industrial growth and a "structural transformation." The former nations experienced high export-oriented growth specializing in primary goods—minerals, timber, and wheat in Canada and wheat and beef in Argentina's case. As economic growth proceeded, the structure of overall employment gradually shifted into more industrial pursuits, especially in Canada.

Modern research has returned to Bairoch's question. Did tariffs and lower engagement with foreign markets lead to higher or lower income per capita? One influential set of studies for a larger number of countries between 1870 and 1914 suggests that growth of GDP per capita was higher in the years following a rise in manufacturing tariffs.[8] However, one objection to this finding is that countries only applied tariffs cautiously when growth was not at risk. Any drag on growth caused by these tariffs may have been offset by other positive forces contributing to growth. Moreover, the latter set of studies only identifies a short-run effect. Tariffs may have inefficiently reallocated demand to domestic production at the cost of foreign production. It is then no surprise that we find a positive short-run association between tariffs and growth in GDP per capita. Figure 7.5 illustrates, however, that there may even be a long-run relationship. Growth in GDP per capita between 1875 and 1910 is positively related to the level of tariffs in 1870.

The question remains whether a policy of high tariffs helped or hurt long-run economic growth or simply induced a short-run "sugar high" juicing the economy through a redistribution from foreign to domestic demand. While no definitive quantitative evidence exists on this, most studies conclude that long-run growth and overall "welfare" would be hampered by sheltering markets from foreign competition and engaging less with other markets.

---

[7] See Inwood and Keay (2013).
[8] See O'Rourke (2000), Clemens and Williamson (2004b), and Lehmann and O'Rourke (2011).

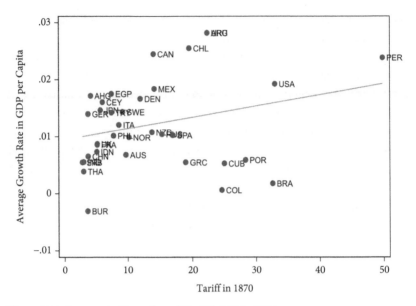

Figure 7.5 Economic Growth and Tariffs, 1870–1910
Source: Author's calculations based on data underlying Clemens and Williamson (2004a)

Evidence from a number of studies in the late 19th century overwhelmingly shows that "market access" (also referred to as "market potential") and general openness-to-trade, whether at the regional or sub-national level, was strongly and positively related to GDP per capita (Figure 7.6).[9] Based on the historical literature, it is prudent to conclude that many other policies and circumstances contribute to economic growth. Industrialization via high tariffs and limitations on foreign competition is neither guaranteed nor is it impossible to achieve without such policies.

The Impact of Immigration

The first wave of globalization unleashed a convergence in real wages as the barriers to the movement of people declined. International trade, where the Heckscher–Ohlin model was relevant, further drove convergence. This

[9] Market potential measures the effective demand for an economy's output and products. After adjusting for trade costs with partner economies, which reduce market potential, it is higher when an economy's trade partners have higher incomes.

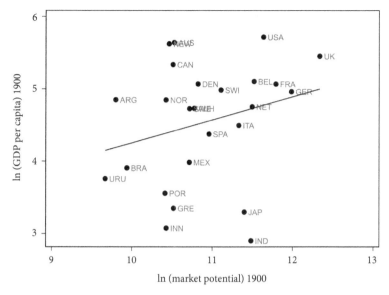

Figure 7.6 GDP per capita and Market Potential, 1900
Source: Author's calculations based on data from Liu and Meissner (2015)

convergence parallels the decline in price gaps in commodity markets previously discussed. In the goods market, arbitrage equalized prices via supply and demand. The impact of migration on local wages can also be understood using some simple economics of the aggregate labor market.

A country's "supply" of total workers available depends on the supply of domestic and foreign workers. Immigration increases the number of hours offered/supplied at each wage. Immigration flattens the aggregate labor supply schedule, and lower wages prevail for all workers at any given level of labor supply. Ostensibly, for this simple reason, organized labor fought to limit immigration in 19th-century America.

It is also immediately obvious why landowners or business owners who receive the proceeds of capital might desire greater immigration. More labor makes land (and capital) more productive. In Brazil, Argentina, Canada, Australia, and New Zealand, subsidies and policies to facilitate European immigration reflected the desire by landowners to lower their wage bills, since labor was a scarce, but key, input in the agricultural/primary sector. Similarly, capitalists in the United States for many decades prior to the 1890s recognized the potential for higher returns to their investments (and hence higher incomes for owners of capital) with more abundant labor.

Many theories assume immigrants are perfect substitutes for domestic workers. In this case, immigration tends to strongly reduce domestic wages. However, when immigrants and locals are "complements" in production, wages of domestic labor decline less when immigration occurs. In fact, in some cases, immigration can actually raise the productivity and incomes of domestic workers. What do we know about the complementarity between foreign and domestic work in history?

In the United States, there is some evidence for complementarity. One estimate by Tim Hatton and Jeffrey G. Williamson suggests that, due to immigration, wages in the United States were 4.5% to 5.5% lower in 1913.[10] Despite massive immigration, this is not a large decline. Immigrants raised the US labor force by as much as 11.6% between 1890 and 1913. This implies an elasticity of substitution between domestic and foreign-born workers of about 3 which is consistent with significant complementarities. It is entirely possible that the relatively small negative impact on wages noted by Hatton and Williamson, despite such strong inflows of labor, was because of such complementarities.

Prior to 1914, formal barriers to migration were extremely limited. However, anti-immigrant sentiment was not unknown. In 1882, the United States established its first limits on immigration based on national origin with the Chinese Exclusion Act. The Chinese Exclusion Act suspended new immigration from China and severely limited the ability of those already resident to reenter the United States. Chinese immigration slowed to a trickle in the following decades to those who could prove to the government they were qualified to immigrate largely for family reasons or those who could evade the border controls.

Where native workers felt economically threatened by the increase in labor supply or where cultural biases persisted, anti-immigrant sentiment remained strong. Organized labor in the United States lobbied strongly and persistently in the closing decades of the 19th century for limits on immigration. The Immigration Act of 1891 denied entry to immigrants with contagious diseases and required immigrants to pass certain other physical and psychological criteria to be admitted.[11] In 1897 and 1898, the US Congress

---

[10] See Hatton and Williamson (1998).

[11] "That the following classes of aliens shall be excluded from admission into the United States . . . All idiots, insane persons, paupers or persons likely to become a public charge, persons suffering from a loathsome or a dangerous contagious disease, persons who have been convicted of a felony or other infamous crime or misdemeanor involving moral turpitude, polygamists, and also any person whose ticket or passage is paid for with the money of another or who is assisted by others to come."

narrowly failed to implement a literacy test that could have decreased immigration by 25% overall and by up to 40% for those arriving from Southern and Eastern Europe.[12]

In 1907 a "Gentlemen's agreement" initiated by the United States "proposed" that Japan place limits on emigration to the United States. The inflow of Japanese was practically halted. Earlier in the 19th century, other limits to emigration are more notorious. In England, up until 1824, emigration of skilled artisans, and engineers with knowledge of advanced industrial techniques, was a criminal offense. The Atlantic slave trade was limited by British (1807), American (1808), and French (1815) laws in the first two decades of the 19th century, but some traffic persisted. By the 1850s, British naval patrols and other forces had largely stopped the outflow of African slaves to the Americas. Religious activists and humanists triumphed, putting an end to one of the most atrocious aspects of globalization.

Summary

Between 1820 and 1914, the world witnessed a dramatic and unprecedented process of integration. International trade led to strong convergence between countries in Western Europe and several key economies in North and South America. However, at the same time, there was also a rapid de-industrialization for a large share of the world's population. De-industrialization, a process partly driven by falling trade costs, harmed economic growth in many non-European economies, especially in Asia and Africa. Empire also played a role in globalization. Extractive colonies emerged where disease and climate limited European settlement. This type of colonization made a negative impact on long-run economic growth. In parts of Western Europe, international competition super charged a politics of dissatisfaction with globalization while other nations steadfastly adhered to free trade.

As for foreign investment, capital flows offered the possibility of significant investment in infrastructure and local enterprise. Capital flows allowed investors to reap rewards from higher returns and diversification. Risk sharing also improved to a degree. Some countries were, however, tempted to invest in unneeded projects, borrow instead of raise taxes, or to simply

---

[12] See Goldin (1993).

"over-invest." This type of borrowing often led to financial crises in moments of economic shocks. The rules of the game of the classical gold-standard era also made it challenging for many countries to maintain stability when these shocks hit and capital flows reversed course. These financial and economic crises inflicted significant damage on participating economies.

The impact of immigration was to promote convergence in wages. A number of smaller European nations "lost" 20% to 50% of their local populations to emigration, putting upward pressure on wages in these low-wage economies. Oppositely, New World economies received over forty million European immigrants, leaving wages somewhat lower than they would have been otherwise. In Asia, tens of millions of migrants participated in the new global economy, raising their living standards at the same time. In some of the receiving countries in the West, especially in the United States, there was eventually a backlash to the free movement of labor across borders.

It is evident then that greater trade, investment, and migration brought gains as well as losses. Some countries were able to manage the disruption of globalization better than other countries. While some nations simply stifled dissent, many other nations eagerly and actively sought out greater integration with the global economy. Nations like Denmark, Belgium, Japan, and Great Britain maintained free trade. Other nations erected tariff barriers (Canada, France, Germany, the United States). A host of economies eagerly adopted the gold standard, adhering to the monetary orthodoxy of the time. Argentina, Russia, Australia, and Canada borrowed and benefitted from foreign investment. Other economies rejected the gold standard and defaulted on debt, effectively cutting themselves off from foreign borrowing for long periods (e.g., Mexico, Peru, Egypt, and Turkey). A vigorous debate opened up about the perils of foreign investment (the United Kingdom) while Germany, France, and the United States used foreign investment to further their geopolitical ambitions. Argentina, Brazil, and Australia took great pains to welcome immigrants, but sentiment turned sour in the United States.

The idea of a golden age of globalization is not to be rejected, but it is also important to recognize that it is not always easy or comfortable to reap the gains from globalization. In this period, some economies were victimized by exploitative and extractive colonization, but de-colonization may not have been an economic magic bullet. A long debate in this area is still unsettled—suffice to say that internal and external issues both matter. In the economies that were not colonized, what can we learn?

Having a responsive political system that can ensure economic opportunity or "compensation" for those who lose from integration is important. Managing the global economy by using the social safety net had only just begun in this period, but pioneering nations like Belgium and Germany led the way in some regards. Both of these countries began offering government pensions, health insurance, and worker's compensation, among other components of the social safety net. Recent research also shows that the first wave of globalization witnessed a wave of increase in labor standards. Leading countries used their economic muscle and influence to cajole trade partners to improve their standards.[13]

Other countries were more aware of the pitfalls and took advance action by improving financial regulation, negotiating favorable trade deals, imposing rules and modifications to free immigration, or simply adapting to the new environment.

From a policy perspective, the first wave of globalization required active management of economic policy within a context of awareness and recognition from responsive and responsible leadership at all levels of society. When societies fail to adapt and sensibly recognize the challenges, they also fail to reap the rewards that integration promises. The years between 1914 and 1945, which include two World Wars and the biggest economic crisis in history, the Great Depression, dramatically illustrate this.

[13] See Huberman and Meissner (2010).

8

World War I and Its Legacy
(Prologue to the Great Depression)

1914–1928

The global economy had reached maturity by the early 1900s. While the globalization process brought improvements in the standard of living, gains were unevenly distributed. Across many countries, backlashes to immigration, trade, and finance had sprouted across the political landscape. World War I shattered the delicate economic connections of the global economy, disrupting trade, migration, and financial flows.

The war strongly curtailed integration in many key markets. The rest of the world was also directly affected as global demands shifted to feed the war effort. By 1920, many of Europe's largest economies were hobbled and devastated, having lived through a war of unimaginable destruction.

The efforts to rebuild the global economy after the war were not entirely successful. Policymakers yearned to rebuild the stability and growth of the first global economy and to foster greater international cooperation. Great Britain and the United States competed for international status and influence, which hindered cooperation. The Treaty of Versailles punished Germany, leading to resentment, nationalism, and ongoing economic challenges. In short, international cooperation and mutual understanding were strongly limited. A new economic leader, or hegemon, emerged in the form of the United States. The United States replaced Great Britain as the most productive and the most central nation for financial markets.

Financial instability was rampant in the inter-war period. Credibility, the key to financial stability prior to 1914, fizzled. Many countries extended the franchise to larger segments of the population. Political parties representing labor rose in popularity and influence. A restricted franchise had allowed governments to play by the rules of the game, sacrificing the economy, when necessary, with high interest rates for the sake of holding on to gold reserves.

One from the Many. Christopher M. Meissner, Oxford University Press. © Oxford University Press 2024.
DOI: 10.1093/oso/9780199924462.003.0008

Workers, directly harmed by high interest rates, deflation, and unemployment, were now in a position to hold politicians accountable. For many countries, the commitment to the gold standard was now much less credible.[1] The repercussions would be fully felt at times of financial stress as occurred in the 1930s. The Great Depression of the 1930s would forever alter the shape of the global economy.

World War I Disrupts the Global Economy

The first global economy came to a crashing and decisive end in late July 1914 when World War I broke out. The ostensible cause of the War was the assassination of the Archduke of Austria Franz Ferdinand by a disgruntled revolutionary in Sarajevo, Bosnia. In reality, Eastern Europe, an ethnically fragmented patchwork of communities, had been ripe for conflict for some years. Nations in Eastern and Central Europe fell further behind Western European nations in the late 19th century in terms of economic development. Nation-building, democracy, and economic modernization were a distant dream for the myriad ethnic groups (e.g., Hungarians, Poles, Czechs, Slovaks, Serbs, and Bulgarians) under the grips of Imperial rulers in Germany, Austria-Hungary, Russia, or Turkey.

The foundation for the war also lay in the decades before 1914 as the Great Powers like France, Russia, Germany, and Great Britain competed for influence and extended their quasi-colonial reach, developing client-states in Eastern and Central Europe, Africa (with formal colonies), and East Asia. Traditionally France was aligned with the Slavic world (Russia, Romania, and Greece especially). France had major investments in these areas as well, which were corollaries to the diplomatic ties.

Germany and Austria-Hungary attempted to make economic and political connections with the Ottoman Empire. Meanwhile, the British exercised some influence on places like Malta, Egypt, and other parts of the Middle East. Nationalism, socialism, Great Power politics, and economic disparities made the situation ripe for extensive conflict.

---

[1] This argument was first articulated and elaborated by the economic historian Barry Eichengreen. See Eichengreen (1992). Earlier, Karl Polanyi (1944) drew attention to the connection between political economy and the fiscal austerity often demanded of deficit countries by the gold standard.

Was the war expected? John Maynard Keynes argued that, prior to the war, few would have predicted such a disaster. In his essay "The Economic Consequences of the Peace," he wrote:

> The inhabitant of London could order by telephone, sipping his morning tea in bed, the various products of the whole earth, in such quantity as he might see fit, and reasonably expect their early delivery upon his doorstep . . . most important of all, he *regarded this state of affairs as normal, certain, and permanent, except in the direction of further improvement,* and any deviation from it as aberrant, scandalous, and avoidable. The projects and politics of militarism and imperialism, of racial and cultural rivalries, of monopolies, restrictions, and exclusion, which were to play the serpent to this paradise, were little more than the amusements of his daily newspaper, and appeared to exercise almost no influence at all on the ordinary course of social and economic life, the internationalization of which was nearly complete in practice. (emphasis added to original)

A belief existed that international commerce was "civilizing" and that when trade relations were intense, nations did not go to war. However, Great Power geo politics pressurized the local desire for greater autonomy by insurgent ethnic groups, ultimately culminating in a disastrous international conflict.

The war fundamentally altered the global economy. The war also transformed the economic and strategic positions of all the leading nations, including Great Britain, France, Germany, Russia, and even the United States. The war created new, independent nations from the rubble of former Empires (e.g., Poland, Hungary, Czechoslovakia, and Yugoslavia), allowing a form of economic nationalism to emerge that drove international integration downward due to the new international borders. Further afield, East Asia and Latin America were also affected by the economic impact of the war. Most of all, the war destroyed the global economic order known to some as the *Pax Britannica* of 1815–1914. While the war lasted from 1914 until November 1918, the economic disruption stretched into the 1920s and arguably helped sow the seeds of the Great Depression, which commenced in 1929.

International Financial Markets

In August 1914, financial markets around the world simultaneously collapsed. The international financial system suffered a disastrous bout of disintegration. The global demand for gold surged. Gold offered market participants protection from inflation and a reliable store of value. Fire sales of equities and bonds in exchange for gold occurred in London, Paris, Berlin, and other leading financial markets. National authorities reacted promptly by prohibiting international gold flows. Stock market trading was halted, limiting the gyrations associated with rising uncertainty and staunching stock market crashes. By closing off normal avenues for investment and imposing capital controls, borrowing costs remained lower than they would have been. This benefitted governments that would shortly need to finance large war expenditures.

In a matter of days and weeks, global financial markets had come to a grinding halt. The London Stock Exchange fell by about 7% between the end of June and late July 1914. The market remained closed until January 1915. Global migration began to dip. Other markets followed suit, crashing and then closing for extended periods. Trade between belligerents fell while inter-allied orders for materiel and supplies skyrocketed.

International lending for economic development, a hallmark of the first global era, dwindled to nothing as the supply of loanable funds was directed toward national war efforts. International capital market integration declined precipitously. Interest rate differentials, an obvious measure of integration, once minuscule between the leading nations, now averaged hundreds of basis points. The fundamental problem was that capital movements were strictly limited. Gold movements had also ceased. Arbitrage was next to impossible.

International capital markets staged a recovery from the early 1920s but on a fundamentally and dramatically different basis from the pre–World War I era. Leading creditor nations like the United Kingdom and France liquidated large shares of their foreign assets between 1914 and 1919 in order to finance war expenditures. France nearly exhausted its accumulated foreign assets, while it is estimated that the United Kingdom ran down a large share of its foreign assets too. In 1920, both countries attained debt-to-GDP levels of about 140%.

The Treaty of Versailles imposed a massive debt on Germany. Germany was served with a reparations bill that came in three types: reparations to cover allied debt accumulated for the war; war damages; and an extra tax to satisfy vengeful parliaments among the allies. The amount totaled an astonishing 250% of German GDP in 1920. A more realistic figure of the amount that could ever be collected was 100% of 1920 GDP. In either case, the treaty imposed significant international liabilities on Germany.

Throughout the 1920s, Germany would finance its international payments by piling on yet more debt, with German banks borrowing from abroad. Local and state governments also issued bonds, largely purchased by American households and financial institutions. This type of finance was precarious since funds were lent short-term. Ultimately, the huge reparations bill was whittled down over time through renegotiation and recognition that initial allied demands were unsustainable. Throughout the early 1930s, reparations also served as a focal point for political battles. Should the foreign debt be honored and, if so, who should bear the burden of repayment?

The United States emerged as the world's largest economy. New York was quickly earning the title of the most important financial center in the world. The City of London was increasingly marginalized as a player in global finance. The United States had escaped relatively unscathed from the war, emerging in a stronger international position in the 1920s than Great Britain and also relative to its own recent past. The United States was now a reliable source of funds with an increasingly sophisticated financial market. The United States had become a net lender, and it now held the firm position of the world's largest and most productive industrial economy.

Coincidence also played a role in this move to international creditor status. In 1914, the United States established the Federal Reserve, the nation's first central bank. The Federal Reserve Act helped create a market for bills of exchange and acceptances (drafts or IOUs used to finance international trade) in the United States. These were the means by which international trade was financed, but they also buttressed the liquidity demands of the money markets. First, banks often accepted them as payment since they were low-risk, high-quality assets. Second, the Federal Reserve was now authorized to purchase or "discount" so-called banker's acceptances. The New York, dollar-based market began to supplant the London, sterling-based market for these discounts of "bills of exchange." The Bank of England had anchored this important market in the first wave of globalization, which helped make London the premier global financial center. After the war, the United States no longer had to rely on financing its trade through London as it had throughout the 19th century. Moreover, residents of other countries could now finance trade in the United States and benefit from the market and the low interest rates. The market for "banker's acceptances" denominated in US dollars flourished in the 1920s. New York also emerged as an international financial center, and foreign countries began to issue debt in New York as they once had in London and Paris in the 19th century.

In addition, American banks, once legally barred from operating in foreign countries, could now open affiliates abroad. US banks expanded their international branches between 1914 and 1929, establishing offices in Latin America, Asia, and continental Europe. This increase in the size and character of the US economy and financial system allowed the Federal Reserve to exercise significant control over international short-term interest rates by the mid-1920s. The dollar came to be an international reserve currency, competing strongly with the pound sterling as the currency in which countries denominated their debt and trade invoices. The dollar's newfound status as an international currency came with certain responsibilities. Namely, the Federal Reserve and the dollar money market were now critical for global economic stability. The Federal Reserve was put to the test in the late 1920s and early 1930s. As we will see, it arguably mishandled the crisis of the 1930s.

International Trade

World War I severely disrupted and altered patterns of international trade. As the war progressed and German U-boats threatened to sink passenger and commodity freight lines alike, international shipping into Europe became extremely risky. This raised shipping costs. Freight rates on common commodities like tobacco and wheat between New York and London, Le Havre (one of France's main ports), and Antwerp (Belgium) skyrocketed. One estimate from contemporaries suggested freight rates from the United States to Europe rose fifty times faster than freight rates from the United States to South America. Trade between the allies and the central powers fell to near zero. The contorted shipping industry drove price gaps upward, erasing the welfare gains from integration witnessed in the first wave of globalization.

Not all trade was limited, however. The belligerents needed supplies, including feed and fodder for stock animals as well as victuals for the active troops. Manufacturers and commodity producers in the Americas benefitted strongly from allied demands for war materiel, food, uniforms, and military gear. Trade that would have formerly gone to Germany poured into allied markets. With other markets offline, and major exporters otherwise tied up in conflict, the war also boosted regional integration in the Americas and Asia.

Japan, an incipient industrial powerhouse, due to its geography, benefitted from the changes in global demand patterns. Facing much lower international competition in regional markets, Japanese manufacturers pounced on the opportunity to expand market share in China and the rest of Asia. Japan's exports to Asia increased by 125% but rose by only 66% with Europe. Japanese exports to North America more than doubled during the war. Japan's share of China's imports rose from 13% in 1913 to around 20% during the war, remaining at this level even in 1925. The United Kingdom captured 10% in 1913 and half of that share during the war. The United Kingdom was permanently displaced, since by 1925 its share remained at 6%. The share of Great Britain in India's imports also steadily declined from 76% in 1913 to 51% in 1925. Japan captured 2% in 1913, quadrupling the share of Indian imports to nearly 8% by 1925.

Commodity prices in Great Britain climbed not only due to the general inflation accompanying the war, but also because demand shifted toward several key commodities like coal (fuel), iron, cotton (for uniforms), coffee (for the troops), and wheat. The process culminated with a rise of more than 50% in real global commodity prices. The shortages that sprang up in Europe prompted arbitrage, of course, but high shipping costs during the war associated with increased risks contributed to increased price gaps between markets. High prices also spurred producers to bring marginal lands into production. Consumers and governments placed orders with new suppliers across the world, forging new trade relationships in the process.

Tariffs, already trending upward slightly before World War I, continued to rise after the war (Figure 8.1). New, smaller nations, created from the disassembly of larger empires in Eastern Europe, gained tariff autonomy, hoping to gain a new source of revenue and promote local industrial production. Leading nations like Britain, once the paragon of free trade in the late 19th century, increased tariffs during the war on luxury items in order to dampen consumption, fund the war, and protect the balance of payments. In 1921 the "Safeguarding of Industries Act" extended British tariffs of up to 50% *ad valorem* on a limited range of manufactured products like lace, silk, dyestuff, and cutlery. Still, this was far from promoting total autarky since these tariffs only covered a small share of British imports.[2] The United States raised tariffs with the Fordney–McCumber Tariff of 1922 in order to boost the prosperity of American manufacturers and agricultural interests

[2] See Capie (1978).

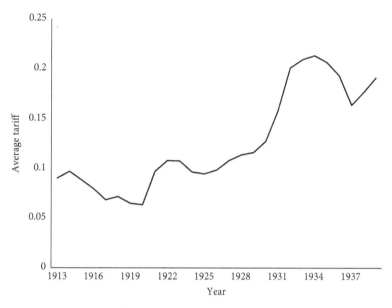

Figure 8.1 Average Tariff, Twenty-three Countries, 1913–1939
Source: Author's calculations based on data underlying Clemens and Williamson (2004b)

alike. Higher tariffs dampened integration, making economic recovery all the more challenging. The ratio of world exports to world GDP stagnated in the 1920s, later taking a nose dive in the 1930s during the Great Depression (Figure 8.2).

Immigration

The war, and then the Great Depression, acted to limit emigration from Europe and other places (Figure 8.3). Prior to World War I, a globally integrated labor market, almost entirely free of significant restrictions on the movement of labor, emerged. Immigration to the United States, one of the largest receiving nations prior to the War, averaged nearly one million people per year between 1900 and 1914. The war reduced these inflows to about two hundred thousand per year. Elsewhere in the Americas, the same risks and market dis-locations that plagued shipping in commodity markets afflicted trans-oceanic passenger lines. Migration dwindled in the Western hemisphere between 1910 and 1920. Wage gaps persisted or reopened.

Figure 8.2 Ratio of World Exports to World GDP, 1913–1939
Source: Author's calculations based on data from Federico and Tena-Junguito (2019).
Notes: constant 1913 prices and borders

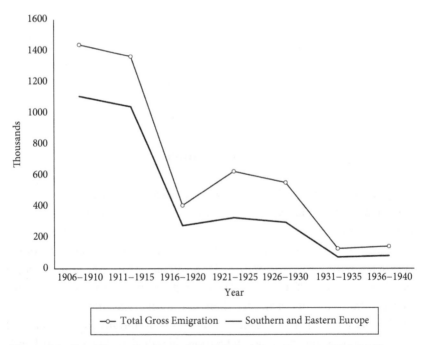

Figure 8.3 Gross Inter-Continental Emigration from Europe, 1906–1940
Source: Chiswick and Hatton (2004). © by the National Bureau of Economic Research

The United States introduced new, severe immigration restrictions beginning in 1921 with the Emergency Quota Act. This act capped annual immigration at about 360,000, less than half of the annual average of 800,000 arrivals between 1910 and 1914. The act divided the total annual quota by nationality, with Southern and Eastern European regions receiving lower shares than those from Northern and Western Europe. In 1924, the Johnson–Reed Act made the quota system permanent. These acts severely curtailed the volume but also affected the main sources of immigration. Also, since the quotas did not apply to the Americas, Canada and Mexico took a larger share of immigrant arrivals. Overall, immigrants to the United States during the 1920s were increasingly high-skilled. This induced wages of the (high-skill) native-born to grow more slowly than they might otherwise have. The foreign-born share of the US population peaked at 15% in 1910 and it declined continuously to 1940, when it stood at 9%.

South American nations imposed fewer restrictions. Three million people immigrated to Argentina in the 1920s (many of them ultimately returning to their home countries). Brazil continued to subsidize immigration. European workers continued to find employment on coffee plantations and in the fast-growing cities like São Paulo. Argentina, like the United States, experienced growing resentment of immigrants. The backlash to immigration had less success than the American policy change. A number of bills and proposals intending to limit immigration stalled out between 1899 and 1923. Argentina remained largely open to foreign workers until the 1930s.

In Asia, migration continued to be strong. By one estimate, fifteen million people arrived (and stayed) in Southeast Asia between 1881 and 1939, with 75% of them arriving after 1911.[3] The principal sending economies of India and China continued to supply millions of new workers for Southeast Asia. Burma, Thailand, and Malaysia were the primary recipients. Immigration to Malaysia had the most significant impact on the local population in the period, with rates of migration of 820 per 1,000 residents. This was nearly five times higher than in Argentina, which itself was an outlier in the Americas. In Burma and Malaysia, net immigration peaked in the 1920s. Immigration began to slow in the 1930s, not due to legal restrictions but due to the global Depression, which limited the opportunities for new workers in this region.

---

[3] See Huff and Caggiano (2007).

Fault Lines in the Inter-War Period

The period between the world wars, 1920 to 1939, is mainly associated with the Great Depression. This economic calamity-cum-international-financial-crisis broke out in late 1929. The root causes of the Great Depression reach back to the 1920s. The severity of the Great Depression depended on the evolution of the global economy and several major policy failures after World War I. The key weaknesses in the global economy were those associated with reparations payments imposed on Germany in the Treaty of Versailles and the precarious reincarnation of the gold-standard system. To some degree, the global economy was also adversely affected by a change in global economic leadership from Great Britain to the United States as well as underlying technological, economic, and political changes. Examples include the increased use of labor contracts in leading economies like the United States and Great Britain, which made wages less flexible. There was also an increased reliance on consumer credit. Borrowing facilitated the purchase of new consumer durables, like automobiles and time-saving home appliances, which were made available and affordable through new mass production techniques. Finally, the extension of the franchise and the increased political power of workers and organized labor made the gold standard less credible.

The Treaty of Versailles and Its Hyperinflationary Consequences

Signed and negotiated in the environs of Paris in 1919, the Treaty of Versailles allowed for the imposition of a nearly insurmountable debt on the defeated German economy. A significant contributor to the debt burden was the need to mollify many political constituencies in the allied countries, who advocated a harsh penalty be imposed on Germany.[4] The treaty itself and the settlements imposed on the Central Powers by the Allies had many dimensions besides the unsustainable financial penalties, including German relinquishment of territory and colonial possession across the world, the return of Alsace-Lorraine to France, and German disarmament.

---

[4] David Lloyd George, leader of the UK Liberal Party, used "Hang the Kaiser and make the Germans pay" as his election slogan in 1918. His coalition was reelected.

However, the single most egregious policy mistake might have been to initially impose reparations payments equal to over five times Germany's GDP in 1913. The initial ask was for 230 billion gold marks (450% of 1913 German GDP) while the offer by Germany was a mere 30 billion marks. The German offer was rejected outright by the Allies. The French soon invaded several important German ports, emphasizing the German inability to successfully bargain for a "reasonable" penalty. The reparations bill was eventually whittled down to 132 billion gold marks (185% of 1925 GDP) or about $33 billion (Table 8.1). This included "A" bonds to pay for war damages (12 bn gold marks or 16% of 1925 GDP), "B" bonds to help the British and French repay their war debts (38 bn gold marks or about 55% of 1925 GDP), and "C" bonds (82 bn gold marks or 115% of 1925 GDP). The C bonds were unlikely to ever be repaid but were used for political purposes to show Allied politicians were punishing Germany.

Why were the reparations so severe? In the 19th century, victors, and even aggressors who had instigated wars, traditionally imposed reparations payments on the vanquished. Such was the case in the Franco-Prussian War of 1870 (25% of French GDP) and the First Sino-Japanese War of 1894–1895 (3.5% of Chinese GDP). Russia avoided direct financial reparations entirely in the Russo-Japanese War, although it was largely forced out of Manchuria, gave up some property rights in Dalian (Port Arthur), and had to cede a portion of Sakhalin Island.

Historians agree that Allied politicians fell victim to a tragedy of the commons—economists would say that they did not internalize the externalities they were imposing on the world economy by assigning

Table 8.1 German Reparations Debt, 1925–1931.

	Debt Value in Reichsmarks	Share of nominal GDP in percent (x 100) by year		
		1925	1929	1931
A Bonds (Net Indemnity)	12	16.88%	13.57%	17.65%
A+B Bonds (incl. 38bn RM for interallied debt)	50	70.32%	56.56%	73.53%
Total: A+B+C Bonds	132	185.65%	149.32%	194.12%
Dawes Plan 1924	46	59%	47.50%	—
YoungPlan1929/30	37	—	41.80%	54.40%

Source: Ritschl (2013)

Germany a heavy, unsustainable debt burden. To be fair, Allied politicians had their own constituencies in mind and their countries had also incurred heavy debts with the United States. France owed 32% of GDP to the United States, the United Kingdom 24%, and Italy roughly 40%.

Germany's reparations debt was to be paid in installments, in gold, via direct transfer to the Allied governments. However, Germany's economy was in tatters due to the war and was facing intense fiscal pressures. Not surprisingly, Germany soon encountered difficulty repaying. Funding the government deficits with new debt was not immediately viable, but raising tax revenue from an economy well below potential output also proved a challenge. The Germans resorted to the printing press.

The hyperinflation which occurred in Germany between 1921 and 1923 was consistent with the maxim enunciated by Milton Freidman: "inflation is always and everywhere a monetary phenomenon." One way to better understand this expression is to study the equation of exchange

$$MV = PY$$

where M equals the supply of money; V is a constant; P is the consumer price level; and Y is real output.

The equation points out that if real output is constant at potential output (i.e., using all its inputs efficiently) and assuming that V is constant, then any rise in the money supply M will be reflected in a rise in consumer prices P. The larger the increase in the money supply, the larger the increase in prices or the higher the inflation. Continuous printing of money will cause continuous rises in prices.[5] Economist Phillip Cagan argued that the German hyperinflation was also driven in part by the public's price/inflation expectations becoming "de-anchored." In other words, even if the printing press had completely halted, there would be tremendous momentum in inflation simply driven by expectations.

Hyperinflation, a situation defined loosely by economists as monthly inflation above 100%, ravaged the German economy. Figure 8.4 shows the exchange rate, prices, and money in circulation in Germany during the hyperinflation. All series rise together exponentially. Between autumn

[5] The German economy was nowhere near potential output in 1921 or 1922 with a gap between GDP per capita and its pre-war trend of about 37%. There was significant room for economic growth without excessive inflation. However, when the money supply grew at rates that were large multiples of the growth rate of real income (GDP), the price effects clearly dominated.

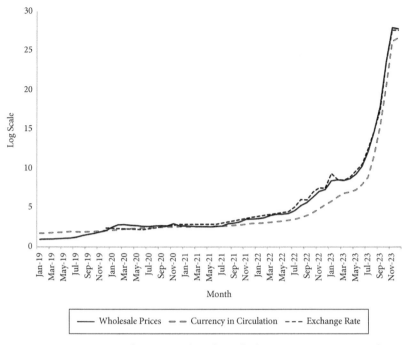

Figure 8.4 Germany: Exchange rate (Mark/Dollar), Consumer Prices, and Currency in Circulation, 1919–1923

Source: Author's calculations using data from Graham (1967)

1921 and early 1923, German consumer prices had risen thousands of times relative to their initial levels. The exchange rate depreciated, with the German Mark price of one US dollar increasing from about 6 at the end of the war to at least 1 trillion at the end of 1923. During the period of hyperinflation, consumers shuffled to the store with wheelbarrows full of cash that would be nearly worthless by the time they arrived at the store. One economist joked that barroom beer drinkers ordered several beers at a time since the beer warmed more slowly than the money in their pocket lost value.

The hyperinflationary process sent the stock market soaring. Real estate prices boomed. But the skewed economic incentives delivered economic costs. People and firms held larger inventories of consumer and producer goods than normal. Firms continually had to change prices incurring so-called menu costs. The costs of changing display prices or menus every day, or even hourly, could be very high in an earlier, non-digital era. Finally, debts were inflated away, violating contracts between creditors and debtors.

By 1923, the German economy was at a standstill, and the financial system had been badly decimated. In early 1923, after some debate, French troops occupied parts of the industrial heartland in the Ruhr valley in an attempt to force (literally at gunpoint) Germany to repay. This occupation failed because German workers passively resisted French orders, refusing to produce the required amounts. Eventually, the hyperinflation ended as Germany imposed a stabilization policy that would restore its financial and monetary system.

The stabilization had multiple components. One key was the 1924 renegotiation of debt under the American-led Dawes Plan. This led to a large reduction in reparations payments (see Table 8.1). In validation of Cagan's momentum theory, stopping inflation required more than stopping the monetary printing presses. Inflation expectations had to be anchored. Stabilization also involved raising tax revenue through "anticipated" taxes (indexation of taxes), raising nominal interest rates, cutting expenditures, and re-denominating the currency at a new lower gold parity. All these conditions made the commitment to lower inflation more credible. By 1925, annual inflation was a mere 8%, and capital (from the United States) was flowing in again, helping to rebuild the German economy.

The roots of the hyperinflation and exchange rate depreciation were the large burden on the balance of payments and the large government deficits all stemming from reparations.[6] From the balance of payments accounting identity, the only way to effect a large transfer of resources would be to sell German marks and purchase foreign currency, with the exchange rate depreciating as a consequence. Exchange-rate depreciation raises prices in an open economy following the law of one price and purchasing power parity (PPP)

$$P^{GER} = eP^{US}$$

where P^{GER} is the German price level; P^{US} is the US price level; e equals the number of German marks per US dollar.

---

[6] The economic issues involved in such wealth transfers came to be known as the *transfer problem*. In modern, open-economy, macroeconomic parlance we are looking for an equilibrium pattern of production, consumption, trade balances, and relative prices consistent with a large transfer of wealth out of Germany to the "Rest of the World." In order to pay reparations in foreign currency, Germany would need to earn foreign currency by selling exports to the rest of the world. John Maynard Keynes, the eminent British economist, held that an impossibly large depreciation of the currency or massive deflation would be necessary to convince foreigners to buy enough German goods and generate enough revenue to pay the reparations. Bertil Ohlin, the eminent Swedish economist argued that Germany could pay by reducing total consumption and transferring the difference between output and consumption abroad. Such transfers would be accompanied by some relative price changes that would not be infeasible nor dramatic under reasonable assumptions about demand and supply.

The scale of the transfers inevitably led to both depreciation and inflation as two sides of the same coin. Moreover, covering the government deficit by printing money also led to inflation, as the equation of exchange suggests, and the theory of purchasing power parity shows.

German hyperinflation can best be understood as a policy choice made under the domestic financial, economic, and political constraints of the time and Germany's international obligations. It is alleged, and widely accepted, that German officials initiated high inflation because balancing the budget through cuts in spending and higher taxes would have led the international community to be less likely to approve a reparations reduction. At the same time, domestic politics was akin to what evolutionary theorists call a *war of attrition*. While labor interest groups might have liked capitalists to shoulder the burden of payment through higher taxes on their wealth and profits, the capitalists would have liked to shove the burden off onto the working classes with lower social spending and higher taxes on wages. Political stalemate ensued. Hyperinflation was seen as improving Germany's international bargaining position as well as providing a solution to the domestic politics of the period.

Hyperinflation, or near hyperinflation, appeared in several other countries in the 1920s, including Austria, Poland, France, and Belgium. Not all these countries had onerous reparations payments, but all these countries did end up increasing the supply of money more rapidly than the rate of economic growth, which in turn led to inflation. Hyperinflation and very high inflation generated a legacy of extreme aversion to floating exchange rates and active monetary policy in most of the countries that sustained it. Citizens learned they could not yet trust governments with the power to print money. In the short term, the pendulum swung in the direction of reinstating fixed exchange rates under the gold standard.

International Financial Flows as a Risk Factor

A closely related risk factor for the Great Depression was the reorientation of international capital flows in the 1920s. The United States displaced Great Britain as the world's banker in the 1920s, becoming an ever-larger source of global lending. New York began to compete effectively with London as the world's financial center. US retail investors, middle-class households from across the country, were lured into international markets by door-to-door traveling bond salesmen. These agents successfully convinced small savers to invest in foreign assets, including German equities as well as corporate and public bonds. A significant amount of US lending was also directed to Latin America. Both types of flows created the potential for instability by raising the probability of a destabilizing sudden stop in capital inflows.

Germany's economy relied on capital inflows during the 1920s. This reliance was one major vulnerability in the period. The triangular pattern of recycled funding was precarious. What form did this "triangle" take? First, foreign investors, many from the United States, funded German borrowing needs. Second, the German economy recycled these funds to repay the Allied reparations bill imposed by the Treaty of Versailles. Third, allies like France, Great Britain, Belgium, and Italy used these inflows to help repay their wartime obligations to the United States. The process was then repeated in order to fund more German repayments.

The fragility of the system arose because a breakage in the links between these economies could lead to default on external financial obligations. From the 1920s perspective, the most fragile link would have been between Germany and the Allies. A German default on reparations would have led to negative political repercussions and financial trouble in the Allied nations. Trouble was averted in the short run. Germany successfully renegotiated its debts under the Dawes Plan in 1924, allowing repayment to continue, but at a more realistic and sustainable level. The risk lurking in the shadows was ultimately the potential cessation of American capital inflows to Germany. Without access to such financing, German banks, businesses, and governments would be forced into austerity (higher taxes, lower spending) sending Germany's economy into a tailspin and potentially creating an international financial shock.

The Unstable Inter-War Gold-Exchange Standard

The gold standard was resurrected in the 1920s after collapsing temporarily during the war. It came to be called the *gold-exchange standard* since countries now augmented their gold reserves with foreign exchange reserves— assets of leading countries with currencies reliably convertible to gold like the pound or the US dollar. This system, described below, was largely unsustainable and fragile for many reasons. The new system lasted only about five years between 1925 and 1930. Compared to the longevity of the classical gold standard, which endured from 1880 until 1914, this regime was a failure. What happened?

Nations universally abandoned the gold standard during World War I. Cross-border gold flows were prohibited, leading domestic currency prices of gold to diverge from their historical "mint parities." The United States ended gold shipments in 1917 but reinstated them in 1919. Germany terrorized Britain with maritime attacks during the war, discouraging significant gold flows. Later, Britain imposed a formal gold embargo beginning on April 1, 1919. While the war ended in 1918, restoration of an international system of fixed exchange rates came only after 1925. Figure 8.5 shows the number of leading countries adhering to the gold standard between 1919 and 1939. Great Britain resumed convertibility of its currency into gold in April 1925, and a number of other countries followed suit around the same time. The United States had restored convertibility by 1919, while France, a late comer, only managed to stabilize its currency in 1927.

Restoring convertibility was more difficult than simply declaring a currency to be convertible to gold. To be convertible, a currency had to declare a

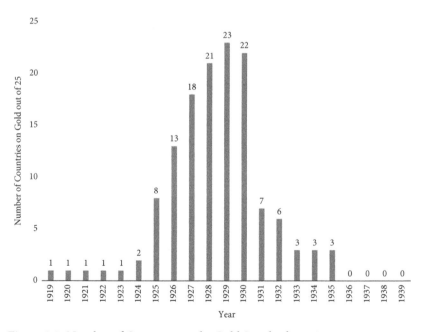

Figure 8.5 Number of Countries on the Gold Standard, 1919–1939

Source: Author's calculations, with assistance from Alain Naef, based on Bernanke and James (1991), Table 1

mint parity (e.g., $20.67 per ounce of fine gold in the United States and £4.25 per ounce of fine gold in Britain). Most countries were expected to return to convertibility at the established pre-war parities. The historical US–UK parity implied a nominal exchange rate ($4.86/£).[7] The purchasing power parity relationship implies that relative price levels have to be "consistent" with this nominal exchange rate or else gold will flow toward the country with the undervalued currency (and low prices) and away from the country with an overvalued currency (high prices).

The war had occasioned massive rises in national price levels, but more problematic were the relative changes. While the United Kingdom resumed convertibility in 1925 at the old parity of $4.86, British prices remained somewhat higher than necessary to achieve *balance of payments equilibrium* especially vis-à-vis France. This led the British real exchange rate to be *overvalued* against its key trading partner, France. One standard indicator of overvaluation is whether the current account is in surplus or deficit. Clearly, the United Kingdom's current account surplus declined after 1925 (Figure 8.6). More broadly, parities were misaligned across the world. Similar imbalances arose in Denmark, Norway, and Italy, among other places.

Meanwhile, across the English Channel, France had resumed convertibility by 1927. But the exchange rate vis-à-vis Great Britain and its other trade partners was *undervalued*. France's current account surplus due to the franc's misalignment continuously pulled gold into France. Between 1926 and 1929, France's share of world gold reserves doubled from about 7% to 15%. This share was much higher than its share in world income. Figure 8.7 shows the persistent current account surplus and the evolution of the trade-weighted real exchange rate (i.e., the real, effective exchange rate, REER). Clearly, France was not playing by the rules of the game. If it had been, the accumulation of gold and the current account surpluses would have declined much earlier. As we have seen, a failure to adhere to these "rules" would lead to persistent imbalances and potential instability. Namely, countries in deficit might eventually lose their gold and hence their ability to convert currencies into gold. An exchange-rate crash could occur.

There were several other systemic fault lines in the inter-war period. As countries rebooted their gold standards, countries began to rely more on

---

[7] The historical parity was $4.866563 to be exact. Prior to the 1930s, there were 23.22 grains of fine (pure) gold per US dollar and 113.0016 grains of pure gold per pound. See Officer (1996) for a thorough introduction to the historical evolution of gold parities and US dollar–British pound sterling exchange rates.

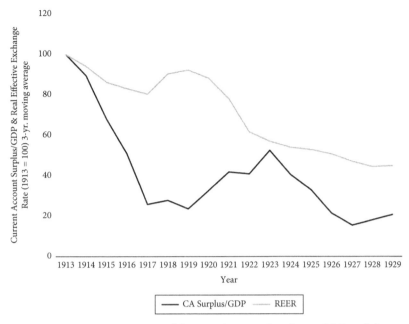

Figure 8.6 Great Britain, Ratio of Current Account Surplus to GDP and the Real Effective Exchange Rate (1913 = 100), 1913–1929

Source: Author's calculations. Current account and GDP based on data underlying Jones and Obstfeld (2000). Exchange rate data based on data underlying Jordà, Schularick, and Taylor (2021) and Jacks, Meissner, and Novy (2008). Notes: Decline in the Real Effective Exchange Rate (REER) is an appreciation

foreign exchange reserves to back their currencies. The approach was not un-precedented. Countries like Japan, India, and Germany had already begun backing their currencies with British bonds prior to World War I to a limited extent. The Genoa Conference of 1922 aimed to encourage countries to "econ-omize" on gold, but no binding commitments were made. Nevertheless, be-cause gold supplies had not kept up with monetary demand, countries began to substitute away from the precious metal. By the mid-1920s, most countries had a substantial component of their reserves held in foreign exchange (US dollars and British sterling) while leading countries like the United Kingdom and the United States held on to gold in order to back up these reserves.

This "pyramiding" led to a potentially dangerous policy dilemma for the leading countries that issued international currencies.[8] Core countries like

---

[8] In the Bretton Woods period this came to be known as the *Triffin Dilemma*. In the 21st century, the problem persists, and economists discuss the supply or shortage of "safe" assets.

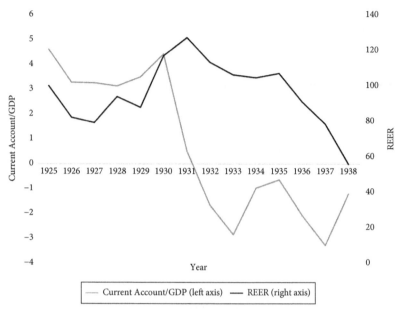

Figure 8.7 France, Ratio of Current Account to GDP and the Real Effective Exchange Rate (1925 = 100), 1925–1938

Source: Author's calculations. Current account and GDP based on data underlying Jones and Obstfeld (2000). Exchange-rate data based on data underlying Jacks, Meissner, and Novy (2008). Notes: Decline in the Real Effective Exchange Rate (REER) is an appreciation

the United States and United Kingdom had to keep increasing their supply of bonds by borrowing more in order to accommodate the natural rate of increase of demand for money. This would help to avoid global deflation. On the other hand, expanding the supply of reserve assets relative to a stock of global monetary gold that was fixed in the short run could engender uncertainty about the convertibility of the dollar or sterling. This situation heightened the potential for a speculative *run* on the key currencies of the system, with gold being the ultimate safe haven. Oppositely, to avoid this run, the supply of bonds could be restrained. This would lead to global deflation as the growth of the global money supply remained sluggish.

Deflation could be economically painful. Why? Price or wage "rigidity" are potential reasons. If commodity prices decline, but (nominal) wages do not, unemployment can occur as real wages rise. Wages were less "flexible" than before World War I because labor unions exercised increasing power to negotiate inflexible wage contracts. Labor unions had strengthened by the 1920s, leading to an increasingly centralized wage bargaining process in some of the advanced industrial economies. These *corporatist* policies tended to create more rigid (nominal) wages than in the pre–World War I period.

Wage (and price) flexibility are generally sufficient conditions to keep output and employment stable in the face of aggregate demand shocks in basic macroeconomic models. The inter-war economy was much less flexible in this regard than the first wave of globalization was. A price decline in the presence of rigid wages can lead labor supply to outstrip labor demand. This is the definition of unemployment. Moreover, unemployment insurance became more prevalent and more generous. With such insurance, unemployed workers had less incentive to "search" for a job. This tended to decrease employment rates, although labor force participation rates remained high. Unemployment insurance undoubtedly contributed to persistent unemployment in the 1920s and 1930s, contributing to social and political dissatisfaction.

Tariffs also impeded smooth adjustment in the balance of payments. In the 19th century, exporters relied on Great Britain's free trade stance. Great Britain was a "buyer-of-last-resort" and the commitment to low tariffs ensured there would be at least one open market to sell to when balance-of-payments adjustment became necessary. In the 1920s, Great Britain began to succumb to tariff protection. Although these tariffs were sometimes as high as 50%, they largely covered only selected, strategic products. Nevertheless, some of these tariffs reduced market access for debtors like Germany on important products such as chemicals and dyes. The United States raised tariffs in 1922 by 64%. Throughout the 1920s, the United States, the world's largest and most important economy, barricaded itself behind average tariffs of nearly 40% on dutiable imports equivalent to an overall average tariff of almost 15% on all imports.

International migration slowed to a trickle in the 1920s as well, erasing yet another margin of adjustment. In the 19th century, when an economy plunged into recession, migrants would leave as employment prospects dimmed. Migration was a safety valve. It released economic pressure, tending to keep wages from falling and unemployment from rising. Consumption could also be maintained as wages stayed stable. Restrictions on trade and migration made individual economies in the 1920s much less capable of coping with monetary, financial, and real shocks in the global economy compared to the 19th century.

Finally, politics mattered. The extension of the franchise weakened the credibility of the gold standard. The vote had been extended to increasingly wider swathes of the population since 1900. Nearly all advanced countries in Western Europe had moved to universal male suffrage by the 1920s, and women were also given the right to vote in many countries during the period. Extension of the franchise generated greater accountability for economic policy. Without the vote, workers could not punish politicians directly at the electoral booth for any perceived (negative) employment effects of "playing by the rules of the game." After all, they had little political voice under the limited franchise.

In the 1920s, voters were perfectly capable of punishing the government at the ballot box for austerity measures required by a fixed-exchange-rate commitment (i.e., the rules of the game) in the face of a trade deficit. Governments became more reticent to play by the rules of the game, implying that their exchange-rate pegs would likely eventually falter. International financial markets perceived this weakness with greater clarity over time. It was now profitable in many cases to bet on the abandonment of a gold-standard commitment. "De-stabilizing speculation" substituted for the *stabilizing speculation* of the classical gold-standard period.

In sum, the global economy of the 1920s had been dramatically transformed. It was now decisively more vulnerable to shocks compared to the first era of globalization. Policymakers and economic participants yearned for the stability and integration of the 19th century but faced many new and unexpected economic and political constraints. Trade policy became more restrictive, international capital flowed less freely, and cross-border labor movement waned. International leaders failed to foresee and forestall the negative impact on the German economy of overly punitive reparations. The transfer of global financial leadership from the seasoned and tested first-mover, Great Britain, to the brash and inexperienced United States also led to potential for policy errors. Structural transformations in labor and financial markets and politics also mattered. Events after 1928 would lay bare how deficient the international economy was in reality.

The 1920s and the Precarious "Credit Boom"

By 1926, the international financial system and the global economy had largely been patched up and sewn back together. A number of countries participated in a global credit boom. Banks across Europe, the United States, and Australia lent not only on the basis of national deposits but also with the help of foreign funding. The financial system in China modernized, and a number of "modern" banks serving a domestic clientele sprang up. These banks managed their business like modern foreign banks, lending to local businesses and governments, taking deposits, and issuing listed equity. Japan emerged as a manufacturing nation with rapidly increasing economic sophistication also supported by a modern financial sector.

The international credit boom can be decomposed into an increase in the supply and demand of loanable funds. On the supply side, banks benefitted from globally low interest rates, which cheapened the cost of funding. Low and stable rates of inflation associated with (temporarily) lower economic volatility also lulled financiers into a false sense of security. Financial innovations emanating from the United States, such as installment credit, fueled a consumer durables binge. Households in the United States financed automobiles and a plethora of new home appliances such as radios, refrigerators, washing machines, and dishwashers on credit. Consumers in Great Britain and Australia enjoyed a similar rise in the availability of credit.

On the demand side, household real incomes began to grow again in the 1920s. Pent-up demand for housing for those denied the option to purchase during the war stoked a housing boom in the early and mid-1920s in the United States. Improved housing quality due to better indoor plumbing and heating also enhanced the demand for housing. A range of new goods that complemented household production and activity also shifted the demand for consumer (and mortgage) credit upward. The move to the suburbs and the ever-expanding road network, partially financed and driven by auto manufacturers, enhanced the demand for automobiles.

The global credit boom might have been unsustainable, however. One indication was the eagerness with which people in the United States bought useless swampland in Florida in the mid-1920s, sight unseen. Many ended up being completely swindled. The US housing boom was one of the biggest on record up to that point. The US housing boom had gone bust before the Great Depression started, having already slowed down by 1927, but many banks remained exposed into the 1930s to the real estate loans made in the mid-1920s.

Stock market booms in Germany and the United States also emerged in the mid-1920s. A period of financial exuberance manifested itself. In Germany, one of the largest banks, the Danatbank made an enormous loan equal to 40% of its equity to the Nordwolle cotton manufacturing company. Such loan concentration emerged for various reasons: poor governance at the executive level, a reach for (high) yield, a lowering of credit standards, and a bet that the government would bail out the systemically important bank in the case of major losses. The latter, an "agency" problem, is known as the "too big to fail" phenomenon and gives rise to what economists call "moral hazard." In the United States, economists and financial analysis stoked the financial frenzy by declaring: "We will not have any more crashes in our time" (John Maynard Keynes, 1927) and "Stock prices have reached what looks like a permanently high plateau" (Irving Fisher of Yale University, September 1929).

Some analysis suggests that price-earnings ratios in the US were not completely disconnected from reality, as they would be in a speculative bubble. Many economists, including Ellen McGrattan and Ed Prescott, argued that new technologies and products, like consumer durables, electrification, better housing, and the automobile, justified to an extent the rapid rise in the US stock market.[9]

By early 1928, some storm clouds had begun to gather over the global economy. The German stock market crashed in May 1927, leading to significant financial losses. The Reichsbank intervention in the market was an ill-fated attempt to curtail "excessive" lending on margin, foreshadowing similar events involving the Fed in New York in 1928–1929. In Germany, higher interest rates and financial volatility prevailed. US investors began to eschew risk, leading to lower capital inflows in Germany.

In 1928, the US Federal Reserve rear-ended global financial markets with a hike in interest rates. The Fed now determined global financial conditions by setting the global benchmark short-term interest rate. Having expressed some worry that the US stock market was over-valued and that investors had taken out too many short-term or broker's loans, the Fed now desired tighter financial conditions. As most of these loans were highly leveraged, borrowers were susceptible to shocks in asset prices. Changes in short-term interest rates could bring such a shock. The rise in US interest rates, a pivot toward tighter monetary policy by the Fed, was the (monetary) impulse that started the Great Depression.

Summary

The global economy was not rebuilt on a solid foundation in the 1920s. World leaders and economic actors yearned to return to normalcy, but they did not

---

[9] See McGrattan and Prescott (2004).

achieve it. A host of factors heightened the chances that economic shocks might disrupt global finance and trade. These included the weakness of the gold-exchange standard in the face of lower credibility, unsustainable debt obligations of Germany due to the Treaty of Versailles, a lack of flexibility in wages, the willingness to impose higher tariffs, and increased restrictions on migration flows. The global economy had begun to reconnect itself, but it had failed to update key institutions for the new environment. Instead of promoting stability, growth, and harmony, the global economy acted as a conduit for the shocks that would hit the global economy beginning in 1928.

9

The Great Depression

An Unprecedented International Economic Crisis

The Great Depression, the worst global economic and financial crisis in recorded history, started in 1929. Between 1929 and 1932, global economic output declined by 10%. Wide variation around this average existed, with the United States experiencing a 25% decline in GDP and Great Britain seeing a decline of 5%. Commodity prices fell at a dramatic pace, international trade collapsed, capital flows dried up, unemployment skyrocketed, and investment crashed. Nearly every country was affected by the Great Depression to some degree. No economic crisis before, or since, had been so widely transmitted, so deep, and so long. Economic integration was the conduit for this transmission. Economic integration promised the same rewards and benefits in the 1920s as it always had, but policy failures interacted with severe economic shocks after 1929. Although the global economy had taken one step forward by the 1930s, it has also taken two steps backward.

The Great Depression: Some Facts and Figures

The Great Depression was an international economic crisis of epic proportions. For the leading countries for which we have reasonable data on GDP, Figure 9.1 shows that the world average level of GDP fell by about 10% between 1929 and 1932. Around this average, there was a wide range of experience. The global downturn started in the commodity exporters such as Australia, Brazil, and the Dutch East Indies.

Figure 9.2 shows the evolution of GDP for four countries over the long run. Germany's downturn began in 1928 after its stock market crash. US industrial production peaked in August 1929, although exports to other countries trended down in early 1928 due to declining incomes in the periphery. France's recession was longer lasting than others, but it started comparatively late, in 1930. In China, the economy was initially protected from a severe

One from the Many. Christopher M. Meissner, Oxford University Press. © Oxford University Press 2024.
DOI: 10.1093/oso/9780199924462.003.0009

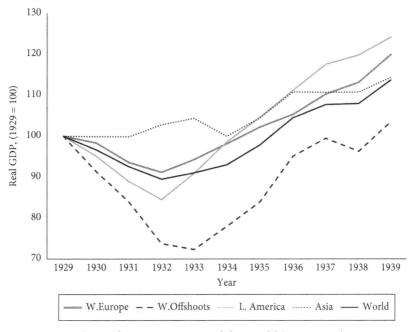

Figure 9.1 Real GDP for Four Regions and the World (1929 = 100), 1929–1939
Source: Bolt et al. (2018)

downturn. Great Britain, which had experienced significant unemployment and slow growth in the 1920s, started recovery sooner than most, in 1931. Once recoveries began in the United States (1933), Japan (1931), and Germany (1933), historically high rates of economic growth prevailed. Even so, the Great Depression was a deep hole out of which it was hard to climb. Unemployment remained at record levels as late as 1939 in countries like the United States, ten full years after the Depression started.

The Great Depression walloped the international economy. World trade collapsed, declining more quickly than global GDP due to a fast rise in trade costs. These included higher tariffs, new preferential trade agreements, commodity price declines, and a falloff in the demand for highly tradeable durable and investment goods. Figure 8.2 shows a 50% decline in the ratio of global exports to GDP between 1929 and 1933. Exports in 1933 were only 56% of their trend value in 1933.

The Great Depression also eviscerated global capital markets after 1929. New foreign investment and long-term lending completely ceased. Short-term trade finance dried up, mirroring the fall in trade but also reflecting

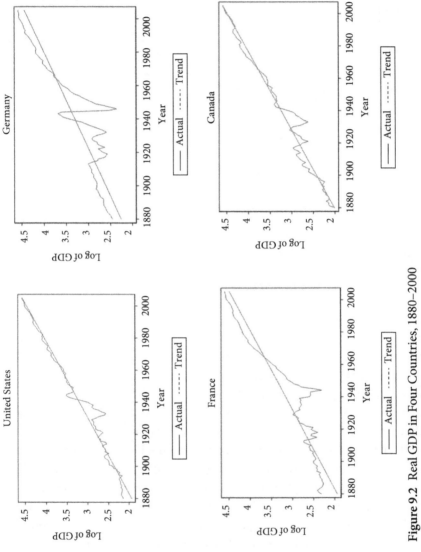

Figure 9.2 Real GDP in Four Countries, 1880–2000

Source: Author's calculations based on data underlying Barro and Ursúa (2008)

Notes: Figures show a constant growth rate trend line and the actual path of real GDP

tight monetary conditions of the period. Global migration, already tightly limited by the 1920s, fell to lows unseen for the greater part of the previous century. Inflows of immigrants to the United States averaged 843,000 people annually between 1900 and 1913 and 450,000 annually between 1920 and 1929. Between 1929 and 1939, immigration averaged 68,000 people per year with a total of only 616,000 arriving in the United States in these years.

The Great Depression exhibited international spillovers due to the numerous linkages between the world's economies. Late-20th-century economists called this contagion. Whatever the name, such spillovers are common in globalized economies. Economists discuss the Great Depression in terms of "real" and "monetary/financial" shocks that were transmitted internationally. Real shocks are the exogenous and endogenous changes in the aggregate demand and supply of commodities and services. Financial shocks emanate from the financial sector and are associated with changes in monetary policy, banking crises, and endogenous and exogenous changes in the supply and demand for loanable funds. Both sorts of shocks were transmitted internationally in the early 1930s. This is most visible in the incessant deflation (outright declines in prices) that affected nearly every country and especially those that operated a gold-based monetary system.

Exchange rate changes were large in the 1930s. There were a number of sharp and unexpected depreciations. In addition, there were the dramatic tariff hikes of the time which impacted the fortunes of trade partners in many significant ways. Monetary policy in the United States and France clearly had a global impact early in the Great Depression. Finally, international financial linkages via banks that lent and borrowed across borders, and also various sorts of outstanding financial obligations like Allied War debts and the German war reparations, contributed to the strength of cross-border spillovers, spreading default and panic beyond their domestic economies.

What Started It?

In 1928, the Federal Reserve Bank of New York began to tighten monetary policy on New York money markets (Figure 9.3). Overvaluation of the New York stock market was cited with the chief concern being the diversion of funding from "legitimate" investment toward financial speculation. By mid-1929, the Federal Reserve Board and the New York Fed agreed that "rampant" financial speculation needed to be thwarted. Monetary policy

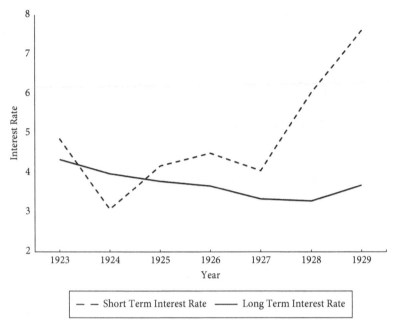

Figure 9.3 US Interest Rates, 1923–1929

Source: Author's calculations based on data in Jordà, Schularick, and Taylor (2021)

turned contractionary again, and interest rates in the United States continued to rise.

The stated goal of the US-based tightening was that the New York stock
market had to be forced down from its heights. No major economic recession was expected. After all, the stock market was successfully deflated in
1920, after a post-war/post-pandemic boom, but no major recession ensued.
On Thursday, October 24, 1929, the New York stock market crashed precipitously, falling by more than 10%. The market would fall by another 12% on
Monday the 28th and again by 11% on Tuesday the 29th. Monetary policy and
economic rhetoric alike seemed to have the intended effect. Stock markets in
other countries like Canada, Great Britain, and Germany also faced dramatic
declines. The stock market crash wiped out about 20% of national wealth in
the United States and led to the bankruptcy of many financial intermediaries
in the New York financial market.

The Fed's policy, while partially coordinated with Great Britain, was
largely made without reference to the impact on the international economy.
Despite ignoring the spillover effects, the US change in monetary policy had

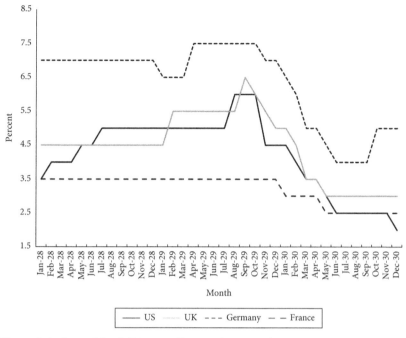

Figure 9.4 Central Bank Discount Rates, 1/1928–12/1930
Source: Author's calculations from data in Statistisches Reichsamt (1936)

a major impact on other countries. First, due to the so-called *trilemma*, most other countries on the gold standard were forced to raise interest rates in step with the American central bank (Figure 9.4). A failure to do so would lead to lower capital inflows and gold outflows toward high-interest-rate countries and eventually unwanted downward pressure on the exchange rate.[1] These disruptions could eventually cause so-called balance-of- payments troubles. A rise in capital and gold outflows could, by the balance-of-payments identity, push the current account away toward a higher surplus (e.g., by raising the trade balance). Finally, such a change could only be effected by cutting consumption (i.e., higher saving) and/or with outright deflation and higher real interest rates. A recession or economic slowdown was almost inevitable

---

[1] The trilemma of open-economy macroeconomics says that an economy must choose two of the following three options: fixed exchange rates, control over the local interest rate and domestic monetary policy, and open capital flows. Countries in 1929 had almost all chosen fixed exchange rates and open capital flows. Hence they lost control over the local interest rate and monetary policy. Later, some countries would impose capital controls or loosened their commitment to the gold standard, which allowed greater control over local monetary policy.

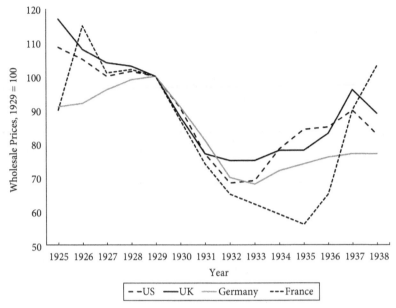

Figure 9.5 Industrial Production in Four Countries (1929 = 100)
Source: Author's calculations based on data from Mitchell (1998a, 1998b)

for the other gold-standard countries in the world economy as they matched
the US rise in interest rates.

The transmission of US monetary policy abroad had several implications
for the global economy. First, higher interest rates would lead to a decline
in aggregate demand, with consumption and investment bearing the brunt
of the policy. Industrial production fell nearly simultaneously in the core
countries (Figure 9.5). Consumers who had been financing their durable
purchases in the 1920s with consumer credit now found it more expensive
to borrow. Despite the housing slowdown already underway in the United
States since 1927, the real estate market became even tighter as credit supply
shrank faster than housing demand fell. Deflation, defined as a fall in the
average price level, set in simultaneously across the major gold standard
countries, with wholesale prices falling by 10% between 1929 and 1930 in
the United States, France, Germany, and the United Kingdom (Figure 9.6).
Falling prices increased the real value of debt and reduced the likelihood of
repayment.

China and Spain, two sizeable countries not on the gold standard, escaped
the initial onset of the Great Depression in 1929–1930. Not being on the
gold standard conferred them some initial immunity to transmission of

Figure 9.6 Wholesale Prices in Four Countries (1929 = 100), 1925–1938
Source: Author's calculations based on data from Mitchell (1998a, 1998b)

the Depression and deflation. Their exchange rates absorbed the monetary shock of deflation. In the case of Spain, the floating exchange rate relieved the nation from following US monetary policy as per the trilemma. Spain's exchange rate depreciated against the gold-based US dollar by 53% between 1929 and 1931. For China, still clinging to a silver standard, adjustment occurred via the relative price of silver in terms of gold. China's silver-based exchange rate depreciated against the dollar by nearly 60% between 1929 and 1931. Immunity did not last. The global crisis would eventually overcome both countries through financial and trade linkages.

The Severity of the Great Depression: Why Was It So Deep? Why Did It Last So Long?

Credibility or Lack Thereof

For gold-standard countries, the orthodox policy response to the global rise in interest rates of 1928–1929 was to "re-trench." This required raising interest rates, reducing the money supply, cutting government spending, raising taxes, limiting consumption, and raising the saving rate. Such changes would invariably lead to lower economic activity, reductions in incomes, lower prices, weak demand, and high unemployment. These were all in the name of improving the balance of payments and maintaining the gold peg. That such policies were not extremely politically popular is an understatement. Doing so was feasible in the 19th century, but this approach was no longer politically tenable.

Given the politics, financial markets were correct in their assessment that very few countries had credibility in their commitment to maintain the gold standard. Investors who bet that a currency would devalue were frequently correct in the 1930s. To place these "bets," investors sold the currency prior to devaluation to avoid making losses when the expected devaluation materialized. Countries under attack tried to deter speculation. They "defended" their currencies with further rises in interest rates, but eventually, most countries felt the economic costs of waging this financial war were too high. Country after country abandoned the gold standard in the 1930s. Dire economic conditions and financial markets squeezed policymakers, leaving them without many other options.

Commodity exporters were among the first to exit the gold standard. Many commodity exporters abandoned the gold standard by 1930. Australia, Argentina, and Brazil ultimately suspended gold convertibility in 1929 and 1930. This major policy change freed countries from the trilemma, allowing policy to have extra room for maneuver. The exchange rate could now move, acting as a shock absorber. In addition, countries could now increase the money supply in order to raise the level of domestic prices. Doing so allowed them to avoid further economic catastrophe and to limit the losses from an already bad situation. These types of countries, and others relying on foreign investment, in the so-called periphery of the world economy, were strongly affected in 1929 and 1930 by tighter monetary policy in the United States.

Higher global interest rates led to a precipitous decline in commodity prices. Terms of trade declines were on the order of 20% as the prices of wool, wheat, coffee, tin, and so on collapsed. Global capital flows declined as well. Repayments on foreign debts in these countries were typically about 15% to 20% of total exports. Nations like Australia, Argentina, and Brazil were in a predicament. With export earnings falling, the foreign exchange necessary to service debts and continue building infrastructure was not forthcoming. Depreciation was a last resort aimed at restoring solvency, raising producer

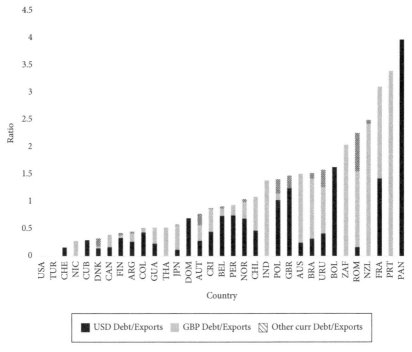

Figure 9.7 Ratio of Public Foreign Debt to Exports by Currency Denomination, 1928

Source Author's calculations based on United Nations (1948)

prices, and boosting incomes. Of course, the issue of foreign currency debt haunted nearly all countries at this time, as it continues to do even today, and as it had done prior to 1914 (Figure 9.7).

Attaining solvency via depreciation depended on exports growing faster than foreign debt service would rise. For countries with large debts denominated in foreign currency and a small elasticity of exports with respect to the exchange rate, default risk loomed. Many economies were in a delicate position in terms of policy. They had to ensure that skittish financial markets did not accelerate a debt crisis by dumping bonds, which would only reinforce the solvency issues perhaps by creating a liquidity or rollover crisis. Policymakers of the time were alert to these matters, which helps explain why unilateral decisions to reflate through depreciation and abandonment of the gold standard were delayed.

Perhaps the leading example of how not to manage such a crisis is Germany. With hindsight, Germany serves as a dark reminder of the negative impact of fiscal and monetary austerity carried out in the name of orthodox policy. By 1933, Adolf Hitler and the Nazi Party had come to power riding a wave of political dissatisfaction. The moderate-center political parties failed to keep their vote share and chaos reigned. Although the SPD (German Socialist Party) and the Communist Party offered an alternative to the far right, these parties appealed more to the urban working class. Ostensibly, the petty bourgeois, shopkeepers, lower-middle classes, and many rural residents became more inclined to give their "protest vote" to the far right. The economic, fiscal, and monetary policies enacted between 1930 and 1932 by the center-right coalition and Chancellor Brüning were, thus, partially responsible for the rise in Nazi vote share. Why were German policymakers unable and/or unwilling to engage in more expansionary, counter-cyclical policy?

Starting in 1930, German localities and states were forced by the federal government to rein in government transfers and spending on new goods and services. Later that year, the SPD (the leading center-left political party) defected from the government coalition in a protest over budget cuts. The Nazi Party vote share surged in the national elections of September 1930. Voters protested contractionary fiscal policies. In places facing greater cuts to government spending and a higher tax burden, the rise in votes for the Nazi Party was higher.[2]

Owing to the government's incessant insistence on "swingeing" austerity, further electoral gains by the extreme right were made in 1932. It was not simply the shock of the Great Depression that brought Hitler to power. Numerous policy errors were made. These errors could have been avoided, even given the understanding of economic policy at the time. Many of them arguably paved the way for the rise of the Nazi Party to power.

Another constraint was monetary policy. Throughout the early 1930s, the Reichsbank proved unwilling to engage in a more expansionary policy, and it failed to accommodate emergency government borrowing. One reason cited for hesitation was that Germany had made an international commitment to maintain the gold standard as part of the recently signed Young Plan for reparations. In addition, assuming Germany would honor its foreign financial obligations, monetary expansion would depreciate the currency and raise the burden of external debt, crushing the economy. The specter of past hyperinflation also haunted policymakers. Finally, financial assistance, by way of new loans, were not forthcoming. Debt relief from the

---

[2] See Galofré-Vila, Meissner, and Stuckler (2021).

Allies was not on the table yet. The options of German policymakers were severely reduced.

What is strange, at least in hindsight, is that Germany did ultimately suspend convertibility of the currency in the summer of 1931, but only after suffering a devastating twin currency and banking crisis. Exchange controls took effect immediately in order to regain some control over the situation, but this simply shifted the burden of policy to domestic residents without ameliorating the debt situation. Outright default or further renegotiation on reparations payments was the obvious solution, but was delayed definitively until Hitler came to power. The Hoover Moratorium was seen as temporary, and it failed to assuage agitated voters in Germany. International leadership was too hesitant and insufficient. Nevertheless, it would seem that domestic political actors sacrificed the economy, many livelihoods, and political stability for their own electoral gains. Indeed, it could be that a set of full-throated expansionary monetary and fiscal policies might have saved both the economy and the political center from collapse.

Global Financial Crises

Real and financial shocks also continued to buffet the global economy. These shocks exacerbated the global economic downturn in late 1930. Although US monetary policy had loosened slightly by early 1930, the Federal Reserve hesitated to do more for the economy. Many decision-makers in the Fed believed that tight money would purge the economy of weak companies, banks, and speculators. Instead, the country soon faced a tidal wave of financial instability and further economic collapse.

In October 1930, the first of three waves of bank failures in the United States occurred, spreading a "contagion of fear" through the US financial system.[3] The banking panic of 1930 led to more than five hundred bank failures, including a sizeable New York–based, commercial bank called the Bank of United States. This was the largest commercial bank to have ever failed up to that point. The panic weakened the economic environment in the American Midwest and led to further generalized uncertainty about the state of the financial system and the economy.

---

[3] This phrase is from the highly influential "A Monetary History of the United States: 1867–1960" by economists Milton Friedman and Anna Schwartz published in 1963 (Freidman and Schwartz, 1963).

In the wake of the Fed's reticence to act, the "appetite for risk" of global investors diminished. Olivier Accominotti and Barry Eichengreen studied the ensuing "Mother of All Sudden Stops."[4] Capital outflows from the United States shrank. In some places that relied on US capital flows, like Germany and South America, nations faced a scarcity of new funding to repay debts. Some countries opted to default on their debt, favoring the dishonor and ignominy of default over a policy of deflation and austerity. Every South American nation except Argentina defaulted between 1929 and 1931 while nearly simultaneously abandoning the gold standard.

Following financial troubles in Germany in June 1931, the Hoover Moratorium gave all European nations a one-year standstill on repayment of their war debts and reparations. By late 1931, international capital markets had ceased to function, since the credit of nearly every country in the world was in tatters and uncertainty gripped the minds of investors.

Germany's default was partially the outcome of a major international financial crisis that started in May 1931. This crisis demolished what remained of international confidence and contributed strongly to the severity and lengthening of the Depression. The global financial crisis of 1931 is an example of international financial contagion. The crisis of 1931 started in Austria but ultimately affected the entire global financial system. Germany, Hungary, and Great Britain were directly affected. However, 1931 would ultimately reshape economic policy across the world. The international financial crisis of 1931 obliterated the inter-war gold-exchange standard.

The crisis came to a head as Austria's largest bank, the Creditanstalt, revealed outsized losses in May 1931. The Creditanstalt was almost certainly "too big to fail." The bank had become larger in the 1920s with important acquisitions of major banks. While its assets had grown, its capital base had not been sufficiently rebuilt in the 1920s. Consequently, the central bank of Austria acted to lend freely to it and other banks that needed liquidity. Despite this, depositor confidence failed, leading to gold reserve losses in the nation's banking system. The ratio of bank deposits to gold reserves fell as depositors withdrew gold from banks. International partners failed to lend sufficiently to the Austrian National Bank. The nation eventually suffered a number of other banking failures. In addition, the surge in credit associated with lender-of-last-resort operations jeopardized the convertibility of

[4] See Accominotti and Eichengreen (2016).

the currency into gold. Investors dumped the Austrian currency in favor of currencies that were likely to remain convertible.

By June, investors in Germany, who had watched the Austrian financial system implode, lost confidence in the German financial system too. The Reichsbank reluctantly assumed its responsibility to act as a lender-of-last-resort but also raised the interest rate at which it lent. The limited policy action came too late. Gold continued to flow out of the banking system and out of the country. By July, the Reichsbank could no longer act as a lender of last resort. Due to the incessant losses of its gold reserves, the ratio of gold to currency outstanding had fallen below the required amount. By July, the Reichsbank severely curtailed its "re-discounts" (i.e., loans) to the now-bankrupt major banks. By mid-July, the entire German banking system was temporarily closed for a bank holiday. On July 15, 1930, the Reichsbank suspended the convertibility of the mark into gold and enacted capital controls. Germany was one of the first countries to impose comprehensive exchange and capital controls in the Depression.

London was also affected by events in Germany. During the early summer, German banks and depositors attempted to cover their obligations by withdrawing funds from London. London's financial markets were now under pressure in a pure case of financial contagion. The British banking system suffered losses over the summer, as gold flowed out of the country. Speculators, anticipating a British abandonment of the gold standard, put greater pressure on the Bank of England to raise interest rates. On September 21, 1931, the government was forced to suspend its commitment to the gold standard. The economic costs of defending the exchange rate with higher interest rates were too high. High unemployment, the obvious side effect of this policy, could no longer be politically tolerated.

The ensuing 25% depreciation of the pound against the US dollar led many countries to follow the lead of Britain. Those that refrained from exiting the gold standard now saw significant real "effective" appreciations of their exchange rates. Prospects for exports to Great Britain and other devaluing countries dimmed significantly. Trade balances for countries relying on British demand worsened as British imports declined. One response to this loss in competitiveness for many gold-standard countries was to raise tariffs. The objective was to reduce the trade deficit. International trade declined to new lows.

An alternative to tariffs was capital controls or "exchange controls," which also acted to reduce integration and commodity trade. These policies restricted access to foreign exchange and limited international flows of capital.

At the same time, capital controls acted as barriers to international trade since because of the balance of payments identity. If capital flows were restricted, trade would now also be limited. In Germany, capital controls were in effect from the summer of 1931. Many other countries followed suit, especially in Eastern Europe. Capital markets could no longer provide the trade finance necessary to clear the multitude of cross-border payments. Bilateral barter agreements for trade, managed by government bureaucracies, became the norm, further disabling the machinery of international finance and trade. Efficiency and welfare suffered.

Banking crises elsewhere haunted the global economy, in the 1930s at the same time triggering bank failures and "financial disintermediation." Banking crises occurred in at least twenty-four major countries between 1929 and the mid-1930s. In the United States, half of all banks failed between 1929 and 1933. Banking crises exacerbated the economic downturn already underway, causing severe "financial recessions." An empirical regularity that holds across the long run, as well as in the Depression, is that recessions accompanied by financial crises (i.e., "financial recessions") are deeper and longer lasting than "normal" recessions.[5]

Banking crises debilitated local economies, which relied on credit to manage the normal flow of orders and payrolls. Crises took a toll on economies struggling to augment local savings for development purposes. Investment collapsed as banks failed. Richard Grossman's landmark, comparative study on banking crises suggested the following key determinants of banking crises: strong competition in the financial sector, a lack of branch banking, declines in industrial production, and whether a country was on the gold standard.[6] The latter factor was decisive because central banks could not simultaneously save banks from panic and liquidity problems and keep their monetary liabilities in line with a legal ratio of money to gold. The Austrian and German crises illustrate this feature. At the same time, defense of the currency often led to a banking crisis, frequently rendering such a defense self-defeating.

Debt Deflation

"Debt deflation" was also a serious issue in economies affected by panic and bankruptcy in financial markets. The standard chain of events in the vicious

[5] See Jordà, Schularick and Taylor (2013).
[6] See Grossman (1994).

cycle of debt deflation is as follows. An economic shock causes withdrawals of deposits from banks. Banks liquidate stocks and other assets to meet demands for cash deposits. Asset prices decelerate or decline. Bank lending dries up. The housing market, a ubiquitous asset, crashes. The expectation of lower profits and lower asset prices due to the credit crunch causes another surge of asset sales, putting more downward pressure on asset prices. Bond prices decline and bond yields (i.e., interest rates) rise, especially for the smallest and riskiest firms. The spread between AAA, rated debt and lower-grade debt rises. Credit dries up. Demand for bonds and houses falls. Price declines for bonds and housing, the very assets typically used as collateral in credit transactions, make the value of collateral fall further. Banks become more unwilling to lend. The supply of loanable funds shifts to the left. Firms, banks, and households are starved for credit and are now more likely to go bankrupt and cut spending. Lenders, especially banks, fail *en masse*. The economy is unable to maintain investment and consumption without banks. GDP falls significantly.

Of course, central banks might have acted to save failing banks and to staunch the deflation by printing more money and buying the assets being liquidated. The singular failure of central banks to act as "lenders of last resort" in the early 1930s is cited as one of the major policy mistakes that caused the severity of the Great Depression. At the time, however, central banks prioritized their commitment to gold convertibility, which was incompatible with extending such liquidity. The traumatic experience with inflation in the 1920s made countries like France, Germany, Poland, and others reticent to abandon the discipline induced by the gold standard. In addition, cooperation, another pillar of stability prior to 1914, failed. In the face of bank failures in Austria in 1931, the Bank of France proved reluctant to lend reserves to Austria, arguing that such a rescue would only be conducive to further financial and monetary "excess." In Germany in 1931, the global community refused to consider a curtailment of German reparations payments, and foreign rescue loans were not forthcoming. The Reichsbank could not bolster its gold reserves and the German economy could not get cooperation on balance of payments relief. An earnest attempt to solve multiple policy objectives suffered from a failure to consider additional policy tools.

In the United States in 1932, the Federal Reserve stated that its hands were tied with respect to easier monetary policy (i.e., to expanding the money supply, offering credit to banks, engaging in open market operations, and lowering interest rates further). Policymakers cited the fact that the ratio of gold reserves to the money supply had shrunk to critically low levels. The great economic contraction continued, despite having gone on for longer than any other recession in American history up to that point. It should be obvious then that one key lesson from the Great Depression is that saving the banking system was paramount to economic stability.

The Gold-Exchange Standard

The gold standard, resurrected as the "gold-exchange standard," also helped to intensify the Great Depression. When banking panics gripped a nation, international capital markets reacted by raising their expectations that a country could soon abandon convertibility. In order to defend against such an outcome and the capital losses that might arise with a 20%–30% surprise devaluation, markets and central banks alike sold the suspect currencies. Sales took the form of exchanging foreign exchange reserves (i.e., the government bonds of countries like Britain, the United States, or France) for gold.

To understand the precariousness of the inter-war gold-exchange standard, one can model the world money supply (M) as follows:

$$M(oney) = G(old) + R(eserves).$$

As reserves (R) were dumped onto markets in exchange for gold (G), the share of reserves backing the world's money supplies fell from 37% in 1929 to about 11% at the end of 1931. In order to rectify the imbalance between a new, lower ratio of reserves to the supply of money (M), monetary policy became tighter, and the money supply decreased again. Depositors also snatched what gold they could from the banking system and placed it under the mattress or in other countries where the currency was expected to be more stable (e.g., Switzerland). The global money supply shrank sharply, causing global deflation. As reserves were sold, the prices of these assets fell in international markets, causing interest rates for anyone borrowing in these currencies to increase. Markets demanded a *risk premium* from suspect countries and the assets denominated in currencies they issued. The natural outcome of such a rise in interest rates was to choke off interest-sensitive spending, leading to unemployment and severe recession.

Perhaps the most illustrative and sensational example of this dynamic at the global level was recently studied by Olivier Accominotti.[7] In 1931, the Bank of France held a large amount of reserves in British sterling assets. Already in 1930, the French had decided to preemptively sell sterling and had been privately trying to insure itself against a British devaluation. Sterling lacked credibility because of its precariously low gold reserves and the apparent unwillingness of the British to raise interest rates with unemployment already in the double digits. French holdings of sterling assets were large relative to British gold reserves, which backed them. Accominotti estimates they accounted for up to 50% of British gold reserves. Not surprisingly, the French sell-off inconvenienced the Bank of England, which was trying to fight a recession already underway. The competitive forces of the market, however, led to higher interest rates in Britain. The Bank of France, through bilateral negotiation, was persuaded to limit sales of sterling, ultimately paying the price in September 1931 when Britain suddenly devalued the pound by a massive 25%. At that point, the Bank of France became technically bankrupt due to the sharp fall in the value of its assets. The Bank of France was soon nationalized. Central banks around the world learned the lesson that credibility of the nation issuing reserves was a concern. The collapse of the gold-exchange standard was complete. The countries that remained on gold, such as France, Switzerland, Belgium, and the Netherlands, held high levels of gold reserves and made sure to keep them with the help of exchange controls, tariffs, and tight monetary policy.

Trade Wars

In a poorly timed policy move, the United States significantly raised tariffs by an average of 50% in 1930 under the so-called Hawley–Smoot Tariff. This policy change was named after Senator Reed Smoot, a Republican from Utah, and Congressman Willis C. Hawley, a Republican from Oregon, but it had been a campaign promise of Herbert Hoover in 1928 intended to help farmers. Hawley–Smoot was not related to the change in monetary policy that occurred in 1928 and 1929, nor to the incipient recession. Still, the move toward higher tariffs was not benign. It quickly led to successive rounds of retaliation. A global trade war ensued, leading to market disintegration and economic losses.

---

[7] See Accominotti (2009).

Higher tariffs in the United States limited US imports and damaged the ability of foreign countries to earn foreign exchange to repay their foreign debts. They exacerbated balance-of-payments problems in many smaller exporters. Nations across the world also retaliated, bringing on second-round effects. Great Britain and many of its colonies conspired to create "Imperial Preferences" through bilaterally negotiated preferential concessions at the Imperial Economic Conference of 1932.[8] The global average of tariffs rose from about 10% in the 1920s to 20% in the 1930s. Additionally, countries that maintained the gold standard lost competitiveness when their trade partners devalued. Many of them attempted to offset this loss in competitiveness by raising tariffs in response. Yet again, this provoked retaliation.

As prices of tariffed imports rose, some of the deflation caused by the monetary process was necessarily diminished. However, tariffs curtailed international demand, lowering revenues and reducing demand for labor. Small, open economies, always with the most to lose from high trade costs, were invariably economically strangled, witnessing much weaker economic growth because of the worldwide hike in tariffs.

Since many tariffs were determined as "specific" tariffs (e.g., 25 cents per ton of coal), global deflation also contributed to rising levels of protection and market disintegration. Furthermore, tariff retaliation also inevitably boomeranged, hurting the very same economy implementing those tariffs. Calculations for Italy suggest that three-fourths of the decline in output between 1929 and 1932 is explained by Italian increases in tariffs in the period. On the other hand, in the United States, a large economy, with very limited dependence on trade, the impact was much smaller. Doug Irwin estimated output losses attributable to tariffs equaled between 2% and 10% of the overall decline in GDP.[9]

Sticky Wages and "Nominal Rigidities"

Institutional changes in labor markets also made the Great Depression very severe. Wages had become less "flexible" across the developed world as industrial labor unions became more powerful. Unemployment insurance in Germany and Britain raised the *replacement rate*, making job search more

---

[8] See Jacks (2014) for an empirical assessment.
[9] See Perri and Quadrini (2002) on Italy and Irwin (1998) on the United States.

lucrative rather than settling for a low wage. In the United States, President Hoover "jawboned" corporations and labor representatives to come together to negotiate high wages so as to keep purchasing power high. It is unclear whether the president understood the ramifications for unemployment and the bottom line for businesses in a period of intense deflation, but some economists have gone so far as to blame Hoover himself for the Great Depression.

Prior to World War I, there is significant evidence that wage and price flexibility prevented large rises in unemployment when negative demand shocks occurred. In this period, when prices fell (nominal) wages would also fall. Unemployment was rare since falling wages would reduce the number of workers seeking employment or actively looking for employment. Oppositely, deflation, in the context of the downwardly rigid wages of the 1930s, caused very high real wages and an imbalance between demand and supply that was not easily eliminated.

The unusually large deflation of 1929–1932 helped create historically high unemployment. Real wages had increased by 10% in the United States between 1929 and 1932, 3% in Germany, and 21% in Great Britain. Unemployment rose to 25% in the United States, 30% in Germany, and 15% in Great Britain. Workers of course actively looked for jobs when real wages were high, but since employers could not afford the cost of labor, and economic activity was limited, job openings remained sparse. Unemployment rates remained high as long as nominal wages failed to fall and the price level stayed low.

Uncertainty

Uncertainty is also cited as another factor for the severity of the Depression. In the early 1930s, some people believed that the "capitalist market system" was finally coming to a catastrophic end. Many leading figures suggested that capitalism was fatally flawed. They viewed the Great Depression as evidence in support of Marxist theory, which had long predicted such a collapse of capitalism. Marxist economists argued that capitalism would experience successively larger and larger crises and ultimately end in a class-based revolution where the people would control the means of production. Reports that the USSR, a regime self-identified as "socialist," and which was operating a command-and-control system for resource allocation, was immune to the

Great Depression and had seen spectacular economic success in the 1920s only strengthened these arguments.

More generally, uncertainty about the future made the economic collapse of the early 1930s even bigger. For many households, especially in the United States, the possibility that a fundamental reset of the economic system was imminent led them to delay purchases of big-ticket items and to become more cautious in their spending. Even if households were less inclined to believe the Marxist theory of imminent collapse of the capitalist order, a prolonged spell of unemployment in a world with only minimal safety nets could lead to big reductions in demand for big-ticket items.

In the United States, the extreme volatility of the stock market reflected this uncertainty. Periods of greater uncertainty between 1929 and 1933 seem to have been associated with lower investment and lower consumption. Christina Romer argued that stock market volatility accounted for a significant amount of the decline in consumer spending between the end of 1929 and late 1932.[10]

Across the world, political and financial uncertainty mushroomed. Spain and China were embroiled in civil war. India's agitation for autonomy and freedom from British rule was becoming more intense and gaining traction. Japan's government became more focused on war and imperial expansion, thus heightening global tensions. In Europe, fascism reared its ugly head. Mussolini proclaimed in an essay in 1932 called "The Doctrine of Fascism" that the people must be "disciplined." The Nazi Party, as early as 1930 and certainly by mid-1932, was viewed as a threat to international peace and stability. Communist, socialist, and worker's parties opposed the fascists advocating their own brand of governance, which following the USSR could have been construed as less than democratic. In short, it would not have been unreasonable to expect the demise of free markets, liberal democracy, and international peace by the early 1930s.

What Got Us Out of It? Economic Policy Changes and Economic Recovery

Monetary and financial factors help explain the severity of the Depression, but monetary factors also explain economic recovery. Specifically,

[10] See Romer (1990).

abandonment of the gold standard reliably predicts recovery in the 1930s. Countries that devalued their currencies relative to gold *and* allowed their money supplies to expand started recovery sooner than the countries that delayed such policy actions.

When Great Britain devalued the pound sterling in September 1931, its economy began growing again almost immediately. When the United States ceased to purchase gold at $20.67 per ounce in mid-1933 under President Franklin Delano Roosevelt (FDR), the dollar fell in value and the US economy experienced a vibrant comeback. Belgium's recovery started in 1936, kicked off by a devaluation in 1935. France's 1937 recovery originated in its 1936 devaluation. Outside of the leading economic countries, recovery consistently followed devaluation.

Going off the gold standard allowed for higher output, higher exports, more investment, and lower unemployment, according to pioneering comparative research by Barry Eichengreen and Jeffrey Sachs.[11] Going off the gold standard typically entailed a large depreciation against a number of key trade partners. A lower relative price of these nations' products for gold-standard trade partners boosted exports. Depreciation boosted exports and increased aggregate demand for domestic products, stimulating higher industrial production, a key component of GDP (Figures 9.8 and 9.9). Naturally, trade partners that did not devalue protested these "competitive devaluations" and often responded with higher tariffs to defensively boost domestic demand.

Abandoning the gold standard helped revive the economy by allowing the money supply to increase. Consequently, real interest rates were likely to fall, boosting interest-sensitive spending like investment. Also, a fixed amount of gold reserves could now buy a larger number of local currency units. This rise in the gold reserve ratio helped raise credibility at the same time that the money supply was expanding. Taking the example of the United States, each ounce of gold reserves formerly backed $20.67, but by 1934 each ounce would legally back $35, allowing for up to a 69% (i.e., 35/20.67 – 1) expansion of the money supply.

The gold-standard orthodoxy requiring a constant parity, supreme for decades (arguably even for centuries), dissolved over the course of five years. As mentioned above, commodity exporters lashed by the twin headwinds of higher interest rates and falling commodity prices abandoned gold early

---

[11] See Eichengreen and Sachs (1985).

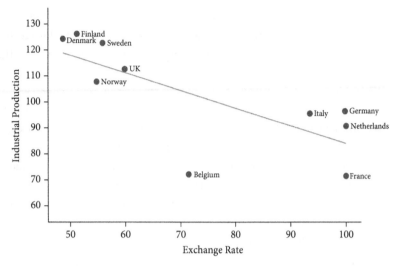

Figure 9.8 Exchange Rates and Industrial Production, 1929–1935

Source: Author's calculations. Exchange Rates: Jordà, Schularick, and Taylor (2021); Industrial production: Mitchell (1998a, 1998b). Notes: Exchange rate is the number of gold-based local currency units at the 1929 gold parity to buy the local currency in 1935 (1929 = 100)

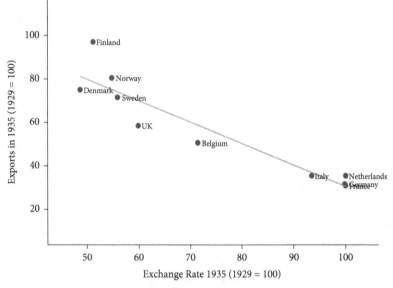

Figure 9.9 Exchange Rates and Exports, 1929–1935

Source: Author's calculations based on Jordà, Schularick, and Taylor (2021). Notes: Exchange rate is the number of gold-based local currency units at the 1929 gold parity to buy the local currency in 1935 (1929 = 100)

between 1928 and 1930. Great Britain, Scandinavia, and Germany, among others, devalued in 1931. The United States waited until FDR was elected in 1933, while a hardcore of France, Switzerland, Belgium, and the Netherlands waited until the mid-1930s.

Evidence shows convincingly that the longer the delay in going off gold the longer a country's Depression lasted. International integration was key to this phenomenon. Any country attempting to maintain a gold standard would see prices evolve in the same direction as other gold countries due to arbitrage. Between 1929 and 1935, prices in gold-standard countries (in terms of local currencies) declined. For instance, prices in the United States fell by nearly 30% between 1929 and 1933. In France, the decline between 1929 and 1935 was 44%. Deflation damaged economies in many ways as articulated above.

A surefire way to offset falling prices was to expand the money supply. Going off the gold standard facilitated this outcome. In addition, prices increased for the simple reason that currency depreciation must raise the local currency price of goods when there is international integration. Such "reflation" (i.e., rising prices) potentially stimulated the economies that chose this policy path. How did this work?

Summarizing, expansionary monetary policy, depreciation, and reflation stimulated economies through several channels. Lower real interest rates allowed firms to begin investing again. Depreciated exchange rates promoted exports, raising national incomes in the process. Higher prices made hiring more palatable. Higher employment prevailed since real wages declined and labor became more affordable for firms. Finally, higher commodity prices sparked recovery in the primary sector.

Abandoning the gold standard also had other indirect salutary effects. Central banks could now act as lenders of last resort to banks caught in liquidity panics. As a matter of fact, no significant banking crises were recorded in any country following departure from the gold standard. A healthier banking system strengthened financial intermediation, promoted investment, helped real estate markets, and stimulated consumer finance.

Abandoning the gold standard also entailed a "regime change" in beliefs and expectations. The dramatic and positive change in expectations about the future level of prices (higher) and future economic policy (more expansionary and benevolent) led to the reverse of the negative uncertainty shock of the early 1930s. In the United States, FDR's policy of abandoning the gold standard immediately set the economy alight, with commodity prices increasing rapidly in the second half of 1933.[12]

But all these benefits beg a question. Why, if recovery was so easy to effect, did nations wait sometimes up to a decade after the start of the Great Depression? There are several potential answers, all of which have some grain of truth in them. First, we might have expected the nations hardest hit by the depression to take early action. For example, Britain, mired in economic doldrums for most of the 1920s, was one of the first economically advanced nations to go off gold. France had a more mild and protracted economic decline, delaying until 1936. The United States, hit hard with unemployment and deflation, delayed four full years from the initial downturn of 1929, however. In Germany, policymakers were reluctant but ultimately were forced off the gold standard amid a severe financial crisis in mid-1931.

Second, political pressure for better policy might have mattered. Unemployed voters and organized labor should have been the loudest voices for expansionary monetary policy, while creditors benefitting from high real interest rates and deflation should have protected the gold standard. Again, the evidence is mixed. In Sweden and Britain, labor was strong and decisively promoted abandonment. Switzerland and the Netherlands were bastions of small savers and sound banks; consequently, their policymakers were more beholden to financial interests. There the delay was long. Again, the United States, with relatively powerful labor unions and a strong democracy, was an outlier in this regard.

Finally, a significant amount of variation in the timing of the abandonment of the gold standard can be explained in terms of historical experience with inflation. The hyperinflations and high instability of the early and mid-1920s generated strong attitudes about proper monetary policy. Many people in these economies associated abandonment of the gold standard with hyperinflation and the social conflict of the post–World War I period. Unsurprisingly, many leaders who had learned the lesson that de-anchoring from gold led to chaos, hesitated to abandon the gold standard. The gold standard was seen as a mechanism to avoid inflation and a policy that would make interest groups across society focus on how to share the burden of economic adjustment (e.g., reparations in the 1920s and the crisis in the 1930s). Opponents of abandonment fretted about opening the floodgates of inflation. In the event, abandoning the gold standard generally relieved economies of

---

[12] See Temin and Wigmore (1990) and more recent research by Eggertson (2008).

the incessant deflation from which they had been suffering. The specter of hyperinflation, while salient in the minds of many, was not a likely possibility in the midst of the worst economic crisis in the history of modern capitalism. Mental models of how the economy was best-managed were seemingly too slow to change despite unprecedented economic devastation.

Could It Happen Again?

Prior to the Global Financial Crisis that began in 2007, most economic historians would undoubtedly have answered "not likely at all!" Presently, and in light of experience in the past several decades, the answer is now "unlikely, but possible." Why should our answer have changed so dramatically in the course of a few years? The answer lies not in what economists know and do not know about how to avoid and combat financial crises and recessions. Instead, there is great unpredictability about policy responses for political reasons.

To demonstrate how much economists thought they had learned from the Depression, Ben Bernanke (then a member of the Federal Reserve Board and who would later become Chairman) apologized in 2002: "Regarding the Great Depression. You're right, we did it. We're very sorry. But thanks to you we won't do it again."[13] Bernanke's apology was on behalf of central bankers and was directed to Milton Friedman and Anna Schwartz. The former authors argued strenuously in their monumental and influential *Monetary History of the United States* that the world's leading central bank, the Federal Reserve, caused the severity of the Depression by not acting to save the banking system from cataclysmic failure. That banking crisis impeded investment and day-to-day business activity, creating unprecedented unemployment and deflation. The lesson learned from monetary economics was that the financial system and the banking system must be saved with the tools of monetary policy whenever a financial crisis and panic sets in. The banking system should not be sacrificed for the objective of maintaining a fixed exchange rate.

John Maynard Keynes published *The General Theory* of *Employment, Money, and Interest* in 1936. The lessons in that treatise were distilled and refined by Paul Samuelson and other "Keynesian" economists after World

---

[13] See Bernanke (2002).

War II. Keynes and Samuelson emphasized fiscal policy could be important too. The fiscal response to a decline in aggregate demand, like that in the Great Depression, was to increase the size of the government deficit by raising spending and cutting taxes. Spending on public works projects and infrastructure, or anything for that matter, would provide salaries for the unemployed when firms failed to hire them. Cutting taxes would stimulate household purchases and business investment by increasing disposable incomes and raising net profits. The government in this case would act as a purchaser of last resort, borrowing from future generations to raise incomes now and thereby acting to smooth incomes over time.

Despite this knowledge, various countries experienced severe economic troubles in the 1990s. Japan suffered a major financial crash and economic slowdown in the early 1990s. Inflation dropped to near zero percent. At times, outright deflation occurred, accompanied by extraordinarily sluggish economic growth. In East Asia, in 1997 and 1998 (see Chapter 13), a major international financial crisis caused losses in output and employment on a scale similar to the Great Depression. Between 2000 and 2002, Argentina's economy shrank by over 20% during a financial crisis reminiscent of the Great Depression. In European nations including Greece, Spain, Ireland, and Portugal, similar events occurred after 2009. Greece, a heavy borrower in the prior decade, faced a major economic meltdown, with unemployment reaching 25% and output hitting a trough equal to 75% of its peak. The numbers are nearly identical to those of the United States in the Great Depression.

In 2009, Barry Eichengreen and Kevin O'Rourke produced a series of charts showing how similar the initial phases of the Global Financial Crisis of 2007–2008 were to the Great Depression.[14] In the event, the depth and duration of the recession following 2007 in many countries was nowhere near as severe as the Great Depression. Despite calls for a fundamental rethinking of economics, obviously unnecessary in its most extreme form, the debates reveal what went wrong and what went right.

What went wrong mainly related to the financial sector and to the monetary regimes in place prior to the crisis. In nearly all the worst-hit countries discussed above, with the possible exception of Japan, small, open economies with fixed exchange rates and heavy capital inflows eventually faced deep downturns. The specifics varied from country-to-country. We will learn more about East Asia in Chapter 13, but Greece is a case in point. Shackled

---

[14] See Eichengreen and O'Rourke (2009).

and bound by the commitment to remain in the European Monetary Union (EMU) and the inability to fund a deficit due to skittish financial markets, Greece made the choice to deflate and reform its economy. The policy of austerity is always an incredibly protracted and painful process, and, unsurprisingly, Greece went years with sub-par economic performance. Had it followed the examples set and the lesson learned in the Great Depression, it might have exited from the European Monetary Union, defaulted partially on its debt, and cleaned up its banking system quickly in order to restore growth. Unfortunately, geopolitics intervened on the way to recovery as it had before in 1931. Germany's Chancellor Angela Merkel, leading the European response, sought to maintain the EMU intact, dismissing breakup of the EMU for fear of stoking fear and financial contagion across the monetary union. Meanwhile, the government in Greece was ultimately convinced to move ahead with a program of deflation and adjustment negotiated with Europe, the IMF, and the European Central Bank.

Fiscal policy as a response to the Global Financial Crisis was relatively timid and faced extraordinary opposition in the rest of Europe and even in the United States as well. In Germany, Chancellor Angela Merkel declared that "one of the first conditions is that you somehow get by with what you earn," implying deficits should stay low in Germany and in partner countries.[15] In the United States, the advice from leading scholars like Christina Romer, President Obama's chief economic advisor, was to undertake a large fiscal expansion. But Nobel Prize–winning economist Robert Lucas disagreed, declaring, "[W]ould a fiscal stimulus somehow get us out of this bind . . .? I just don't see this at all."[16] While the *American Recovery and Re-Investment Act* (ARRA) was intended to stimulate the economy, many economists argued it was far too small for the size of the recession and indeed, government employment decreased under Obama with a cumulative loss of 590,000 public sector jobs.

Monetary policy fared better than fiscal policy. Indeed, Ben Bernanke, now at the helm of the Federal Reserve, led the charge. Bernanke's main objective was to save the financial sector from collapse. His playbook consisted of innovative methods of using Federal Reserve powers and tools to stabilize the American and the global financial system. Federal Reserve action

---

[15] Speech given by Angela Merkel on April 24, 2012, as quoted in *Spiegel International*, April 26, 2012.

[16] Council on Foreign Relations Symposium on a Second Look at the Great Depression and the New Deal, March 30, 2009.

included new lending facilities for banks facing liquidity problems, support for mortgage markets and "asset-backed securities" as well as arranging for funding for all the Wall Street investment banks that were teetering on the edge of bankruptcy. In the end, the Fed was heavily constrained by a lack of information, a new financial environment that had become surreptitiously complex, and by the dire financial straits of an insurance company named AIG. This company was systemically important (i.e., able to bring the entire financial system down itself with a failure), but was not under the regulatory purview of the Fed.

In Europe, the European Central Bank (ECB) was faced with extreme asymmetries. Lowering interest rates would have helped Southern European countries in the monetary union, but northern countries, not in the midst of financial crisis, might have "over-heated." Politicians from the north dismissed expansionary policy while those in the south clamored for an expansion. Tortuous negotiations at the highest levels of the EU ensued. Moreover, financial regulatory systems in Europe were not harmonized, despite cross-country capital flows. This fact hindered political agreements on which country (or countries) should be responsible for resolving the various banking crises that had now spilled over across borders.

In summary, it would appear that the global economy is only one political conflict away from another Great Depression. This conclusion is only strengthened when one recognizes that other factors that cause financial crises remain ubiquitous. As we have seen, these include integrated international capital markets, rapid rises in borrowing and debt, fixed exchange rates, and inappropriately regulated banking and financial systems. While the details and complexity of the international financial system have changed over time, and will continue to evolve, the basic premises laid down here both for the causes and the solutions to them seem to be fairly consistent over the last 150 years and will likely endure.

10

Rebuilding the World Economy
(Yet Again)

World War II interrupted the growth and further integration of the global economy, just as World War I and the Great Depression had done. The devastation of the war was singularly immense and tragic. The war, waged in Europe, Asia, and North Africa, had implications for how trade, capital, and the labor force would evolve over the following decades.

The toll of World War II was staggering. Over forty million people had died. One in twenty were dead in Western Europe. In Germany, coal production and industrial output had fallen to half the pre-war levels. The European economy had broken down. The Soviet Union, an avowedly communist nation, which favored centralized planning, suffered a heavy toll in terms of loss of life. In later decades, the USSR emerged as a superpower. Eventually, the Iron Curtain drew closed across Eastern Europe, forcing these nations to largely disassociate themselves from Western economies.

By the late 1940s, the "Cold War" had already begun to put a freeze on cooperation between the United States and the USSR—two large economies that had just recently allied to defeat Nazi Germany. This geopolitical situation would continue to shape policies and the economy over the coming decades.

Asia was in turmoil too. The incipient push for decolonization and independence in British India (stretching from what is now called Afghanistan to Myanmar) had come to fruition by 1947. In China, the Chinese Communist Party (CCP) assumed power in 1949, after intensive struggle against its nationalist government and Japan. Japan's domestic economy and society were in shreds, and its imperial grip on East and Southeast Asia had totally evaporated. The war did not reach North and South America in any significant way, but both continents were heavily involved in the war effort, supplying material products if not direct military intervention.

In response to the rising power and perceived threat to the "American way of life" (and business) that the communist nations represented, the Truman

One from the Many. Christopher M. Meissner, Oxford University Press. © Oxford University Press 2024.
DOI: 10.1093/oso/9780199924462.003.0010

Doctrine emerged, requiring containment of communism and rapid economic recovery. The Marshall Plan in Europe and other foreign aid programs
concurrently directed to South Korea and Southeast Asia attempted to win
hearts and minds by promoting economic development and the market
economy.

In many of the world's poorest countries, covert forces instigated proxy
wars, and battles raged for political and economic influence. Access to natural resources was also important at times. The first instances of these Cold
War battles, outside of Europe, occurred in China, where the United States
supported the "Nationalist" KMT, and then on the Korean peninsula, which
witnessed yet another devastating war between 1950 and 1953. Such international conflicts were a violent backdrop to the post-war decades.

Despite these choppy waters of international relations, strong economic
growth, improved economic development for a range of countries, and recovery of the global economy prevailed in the three decades following World
War II. This chapter analyzes both economic growth in Europe and East
Asia and the forces driving the resurgence of the global economy prior to
the 1980s.

The Marshall Plan: Rehabilitating Europe

The Americans and the British had already begun planning for the post-
war period by the early 1940s. With the Atlantic Charter of 1941, FDR and
Churchill signaled that it would be vital in the post-war period to orient the
European economies toward the market system of capitalism, instead of
allowing them to fall under the sway of state-led, "communist" economic organization. Business interests and policymakers revisioned the international
economy at the Bretton Woods summit (discussed in Chapter 12) in order to
avoid the international financial failures of the 1920s and 1930s. Most of all,
America, and especially Great Britain, a nation particularly exhausted from
war, aimed to keep Europe from going back to war yet again.

Surveying the damage done in 1946, GDP in the key economies of France,
Germany, and Italy had been reduced by between 25% and 50% relative to the
level predicted by average pre-war trend growth rates (Figure 10.1). Other
countries barely managed to stay on their already sluggish inter-war trend
line. European consumers had fallen behind their American counterparts
in terms of the latest modern conveniences. The interruptions of the Great

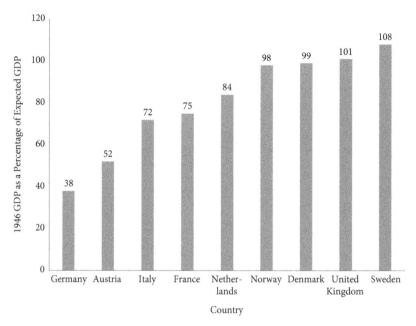

Figure 10.1 GDP in 1946 as a percentage of the predicted level using pre-war trend growth
Source: Author's calculations using data from Bolt et al. (2018)

Depression impoverished millions. Rearmament in the late 1930s generally disfavored personal consumption.[1] Eventually the war itself limited consumption by destroying the everyday lives of populations across entire continents.

On the other hand, in 1947, the United States found itself in a powerful, nearly "hegemonic" position. The US economy, with 6% of world population, accounted for over 25% of world output and more than 65% of world trade. Because of this, it was able to strongly influence the terms of post-war economic policy, even over frequent objections of its ally Great Britain.

In order to kick-start growth in Europe, the US Congress approved the European Recovery Program, also known as the Marshall Plan, in early 1948. The Marshall Plan evokes vivid images and strong preconceptions. Many people envision that the plan deployed vast amounts of resources in order

---

[1] However, according to economic historians Nico Voigtlaender and Hans-Joachim Voth, the Nazi government used the construction of a highway network after 1933 to increase political support and help improve the economy. The highways also complemented automobile ownership and production. Consumers were given tax exemptions for car purchases.

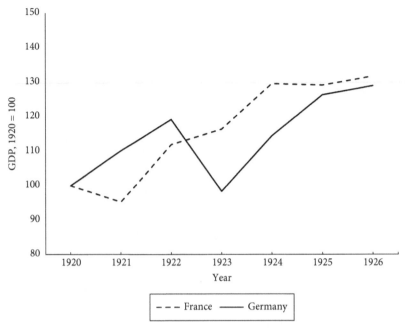

Figure 10.2 Economic Growth in Germany and France Post–World War I
Source: Author's calculations using data from Bolt et al. (2018)

to resurrect Europe economically, but this is more of a myth than a reality. The program transferred only about $13 billion in resources (roughly 2% of recipients' combined GDP) to different countries between 1948 to 1951. The Marshall Plan did not rebuild Western Europe's infrastructure, nor did it provide massive resources.

Instead, the Marshall Plan promoted a market-friendly policy environment, suggesting the least government intervention in the economy possible. US advisors and policymakers argued that international market integration and cooperation would be the best environment for promoting economic growth. Comparing Figures 10.2 and 10.3 shows that growth was more stable and faster in the key economies of France and Germany in the seven years following the end of World War II compared to seven key years (1920–1926) after World War I. The Marshall Plan succeeded by laying a foundation for this strong and solid recovery. Unaccounted for in the raw numbers of dollars sent to Europe and elsewhere is the fervency and passion American policymakers applied to win the hearts and minds of Western European societies and leaders. The objective of such campaigns being that they would

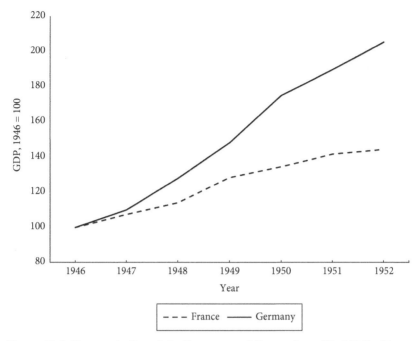

Figure 10.3 Economic Growth in Germany and France Post–World War II
Source: Author's calculations using data from Bolt et al. (2018)

remain in the orbit of the market system of the West and at the same time develop closer economic ties.

What the Marshall Plan Did

Marshall Plan policymakers and other American liaisons "preached a gospel of salvation through improved exports."[2] The United States urged European governments to prioritize the market as a foundation for the welfare state. Many European political parties sought to enhance the latter in these years. According to Barry Eichengreen and Brad DeLong, the impassioned US bureaucrats and supporters of the plan were described by some contemporary observers as economic "Savonarolas," named after Girolamo Savonarola, a medieval friar given to spirited evangelical proselytizing.

---

[2] The discussion of the Marshall Plan is based largely on the interpretation given in De Long and Eichengreen (2003).

Marshall Plan aid was conditional and included matching grants. Both tactics leveraged the American ability to influence the direction of the economic system. When France could not pass a balanced budget in 1948, the United States withheld access to credit until a smaller deficit was approved. The British were informed they would be missing a disbursement due to the fact that social spending (largely housing) continued to increase too rapidly. Extensions of the social welfare state were stymied and discouraged by American bureaucrats.

The Marshall Plan also tried to minimize class conflict. The burden of paying for the war would have to be shared equally rather than shunted off to vulnerable minorities or the voters of out-of-power political parties as governments often attempted to do during the disastrous inter-war period. The Americans would not tolerate delayed action due to political hold-ups, which jeopardized economic recovery. Instead of costly, endless debates; funding a deficit with inflation (often hurting creditors and other financial interests); or imposing inordinate payroll taxes (hitting the paychecks of the working class), the Marshall Plan added marginal amounts of funding for such deficits as may have arisen. Policymakers hoped to extinguish the flames of class conflict and to get immediate action to get economic growth back on track.

The Marshall Plan lasted four years and consisted of many different programs and sub-programs. Aid came in three ways: grants ($9.1 billion), loans ($1.1 billion), and "conditional" aid ($1.5 billion). The bulk of the plan offered straightforward transfers of funds and aid in-kind to assist in feeding impoverished populations, to help industry import crucial inputs, and to promote investment. Conditional aid promoted intra-European trade. Other programs involved training of business executives, giving technical assistance, and promoting competition and productivity enhancement. According to economic historian Michela Giorcelli, one program in Italy allowed hundreds of local business managers and executives to gain advanced training in the United States, resulting in significant increases in productivity and revenues for the companies involved.[3]

The Marshall Plan succeeded in providing a bulwark against communism and central planning in Western Europe. Some countries like Germany also benefitted from additional aid in the period coming from the United States under GARIOA (Government Aid and Relief in Occupied Areas) and also

---

[3] See Giorcelli (2019).

from the United Nations. In Greece and Italy, communist takeovers and elec-toral successes were averted, much to the relief of the State Department. Many in Europe begrudgingly accepted US aid as the cost of maintaining their sovereignty from the USSR, but many also maintained reservations about American influence. To offset American dominance, a number of European initiatives, including the OEEC, the European Coal and Steel Community (ECSC), and ongoing intense collaboration between high-level officials, provided the foundation for what would eventually become the European Economic Community/European Community and ultimately the EU.[4]

What the Marshall Plan Did Not Do

The Marshall Plan did not rebuild enough infrastructure to matter for the European economy. The war ended in 1945, and the Marshall Plan commenced three years later. By then, a majority of railways, bridges, and other infrastructure had already been repaired. In 1947, railway freight volume in the major European nations on the continent was above its pre-war capacity (Figure 10.4).

Nor did the Marshall Plan matter for investment. Suppose, for the sake of argument, that it did. Now follow the logic of Brad DeLong and Barry Eichengreen in exploring this to find a contradiction. Marshall Plan aid totaled 2% of recipients' GDP and investment usually accounted for about 20% of GDP. This implies that aid, if fully spent on investment, accounted for at most 1/10 (equal to 2% divided by 20%) of total investment. A maximum of 35% of Marshall Plan aid was spent on investment properly classified. Given this figure, US aid for investment purposes accounted for less than 1/20 of investment and 1% of GDP at most.

Further, let us assume a historically and abnormally massive rate of return on investment of 50% on this extra 1% of GDP invested in order to strongly overexaggerate the potential impact of the Marshall Plan. We then find that these funds could have accounted for only an extra half of a percentage point of economic growth! Over four years, this might have totaled slightly more than an extra 2% of GDP relative to 1948, but the European economies had grown on average 15% to 20% between 1948 and 1951.

---

[4] Initiatives to extend the "Benelux" (Belgium, Luxembourg, and the Netherlands) customs and economic union to include France and Italy, such as "Benefit," "Fritalux," and "Finabel," did not suc-ceed, despite their flamboyant acronyms.

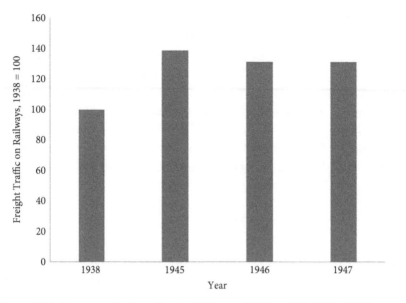

Figure 10.4 European Railway Freight Volumes (1938 = 100), 1938–1947
Source: Author's calculations based on data in Mitchell (1998b)

Much of the literature on the Marshall Plan has focused on relieving production bottlenecks. Crucial industrial inputs like coal could not be imported when countries lacked the foreign exchange to purchase them. This channel has also been overstated. Again, let us consider another thought experiment proposed by DeLong and Eichengreen. Assume that a country was constrained, had no foreign exchange reserves, and could not import coal. Assume also that one-half of total output depends on coal and a technical constraint that coal must be matched 1:1 with other inputs. Imports of coal averaged 7% at the time in Europe. A reduction in coal imports due to a lack of foreign exchange could lead to a maximum decline in output of only 3.5% (equal to 50% of 7%). In other words, even if the Marshall Plan had worked to eliminate the coal shortage, output would only have expanded by several percentage points at most.

In 1947, the prognosis of many leaders in the United States was that the triumph of free markets and democracy in Western Europe was not guaranteed. The European Recovery Program thus helped set the mood and the preconditions for market-based economic growth, rather than simply providing massive amounts of resources and transfers. Some commentators regard the ERP as the first significant foreign economic policy intervention of the United States outside of the western hemisphere, where it had been intervening for decades. Another way to think about the Marshall Plan is that it set a precedent for structural adjustment programs popular with the International Monetary Fund in the post-war period. These programs mandated fiscal austerity (higher taxes, cuts to social spending) and tight monetary policy in exchange for access to IMF loans and assistance. This bears similarity to the blueprint for the Marshal Plan.

Despite its limited direct impact, the Marshall Plan did lay the groundwork for an emphasis on the market approach to resource allocation. Indeed, economic growth from 1950 up to the late 1960s was unprecedentedly high in Western Europe. We turn now to exploring the other forces that contributed to this phenomenon and its implications for the global economy.

The Golden Age: Economic Growth and the Global Economy in Western Europe

The years 1950 to 1973 encompass a "golden age" of economic growth.[5] In these years, Western Europe experienced accelerated economic growth, leading to rapidly rising standards of living. Table 10.1 shows that economic growth in the post–World War II period was faster than in any period before or after. In the first wave of globalization, and the inter-war period, growth of GDP per capita averaged a mere 1.3% per year. In the golden age, the average growth rate of GDP per capita was 3.8% per year. This is almost three times higher than it had ever been since the onset of modern economic growth in the 1800s. The effect on living standards and broader society, as well as the global economy, was unprecedented in human history.

Dramatic social changes were set afoot by new technologies and the demands of the modern industrial economy. The automobile and other durable goods, such as washing machines, refrigerators, the radio, and television, transformed domestic life as they had a generation earlier in the United States. The welfare state became entrenched, and workers became accustomed to the "cradle-to-the-grave" health care and social safety net provided by national governments, reductions in the number of hours in the work week, a "13th month" of pay, as well as the annual (paid) summer and winter vacations, totaling between four and eight weeks. Policymakers had hoped

---

[5] This discussion follows Eichengreen (1996) closely.

Table 10.1 Economic Growth Rates in Europe and the United States, 1820–2016.

Countries	1820–1870	1870–1913	1913–1950	1950–1973	1973–2016
Austria	0.85	1.45	0.18	4.94	1.77
Belgium		1.05	0.70	3.54	1.56
Denmark	0.91	1.57	1.56	3.08	1.36
Finland	0.65	1.44	1.91	4.25	1.71
France	1.01	1.45	1.08	4.02	1.32
Germany		1.61	0.17	5.02	1.44
Italy	0.04	0.94	0.87	4.95	1.24
Netherlands	0.77	0.88	1.07	3.45	1.55
Sweden	0.83	1.78	2.33	3.06	1.58
Switzerland		2.12	0.66	3.08	0.79
United Kingdom	1.14	0.80	0.81	2.42	1.61
European Average	0.79	1.40	1.10	3.75	1.50
United States	1.18	1.82	1.72	2.45	1.62

Source: Author's calculations using data from Bolt et al. (2018)

that the post-war period would be one of economic and social progress and increased integration. Economists and politicians touted the Social Market Economy—fundamentally a market-based system but allowing for government assistance and social insurance in times of need. They also wanted to avoid a global economic crisis like the 1930s. Their hopes were not dashed.

Proximate Causes of Growth

According to neo-classical growth theory, countries should rebound quickly after negative economic shocks like the war and the Great Depression. To understand the post-war growth miracle further, it is useful to characterize the drivers of this rebound growth, also called the "proximate" sources of growth. These include high investment, low inflation, and strong growth in exports.

Finally, to understand these changes more deeply, we need to take one more step and understand the "ultimate" causes of economic growth. These relate to the institutional foundations of economic growth. A grand bargain between workers (i.e., labor) and employers (i.e., capital) proved to be the key ingredient. In addition, several international initiatives cemented and

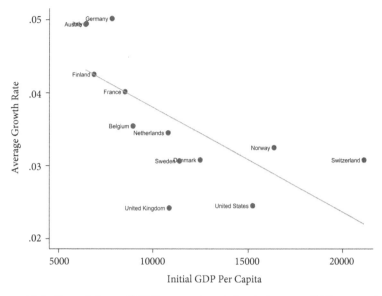

Figure 10.5 Growth Rate of GDP per capita 1950–1973 versus GDP per capita in 1950

Source: Author's calculations using data from Bolt et al. (2018)

supported the achievements in the domestic economies. To understand the process of growth better, we first examine the proximate sources of growth one at a time.

What evidence is there for a strong rebound effect? Figure 10.5 shows evidence for Western Europe that the lower the GDP per capita in 1950, the faster the subsequent growth rate of GDP per capita. The reason given in neo-classical growth theory for this relationship is usually that the rate of return on investment in physical capital (i.e., the marginal product of capital) would be high in Western Europe. Investment therefore can be termed a proximate factor.

Investment was astonishingly high in this period. Investment to GDP ratios averaged nearly 25%, as can be seen in Figure 10.6. While the investment rate was not significantly lower in the two decades following 1970, the rate of return in terms of national income seems to have been higher between 1950 and 1970 than after 1970 at each level of investment. The key questions here, which open the door to investigation of the ultimate causes, are as follows: why were capitalists so willing to invest and why was investment correlated with such high returns?

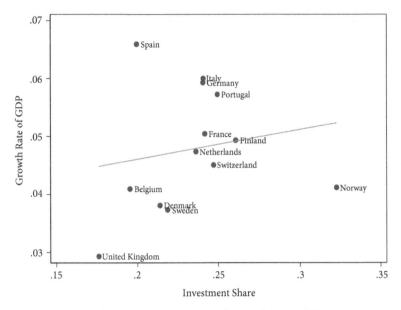

Figure 10.6 Ratio of Investment to GDP and Growth Rate of GDP, Western Europe, 1950–1970

Source: Author's calculations. GDP from Bolt et al. (2018); investment shares from Jordà, Schularick, and Taylor (2021)

A second characteristic of the golden age is the low inflation rate. Inflation rates were low and stable at about 3.5% per year. Gone were the high inflation and instability of the 1920s and the late 1940s. Low inflation is paradoxical, however. Economies on high growth trajectories, with low unemployment and "tight" labor markets, usually tend to generate inflation. Tight labor markets require employers to offer higher wages to attract "scarce" workers, and workers often exercise greater bargaining power over their wages in such environments. Producers in turn cover higher labor costs with higher output prices. The Phillips curve trade-off is a classic representation of this dynamic. Lower unemployment is typically accompanied by rising inflation.

A third fact about growth between 1950 and 1973 is that exports grew very quickly. International integration supported faster growth by allowing countries to specialize along the lines of comparative advantage and by forcing greater competition in product markets. While the average growth rate of (nominal) exports for Western European economies was about 9.5% per year after 1973, the growth rate was on the order of 13.5% per year between 1950 and 1973. Countries that grew faster had stronger growth in exports in the

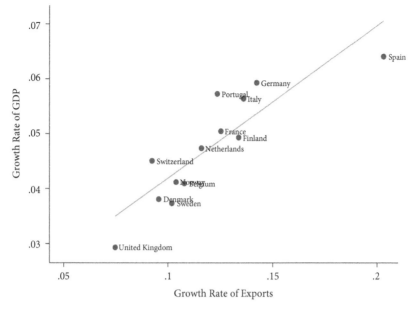

Figure 10.7 Growth Rate of GDP versus Growth Rate of Exports, Western Europe, 1950–1973

Source: Author's calculations. GDP from Bolt et al. (2018); exports from Jordà, Schularick, and Taylor (2021)

period (Figure 10.7). To support this increasing integration, important institutional changes mattered.

The Institutional Foundations of Post-War Growth

Economic historian Barry Eichengreen makes a persuasive case that institutions mattered for post-war European economic growth. To understand these ultimate or institutional causes for the golden age growth miracle, consider a "game" (as in game theory). One of the players represents firm owners (i.e., capitalists) and the other represents workers (labor). Each player (capital and labor) has two available actions. Capitalists can invest heavily in plant and equipment or limit investment. Labor can limit demands for wage growth or instead exercise their collective voice and demand high wage growth. Given these options, we need to understand how Western Europe achieved the observed outcome of high investment and low inflation of wages and prices. Was this an "equilibrium" of the game? Crucially we need to understand the observed actions as a function of the payoffs to each player in this game.

Investment is, of course, beneficial for incomes and economic growth because more productive workers receive higher wages. Firms will also earn higher revenue if they can become more productive with investment. In the short run, however, it might be profitable for the capitalist to skimp on investment and lower costs. Capitalists could simply take high profits now and not worry about the future. Moreover, you might have thought workers would always prefer higher wages now versus waiting for higher wages later. However, a higher payoff to workers is available through wage restraint today if keeping wages low incentivizes capitalists to use the savings toward investment.

What factors helped avoid the "low-growth" outcome where capitalists did not invest and labor demanded high wages? To achieve the outcome of high investment and wage restraint, we might only require that workers and capitalists are somehow sufficiently patient, a key variable related to "time-discounting" in economic games that are repeated over time. Appealing only to the patience of both sets of players would not be satisfactory, nor would it be consistent with the historical record.

Why would the players have suddenly become more patient and willing to make sacrifices now, when hunger and poverty were so prevalent? In essence, the credibility of the commitments to low wage growth and high investment is in question. Under this "good" outcome, each player would assess the costs and benefits of adhering to the arrangement. It is entirely possible that each side would attempt to take advantage of the other side after such an agreement.

For example, workers might persuade capitalists to invest a lot, but then, *ex post*, they could demand a larger share of profits from the firm *after* investment was made. After all, now that the firm has invested in plant and equipment, not investing is no longer an option. That choice was irreversible. Similarly, if a capitalist were to spend the profits gained by delayed wage increases, say by taking a trip to Club Med in sunny southern France (without the workers, of course), then there is no way that workers could regain their fair share. The money has already been spent (largely spent on luxurious seafood and fine wine, of course) by the capitalist. How then can the two parties constrain themselves to adhere to the bargain?

It turns out that policy and institutional arrangements facilitated the agreement. Four factors made a difference. We will categorize them as *monitoring* mechanisms, *bonding* policies, *coordination* devices, and *international* institutions. All these mechanisms kept the players to their promises and made the agreements credible.

"Monitoring" allowed workers to keep their eye on high-level managerial decisions, including investment policies. In post-war Europe, firms and industries typically reserved a seat for workers on company boards. Such participation enhanced the informational environment. Workers could now know if management was adhering to its side of the bargain. Monitoring was specifically allowed through the Works Councils and other similar collaborative institutions, such as co-determination agreements. In Germany, Works Councils date back to the 1920s, traditionally enabling labor to have voice and facilitating local adjustment to nationally negotiated contracts. In the post–World War II environment, nearly all countries in the region adopted similar practices, often called co-determination as well.

"Bonding" refers to a financial incentive. Reneging on commitments becomes more costly when such incentives are in force. In this instance, Western European governments offered valuable tax breaks, investment subsidies, and marketing arrangements to companies and sectors that maintained investment. The social security system (accident and unemployment insurance or pensions) and social services (education, housing, health care, transportation) benefitting workers could also be interpreted as a political strategy to keep labor unions from becoming too militant in their wage demands.

Coordination of wage bargaining at the national level also kept wages from rising too quickly. Implemented in many Western European countries, coordination minimized the potential of a destabilizing cost-push inflation by internalizing the externalities associated with industry-by-industry wage bargaining. Assume there is no coordination. Then, a wage rise in the coal industry would lead to a higher coal price, so that coal companies can maintain their profitability. Since coal is a key input for nearly all other industries, this rising cost of an input could easily lead to higher prices in many other industries, and so on until all final goods and services prices are higher. The fundamental problem without coordination is that the coal industry would not take into account the effect on the overall macroeconomy, instead only considering its own costs and benefits. When wages were coordinated and negotiated nationally, however, and the objective was to keep prices from rising too quickly, wages could be set to be consistent with this objective.

Integration with world markets, as measured by the average ratio of exports-to-GDP in Europe, started lower but on a similar path to the rest of the world, but it rose more quickly in Europe from the late 1950s (Figure 10.8). International institutions within Europe played a role in boosting growth by promoting international integration. These efforts were nearly continuous throughout the 1950s and 1960s.

One early example of such policies is the European Coal and Steel Community (ECSC), which sought to induce access to key inputs by lowering tariffs and other trade barriers. The ECSC ensured that French steel producers could purchase high-quality coal from the German Ruhr valley at low cost. Oppositely, the German steel industry relied on iron ore from the Lorraine valley on the French side of the border, which it could now readily obtain at lower cost. Six nations signed up for this European-led initiative in 1951. They included West Germany, France, Italy, Belgium, the Netherlands, and Luxembourg.

Figure 10.8 Ratio of Exports to GDP in Western Europe and the World, 1950–1973

Source: Author's calculations based on data Federico and Tena-Junguito (2019)

Other plans for greater economic integration, long having been on the policy agenda in Europe but stymied by global conflict, political turmoil, and depression, received further impetus in the late 1950s. The Treaty of Rome, signed in 1957, established the European Economic Community (EEC) from January 1, 1958. Again, the same six countries that had participated in the ECSC were the founding members.

The EEC marked the beginning of what we now call the EU. The EEC aimed to establish a "common market" in goods, services, labor, and capital by reducing customs duties and other non-tariff barriers to trade within the group of member nations. The EEC also initiated the common agricultural policy (CAP), which provided price supports for the agricultural sector and harmonized such intervention across national borders. The CAP would become an important piece of the puzzle in later rounds of European integration and expansion of members, including the United Kingdom.

The EPU, in effect from 1950, fostered international trade by promoting multilateral clearing of trade imbalances. Barter exchange and bilateral clearing became common with the exchange controls implemented in the 1930s and persisted into the post-war period. International trade was limited under such arrangements because trade rarely balances between any two countries. Forcing trade to balance bilaterally led to major distortions in the international economy, inefficiently limiting trade and hindering growth. The EPU incentivized membership by offering larger trade credits to participants, which adhered to multilateral clearing and, in so doing, promoted economic growth. Dropping out of the EPU was not credible since it would have led to lower income via lower trade. By further incentivizing investments and growth, the EPU supported and reinforced the bargains outlined above.

By the late 1960s and early 1970s, economic growth began to slow. Inflation in the 1970s averaged 10%, almost triple the average rate of 3.5% witnessed between 1950 and 1970. Had the institutions that served the purpose of growth now become obsolete or did other forces limit growth?

Several explanations have been put forth, including exchange-rate instability and political decay. The end of the Bretton Woods system of fixed exchange rates occurred in 1971, leading to a more variable and uncertain macroeconomic environment. Alas, the slowdown in economic growth is evident prior to 1971, so this explanation does not go so far. Another potential cause of slower growth may have been institutional "capture." Capture erodes the efficacy of an institution. The parties affected by a binding regulation tend to hijack the governance mechanisms of the system. Then they avoid being constrained by the rules. The explanatory power of this argument seems limited. If true, why did it take so long for this to happen?

Barry Eichengreen proposes that the fundamental problem was that growth was bound to slow down eventually. Slower growth implied that the benefits of adhering to the bargain diminished over time. Why was growth bound to slow? In the short run, growth is due to investment as countries raise their capital-to-labor ratio to a level determined by demography, savings rates, and overall economic efficiency. Economists call this "catch-up" growth or convergence, following the implications of the Solow/neo-classical growth model.

In the long run, growth depends on the pace of technological change or the growth rate of total factor productivity (TFP). Europe, while technologically advanced, relied on a large amount of technology transfer from the United States and other nations after the war. The Marshall Plan, in part, encouraged managers to attend training classes in the United States to learn best practices in inventory management and personnel. These courses diffused state-of-the-art, managerial knowledge and significantly raised productivity in associated Italian firms, according to a study by economist Michela Giorcelli.[6]

A backlog of other technologies, processes, and know-how existed in 1945. European producers adopted these in the 1950s and 1960s. By the late 1960s, technology adoption, updating of processes, and economy-wide structural change had gone as far as possible. The convergence process had been largely exhausted. Western European economies now had to push the frontier to grow faster as in any mature economy. The end of catching-up diminished the benefits of adhering to the post-war bargain. The incentives to maintain wage restraint or to invest for the future had disappeared.

Ultimately, while the golden age could be simply attributed to convergence and catching up to the United States, such a description fails to consider a counterfactual. For example, in eight of the largest economies in Latin America, growth in GDP per capita averaged about 2.5% between 1950 and 1973. Even very poor countries like India (1.5%) and China (3%) grew more slowly. Nothing guaranteed that the European economies would grow so fast after World War II. Instead, conscientious policymakers, a certain amount of political harmony, and an agreement that economic growth would help defend against the Soviet threat from the East are ostensibly responsible for the economic miracle of the period.

[6] See Giorcelli (2019).

Table 10.2 Relative Growth and Levels of GDP per Capita, South Korea and Taiwan.

Country	Per-capita GDP, 1960 (1985 dollars)	Per-capita GDP, 1989 (1985 dollars)	Per-capita GDP Growth Rate, 1960–1989 (%)
South Korea	883	6206	6.82
Taiwan	1359	8207	6.17
Ghana	873	815	−0.54
Senegal	1017	1082	0.16
Mozambique	1128	756	−2.29
Brazil	1745	4138	3.58
Mexico	2798	5163	2.36
Argentina	3294	3608	0.63

Source: Rodrik (1995), p. 56, Table 1

East Asia: Export-Led Economic Growth in a Set of Newly Industrialized Economies?

From the mid-1960s until the 1990s, the economies of South Korea, Taiwan, Singapore, Hong Kong, Thailand, Indonesia, and Malaysia also experienced their own growth miracle.[7] In the late 1950s, no one would have predicted the subsequent economic success of many economies in East and Southeast Asia. After all, the level of GDP per capita in 1960 of South Korea and Taiwan was lower than those of African countries like Ghana and Senegal and much lower than the leaders of Latin America like Argentina, Brazil, and Mexico (Table 10.2).

South Korea suffered from political instability and was recovering from the devastating toll of the Korean War. Taiwan, incorporating a large band of political refugees from the Chinese Civil War and with a legacy of Japanese colonial exploitation, was embarking on a period of martial law. The economy was tightly regulated and controlled, and it suffered from high inflation and a persistent trade deficit. Farther south, Indonesia and Malaysia, like the Philippines and Vietnam, faced internal political struggles and the dual disadvantages of tropical geography and extractive colonial legacies.

[7] Japan grew quickly in the 1950s through the 1980s, too, but its process of development and modernization had already started in the late 19th century.

Amazingly, between 1960 and 1989, Korean and Taiwanese growth outpaced Latin American countries by a factor of two. By 1989, South Korea and Taiwan registered incomes per capita 50% to 100% higher than most Latin American countries. African economic progress was limited. Asian economies, once comparable to places in Africa, now had a ten-fold advantage in income per capita by 1989. As of 1997, East and Southeast Asia accounted for over 18% of global manufactured exports, a share that was only 3% in 1955. Since 1989, these economies continued to grow faster than average, especially Hong Kong, Singapore, Taiwan, and South Korea.

By the late 1990s, growth in Thailand, Malaysia, and Indonesia had slowed down as a consequence of the 1997 financial crisis, and because mainland China was starting to displace their exports, competing directly and effectively with them in global markets. The process of economic liberalization in China began with agricultural markets in the 1970s. This helped raise agricultural productivity. Next, the government, led by Deng Xiaoping, promoted Special Economic Zones from the late 1970s. These boosted investment and exports in the modern sector with a focus on light manufactures and assembly from imported components. The structural transformation and modernization of China continued into the 21st century. In the late 1990s, Vietnam also started a process of opening up to global markets, experiencing faster growth. Meanwhile, North Korea, Laos, Cambodia, Mongolia, Myanmar, and the Philippines (among others) failed to change their economic policies and grew more slowly.

Growth "accounting" exercises for East Asia by Nick Crafts and Kevin O'Rourke reveal that a significant percentage of growth between 1960 and 1990 is accounted for by capital deepening and investment.[8] South Korea's investment-to-GDP ratio was about 35% in the 1970s and 1980s compared to an average of about 20% to 25% in Europe in the 1960s. Crafts and O'Rourke also report that between 1960 and 1980, growth in the capital-to-labor ratio explains roughly half of economic growth of per capita GDP. This contrasts sharply with the European experience of the 19th century, when TFP growth mattered more, and capital deepening only explains about one-third of the advance in labor productivity. It is clear then that the East Asian growth experience represented an economic breakthrough. The question is this: what were the main causes?

---

[8] See Crafts and O'Rourke (2014).

The initial conditions in Korea and Taiwan were relatively favorable in some dimensions. First, in the 1950s, both places had unexpectedly high levels of human capital. High rates of primary and secondary education attainment created a relatively highly skilled labor force that was able to accommodate the technologies of advanced economic growth. The so-called dependency ratio was also favorable. High labor force participation and long working hours driven by a relatively small share of the elderly and children in the population boosted GDP per capita. Finally, both South Korea and Taiwan had low income and wealth inequality. Political squabbles over the distribution of rents can lead to poor policies as the majority tyrannize the wealthy minority (as had happened in Latin America and earlier in inter-war Germany and Europe) with punitive tax rates on high earners and overly restrictive labor market policies. Avoiding distributional battles was key in post–World War II Europe, as it was in East Asia. Aside from these initial conditions, what dynamic forces were at play?

The Deep Determinants of the Asian Growth Miracle

Economist Dani Rodrik highlights that an overall strategy, focusing on a coordinated "big push" for industrialization, allowed for strong growth.[9] This contrasts with a view from the 1980s. At that point, leading mainstream economists fetishized East Asian growth as a triumph of market-oriented policies and openness to international trade. The very same economists blamed distortionary and protectionist policies called Import Substituting Industrialization (ISI) for "failure" in Latin America. As it turns out, both regions engaged in heavily distortionary policies, so this cannot be the decisive factor.

What was ISI? After World War II, countries in South America as elsewhere strengthened economic policies favoring domestic manufacturing as a means to kick-starting structural change. Limiting dependence on the primary sector—an ostensible economic dead end—was another goal. Overvalued exchange rates coupled with exchange controls cheapened key industrial inputs and made foreign finished goods more expensive. Tariffs, quotas, and other highly specific but arbitrary regulations were set up to

---

[9] This discussion follows Rodrik (1995) closely.

shelter domestic industry from foreign competition. Economists argued that ISI policies provided weak incentives to improve technology.

In addition, macroeconomic mismanagement (high inflation and public deficits), behind a wall of capital controls and financial repression, contributed to low investment in industry and eventually to devastating financial crises. Subsequently, growth was sluggish, and these nations failed to build world-class, internationally competitive industries. When is the last time you saw someone driving an Argentinean car instead of a South Korean Hyundai or Kia? Farmers do not regularly use Argentinean tractors. Some of the leading producers of microprocessors are located East Asia. None of them are based in Latin America. Countries like Brazil, Chile, Bolivia, Colombia, and Mexico are still better known for their primary goods like coffee, copper, and petroleum.

So how did these economies in East Asia succeed in becoming manufacturing powerhouses, whereas Latin America largely failed? In fact, there are many superficial similarities between policies in East Asia and Latin America. In reality, both Latin American and East Asian governments intervened and interfered in the operations of the market economy. The key difference was not in the degree of government intervention but in the overall strategy. Ostensibly, the goals of the given interventions and the type of interventions made the difference. The net impact, combined with potentially more favorable "initial conditions," was arguably more positive. In East Asia standards of living and manufacturing capacity continuously rose while long-run results proved disappointing in most of Latin America.

One contrast from Latin America is that East Asian governments ostensibly never shied away from global markets. Imports of machinery and equipment in Korea and Taiwan formed the basis of a growth miracle. To pay for these crucial imports, East Asian governments promoted and incentivized household saving. Saving was then funneled to investment in key industrial sectors. Investment in Korea benefitted from tax credits. The government gave subsidies to borrowers. Development economist Dani Rodrik argued that these sectors required a range of key inputs to be profitable, but demand for a range of final products also has to be present. This is an older idea from the macro-development literature called the "big push." Development can occur when demand is large enough to ensure suppliers generate sufficient revenue to cover their costs. The Korean version of the story adds upstream linkages to inputs which were scarce and expensive at first. Although inputs would have to be imported at first, soon, local producers could do it themselves. Once a range of inputs was available, downstream domestic producers had to rely on demand in order to cover the costs of necessary investments. The government ensured sufficient demand was there.

Rodrik's review of the evidence provides colorful anecdotes from some of the most successful Korean companies. For instance, Lucky Goldstar (LG), now a global brand known for its leadership in electronics and appliances, started as a cosmetics manufacturer. Finding high-quality plastic caps for their tubes and pots of cream proved challenging. Lucky Goldstar found that through "economies of scope," it could start its own plastics company, manufacturing a range of related products. Subsequently, management noticed that products in the electrical and electronics industry were similar in nature. Lucky Goldstar expanded into those products. Eventually, the company started refining its own oil, transporting the petroleum in-house, and providing insurance through a wholly owned insurance subsidiary.

Hyundai, today a world-renowned manufacturing company, benefitted from government coordination as well as early experience in other industries. The company was originally a cement producer in the 1960s. Accumulated knowledge of distribution, organization and management, and quality control from its early years helped Hyundai achieve great success later in more advanced industries like automobile manufacturing and shipbuilding. The shipbuilding industry required a talented and experienced workforce to design ships to local specification. It also relied on the helping hand of the government. At one point, the Korean government guaranteed the market for ships and, in at least one case, stepped in to force Korean companies to ship in Korean-owned vessels when market demand was low.

In Taiwan, industrial enterprise tended not to be as horizontally and vertically integrated as in South Korea. Still, the government emphasized that key inputs and markets needed government assistance. Companies advanced with the help of government in the early stages (Rodrik discusses the case of PVC manufacturers), but quickly, competition in the private sector was encouraged. The very same dynamic is visible in the synthetic fiber industry, where joint ventures between American companies and the government kick-started production in the 1960s. Later on, when specific know-how had accumulated, private firms entered the market. Finally, the ERSO (Electronics Research and Service Organization) is cited as an example of government-led investment in the silicon wafer industry. That industry grew with the further entry of private firms shortly thereafter.

Broadly speaking, then, the Korean and Taiwanese governments emphasized coordination across sectors. Specifically, the development strategy aimed to build capacity in industry that relied on "forward" and "backward" linkages between industries. Because profitability would be low in any one of the industries without the presence (and supply) of the upstream industries and downstream demand, the government's vision was to ensure the existence of all the sectors as rapidly as possible and to use imported inputs when domestic suppliers were unavailable.

They did so by subsidizing investment and leading research and development (especially in Taiwan). In Korea, the conglomerates of industry known as the "Chaebols," large, horizontally and vertically integrated companies, also internalized some of the externalities associated with setting up an entire industrial ecosystem of suppliers. Without such a basis, each industry would never invest, as profitability would be too low in isolation. Governmental policy in these countries focused on and solved the "coordination problem" that can limit the emergence of complex modern industrial sectors that rely on many different types of inputs or "downstream" demand.

These two success stories, South Korea and Taiwan, did not eschew the global economy. Instead, policies aimed at importing foreign investment goods and know-how that would improve the profitability of local industry. This approach was decidedly different from that seen in Latin America, where policymakers are characterized as chasing after the goal of domestic production of many of the steps in the production process and excluding foreign supplies of such products.

Rodrik's thesis is that early investment drove the export boom of the 1970s and 1980s. The strategy paid off handsomely, and exports contributed to sustained economic growth. If this thesis is true, then the traces of these policies should be visible in the data. Figures 10.9 and 10.10 show some support. Investment appears to rise in advance of an acceleration in exports. Thus, calling this "export-led" growth is unwarranted.

In the 1960s, both Korea and Taiwan relied heavily on imports of machinery and equipment. Only after local industry was able to become competitive and productive did exports boom. Prior to Rodrik's exploration of these issues, economists had surmised that reliance on the global market via exports was the key factor determining the profitability of local industry. One pitfall of these earlier analyses was that they failed to consider the historical dimensions of the dynamic process at play, relying too much on abstract argumentation and insufficient knowledge of facts on the ground.

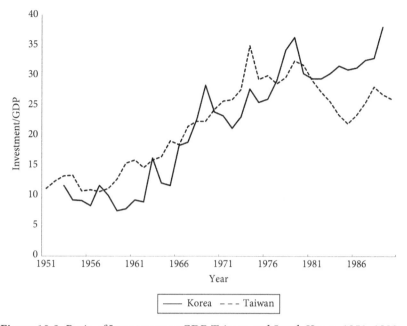

Figure 10.9 Ratio of Investment to GDP, Taiwan and South Korea, 1951–1990
Source: Author's calculations based on Rodrik (1995), p. 59, Figure 3

Figure 10.10 Ratio of Exports to GDP, Taiwan and South Korea, 1952–1990
Source: Author's calculations based on Rodrik (1995), p. 58, Figure 2

Summary

The period between 1950 and 1980 witnessed strong economic growth in Western Europe as in many economies of East Asia. The proximate drivers in Europe and Asia were investment, human capital, and accumulation of technology. The ultimate drivers, perhaps the most crucial, were high-quality policy interventions and institutional innovations. In Western Europe, policymakers made significant progress by creating the Social Market Economy as a viable economic system. All the successful economies relied on the global economy as a source of growth, and the global economy was itself transformed by these growth miracles. We now explore the dimensions of these changes in the global economy during these years.

11

The Global Economy in the Post-War Era

In the three decades after 1945, the world experienced a wholesale reconstruction of the global economy. In the 1940s, the global economy lay in a
heap, browbeaten by the legacy of 1930s protectionism and disfigured by the
demands of the war economies. By the 1970s, trade integration had regained
the level it had achieved in the late 19th century (Figure 11.1). The fundamental drivers of higher trade integration were, of course, lower trade costs.
New technologies, higher incomes, and a new, multilateral approach to trade
policy drove these declines.

   The global economy also witnessed a resurgence of economically
motivated migration in the 1950s and 1960s. Western European nations were
especially dependent on inflows of manufacturing workers. In the Americas,
migration restrictions remained, although by the 1960s the United States and
several other "new world" nations began to see modest increases in the numbers of foreign-born. Nevertheless, during the 1950s and 1960s, migration
rates would never attain the levels they had prior to World War II in these
former "receiving" nations.

Trade Policy in the Post-War Era

By the end of the war, the world required a new paradigm to govern trade
policy. The United States and other leading nations under the GATT led a
push to reduce tariffs. Average tariffs in the first wave of globalization were
roughly 10% with near-zero tariffs in countries like Great Britain, Belgium,
and Denmark. By the 1930s, average tariff rates had risen to roughly 20%.
Lower tariffs would ultimately prevail due to GATT with the global average
among industrialized countries falling from 15% in 1947 to 11% by the late
1960s and to barely 2% by the 1990s (Figure 11.2).

   Although commitment to free trade and liberalization were the hallmark
of the first wave of globalization, by the 1930s, a multitude of trade barriers
emerged as nation-after-nation fought destructive trade wars. Higher tariffs

One from the Many. Christopher M. Meissner, Oxford University Press. © Oxford University Press 2024.
DOI: 10.1093/oso/9780199924462.003.0011

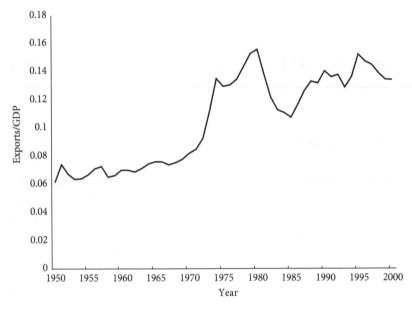

Figure 11.1 Ratio of World Exports to GDP, 1950–2000
Source: Federico and Tena-Junguito (2019)

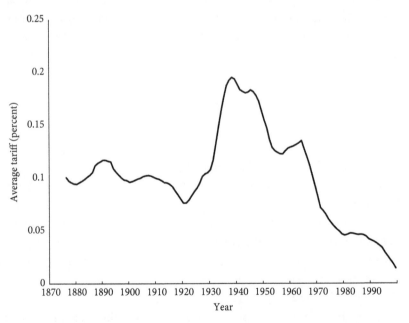

Figure 11.2 Average Tariff (Moving Average, Twenty-three Countries), 1870–1998
Source: Author's calculations based on data underlying Clemens and Williamson (2004b)

were politically expedient, and some countries claimed tariffs aided their ec-onomic recoveries. Others used tariffs (and exchange restrictions) to exert greater control over the economy.

By the mid-1930s, initial attempts to negotiate lower tariffs had begun. In 1934, the United States, in the midst of its recovery from the Depression, attempted to reverse the trend of trade restrictions by devising a new tactic aimed at liberalizing international trade. The United States was now offering "reciprocity" under the Reciprocal Trade Agreements Act (RTAA). This new approach promised lower tariffs in the United States in exchange for reductions by trading partners. The job of tearing down the tariff walls of the early 1930s was, however, left unfinished by the outbreak of the war.

When the war ended, the United States and its allies together pursued a similar but more ambitious tactic. The pillars were "reciprocity" and "non-discrimination." Reciprocity required mutual reductions in trade barriers. Non-discrimination ensued from the insistence that partners adopt the un-conditional MFN clause in their trade agreements.

In the late 1940s, a small group of leading nations began negotiating lower trade barriers among themselves in the so-called GATT. GATT negotiations aimed to limit quantitative barriers to trade, export subsidies, and other policies that restricted international trade. The International Trade Organization (ITO), an international body with wider membership, was also envisioned to approve such changes for all other countries.

The ITO was never ratified by the US Congress, stymying a universal/global reduction in trade barriers. Still, a large coalition of interest groups in the United States, now the world's most important economy, believed that free trade would promote growth, benefit consumers and exporters, and crucially help to contain the communist threat. The latter helped con-vince Republican leaders, traditionally advocates of high tariffs, that free trade was acceptable. The American strategy on trade policy would still have to be driven by international agreements and negotiations, but US voters and interest groups did not approve of an unaccountable and une-lected international organization governing trade policy. After the failure to ratify the ITO in the United States, the GATT became more inclu-sive and continued in successive rounds to negotiate reductions in trade barriers.

The United States played a central role in organizing international co-operation and agreements to lower tariffs. The successive "rounds" of tariff negotiations were held under the auspices of the GATT beginning in 1947.

Early rounds consisted of many preliminary "bilateral" negotiations about tariff levels using the bargaining tactic of reciprocity that had begun in the 1930s. By the 1960s, a new global network of trade treaties led to rapidly declining tariffs (and rising trade). Many of these deals were supported by the unconditional MFN clause.

In later decades, the rules and norms supporting global trade evolved to become significantly more complex than previous global trading regimes had been. Several aspects are worth highlighting. First, many developing countries benefitted or survived global competition by negotiating special privileges. Former colonies received exemptions from tariffs—West African bananas received lower tariffs than Caribbean bananas in France, for instance. After 1979, the Generalized System of Preferences (GSP) allowed wealthy countries to offer lower tariffs to less developed economies even without reciprocal changes and without reference to other partners despite the MFN norm. This was referred to as "special and differential treatment." In 1974, advanced countries began enforcing quotas on footwear and apparel imports from poorer countries under the Multifiber Agreement (MFA). The MFA benefitted LDC exporters with higher prices due to reduced supply and allowed advanced nations to forestall employment losses in politically sensitive textile industries. Average tariffs in LDCs consistently remained higher than the MFN tariffs of advanced economies (AEs) throughout the post-war period.

Free trade agreements (FTAs) and regional trade initiatives would also now become feasible under the agreed principles of the GATT.[1] The number of such agreements rose from less than a dozen in the 1960s to 250 by 2010 and over 300 by 2020. The sharpest acceleration occurred in the 1990s, when there was a wave of enthusiasm for regionalism. The most significant customs union was the European Economic Community (EEC), established with the Treaty of Rome in 1957. The EEC created the "common market" for six founding countries but expanded over the following decades. The European Free Trade Association provided a bridge for European nations that had not yet fully integrated into the EEC. With the passage of the Treaty of Maastricht in the 1990s, the EU was born. Expansion over the years has brought together twenty-seven nations, which trade freely among

---

[1] Some terminology: A preferential trade agreement (PTA) is a treaty that involves lower tariffs for members of the agreement than GATT/WTO/MFN tariffs. A regional trade agreement (RTA) is a PTA that focuses on a region. A customs union is a PTA that binds the group of countries involved to have unified external tariffs. All of these are examples of FTAs.

themselves. Other free trade agreements and initiatives include the Canada-US Free Trade Agreement, later becoming the North American Free Trade Agreement (NAFTA) in 1992, the ASEAN (Association of Southeast Asian Nations) sponsored AFTA (ASEAN Free Trade Agreement), APEC (Asia Pacific Economic Cooperation), and MERCOSUR (Southern Common Market) in South America.

The Uruguay round of GATT also established a formal "dispute settlement" mechanism. Trade disputes arise when countries claim that trade partners are not abiding by WTO rules or not offering the market access promised by treaty. Under GATT, nations agreed that local action in the form of retaliatory or compensatory tariffs could be permissible in the case of a favorable decision. The WTO now governs such disputes with each case being decided by an ad hoc panel chosen by the countries involved. If a ruling is in favor of the complaining nation, then the policy must be reversed, or compensation must be applied. Tariff retaliation is also possible if the partner does not respond to the formal decision.

The idea of an "escape clause" was pioneered by the United States in the 1930s. These allowed the United States to revise tariff concessions in the case of economic hardship at the industry level or persistent deficits with a partner. Later, the United States created, and began to use, other formats. In the 1970s, the US Congress introduced "Section 201" and "Section 301" after the Trade Act of 1974. Section 201 allowed upward revisions to US tariffs in the case imports were a "substantial cause of serious (economic) injury." Section 301 allowed exporters to complain to the administration about unfair trade practices in foreign markets, potentially triggering US tariff retaliation.

In recent decades, trade agreements have become more encompassing, including labor and environmental standards, intellectual property protection, regulatory harmonization, and investor-protection clauses. The most significant of the recent agreements and negotiations, the TTIP (Transatlantic Trade Partnership), TPP (Trans-Pacific Partnership), and the USMCA (United States-Mexico-Canada Agreement) all included these issues. For example, the USMCA prohibited imports of goods made with forced labor and attempted to limit other coercive practices. Beyond that, as part of the agreement, Mexico agreed to strengthen worker rights with a series of new labor laws. European negotiators took a tough line on environmental standards during TTIP negotiations. While the United States wanted to see the removal of myriad public health regulations and restrictions on certain types of pesticides, the EU stood pat. While the United States abandoned the TPP in

2017, the EU and Japan continued, making it less likely that America's preference for an investor-state dispute settlement clause would be included, since the EU was largely opposed. Trade economists generally agree that while tariffs have fallen thanks to GATT and the WTO in recent decades, greater "regulatory coherence" can lower remaining barriers to trade.

Because these issues are so very politically sensitive, it is unclear whether negotiated trade agreements and treaties will be the best avenue for addressing these differences. Moreover, the WTO and recent negotiating rounds have failed to deliver substantive changes due to the many complexities involved. The USMCA shows that there is still some possibility that greater integration and trade agreements can drive regulatory changes, helping to avoid a free-for-all/race-to-the-bottom.

New Technology and Trade Costs

Other technological and political changes affected trade patterns in the postwar period. These included the diffusion of container shipping, better telecommunications, air travel, and decolonization. The first three dramatically altered the international division of labor and the location of production. Decolonization impeded trade that once thrived under the umbrella of imperial preference, but the sometimes violent and often acrimonious breakups also tended to change trade patterns.

Container ships are commonplace today, especially on long-distance routes between Asia, North America, and Europe. Containers are "intermodal" meaning a crane can off-load them from a ship directly onto a flatbed train car or a semi-truck trailer. They can then be shipped inland from the container port at high speed. Prior to the container, shipping was expensive with most products packed in bulk. Unloading a ship was labor intensive, slow, and costly. These trade costs limited international exchange.

The US military first capitalized on the innovation of the container in the mid-20th century, but it did not take long for the container to attain commercial dominance. As nations adapted their ports and harbors to the larger ships that carried these containers, containers quickly became the preferred method to transport most non-liquid commodities. In 1960, the share of imports to the port of New York arriving in containers was about 6%. By 1970 this figure was 31%. One empirical study suggests that the container raised global trade in these years by roughly 15%.

Air travel and telecommunications transformed the global economy in the post-1945 period the way the telegraph and the railway did in the 19th century. After World War II, international and transoceanic telephonic connections increased dramatically. Better technology and deregulation of the telecoms industry drove the cost of a telephone call from New York to London down from about $25 per minute to $0.75 per minute by 1982.[2] In 1927, transoceanic telephone calls like these were placed via high-frequency radio transmission. In the 1950s, new transatlantic cable infrastructure was laid, and from the 1960s, communications satellites helped connect nations directly and efficiently.

In the 1990s, fiber-optic cables combined with advances in computing hardware and software stoked the ICT (information and communications technology) revolution. The "internet," developed through early efforts at the US-based DARPA and other laboratories in the United Kingdom and France, was commercialized from the late 1980s and early 1990s. The length and number of high bandwidth fiber-optic cable connections increased exponentially in the 1990s and in the first decade of the 21st century. Cellular and mobile communication technologies, rolled out extensively in the 1990s and 2000s, enhanced mobility and access to information with successive generations of technology. Improvements, including 3G, 4G LTE, and 5G made communication between almost any two points in the world instant, nearly free, and highly effective.

Similar to telecommunications, immense technological changes helped spur long-distance/long-haul flight connections. Better flight connections decreased the cost of face-to-face meetings and interactions, enabling the flow of information, reducing the costs of doing long-distance trade, and enhancing the monitoring of overseas subsidiaries by HQ. Executives, commercial agents, and tourists benefitted from the Boeing 707 introduced in the 1950s. The 707 permitted regular, non-stop commercial transatlantic air travel. By the 1970s, Boeing's 747 connected San Francisco and Sydney, then the world's longest non-stop flight. By the 2000s, daily non-stop flights connected every continent and every major city as well as second-tier cities. Airfares had fallen with deregulation in the United States, Europe, and other markets. Air travel generally promoted trade, but country pairs with

---

[2] See *New York Times*, May 19, 1982, Section C, Page 14 of the national edition with the headline: "Rates on Overseas Phone Calls Decline," https://www.nytimes.com/1982/05/19/garden/rates-on-overseas-phone-calls-decline.html, downloaded September 23, 2021.

non-stop flight connections witnessed significantly faster growth in trade and economic growth than country pairs without such connections.[3]

New Patterns of Specialization

The dominant paradigm to explain international trade prior to the mid-20th century was the factor endowment approach of Hecksher and Ohlin. This workhorse trade theory became increasingly obsolete in the 1950s, as technology and economic growth altered the way many nations traded. The downfall of this once-dominant theory may have started when Wassily Leontief demonstrated a "paradox" in 1953. Leontief showed that the United States, ostensibly the most capital-abundant country in the world, had imports that were more capital-intensive than its exports. Under the Heckscher–Ohlin model, the reverse should have been true. US exports should have been more capital-intensive than US imports.

Economists who favor the factor-endowment approach were not deterred by these negative findings. Instead, they suggested a more granular set of factor endowments, deciding that input "quality" could matter too. Making such adjustments allows a country like the United States to specialize in products relying on (non-renewable) natural resources such as automobiles and other manufactures of steel, or even products that intensively use "research and development" (R&D). Meanwhile, middle income countries like Turkey, Mexico, Brazil, or Indonesia can export products using factors based on their particular climates or using "semi-skilled" labor. Empirical models that enrich the range and quality of factor endowments have been somewhat more successful in explaining trade and patterns of specialization than the original models.

Still, Leontief's findings spurred further research into the drivers of international trade. For advanced countries, economists eventually discovered that intra-industry competition and trade were increasingly commonplace. As nations developed, they began to trade more intensively in similar products. An example is tennis shoes. Japan produces Asics/OnitsukaTiger, the United States produces Nike, and Germany/EU produces Adidas. All of these "varieties" of shoes are popular in all these countries. Trade in automobiles and aircraft are other examples, although since the 1970s such

---

[3] See Campante and Yanagizawa-Drott (2018).

products are now produced from components made all over the world, as we will see below.

As discussed above, "new" trade theory, developed in the 1970s and 1980s by Paul Krugman and others, argues that trade is largely driven by (lower) trade costs and consumers' preference for "variety." Comparative advantage plays a small role. In "new" trade theory, trade cost declines raise the foreign share of consumption within each industry. Intensified foreign competition eliminates some local producers (i.e., firms), but a majority of incumbents expand their exports to trade partners. These models allow for gains from trade driven by lower import prices and higher export prices. There is an additional gain from the enhanced variety generated by lower trade costs. Firms expand the range of their inputs, making them more productive. Consumers achieve higher welfare due to the wider range of final products now available. One prediction is that trade of similar products (Adidas for Nikes, Rossignol skis for K2 skis, etc.) would expand.

Intra-industry trade rose as a share of total trade from about 30% to 65% for trade within the G7 countries between the 1960s and 2000 (Figure 11.3). The rise revealed that trade was increasingly driven by a "love of variety" rather than exclusively by relative factor endowments. Although many

Figure 11.3 Grubel-Lloyd Index of Intra-Industry Trade, 1962–2000

Source: Author's calculations from National Bureau of Economic Research (NBER) and United Nations Trade Database

European nations had been trading with each other intensively since the 19th century or earlier, the products that they traded became even more similar. The implication was that trade patterns were increasingly consistent with the predictions of new trade theory. This implies that variety as well as a terms-of-trade effect provided the gains from trade. Another implication was that trade had less of an impact on the factors of production so that international competition was more likely to be felt at the sector or industry level.

Migration and Movement of People Post-1945

International migrations after World War II were also significant. Although transportation and communication costs had fallen immensely, many nations imposed restrictive immigration policies, especially in the advanced countries that were the main receivers of immigrants prior to 1945. These nations would no longer accept a steady stream of workers and migrants since the political power of labor, which viewed immigration as an economic threat, had increased over time. Additionally, the frontiers in the so-called New World countries were now closed, largely limiting the once-heavy flows of people to the Americas and Australasia.

World War II generated tens of millions of refugees in Eastern Europe. In the following years, official "exchanges" moved a sizeable number of people across international borders. Ethnic Germans were moved back to Germany from territories now belonging to Poland, while ethnic Poles were moved out of the USSR. Roughly eight million ethnic Germans were moved from Poland to Germany, and in their place came two million ethnic Poles who had been living in territory (Kresy) now claimed by the USSR. The Poles took over the farms and acquired capital, including housing vacated by the Germans.

Similar exchanges of population occurred in Bulgaria (160,000 Turks were sent to Turkey), Hungary (trading over 100,000 Slovaks for a similar number of Hungarians living to the north in Czechoslovakia), Lithuania, Yugoslavia, and the USSR. In Asia, up to nine million people were affected with up to three million Japanese repatriated out of former territories in Manchuria and other parts of Northern China. More than two million ethnic Koreans returned to Korea from Japan and China. Millions of people were reshuffled across newly drawn borders. A closer correspondence between ethnicity and nation prevailed.

After the immediate trauma of the war and into the 1950s and 1960s, many fast-growing European nations faced labor "shortages." Nations sought to alleviate these "bottlenecks" in a bid to keep wage growth low, thereby enhancing profitability. West Germany relied heavily on immigrants to help staff mines and factories. The vast majority of these "guest workers" came from Italy and Turkey, but the German employers recruited far and wide, including from places like Greece, Morocco, Portugal, Tunisia, and Yugoslavia.

Belgium also received a large influx of Italian workers, who found employment in the southern industrial heartland of Wallonia. France, following the acrimonious civil war in Algeria and decolonization in the 1960s, began to receive migrants from its former colonies in Africa and the Caribbean as well as Southeastern Asia. Great Britain was in a similar position, also receiving new residents from former colonies—including India, Pakistan, and Bangladesh.

Movement of people within Europe in the 1950s and 1960s was not insignificant. For instance, nine million Italians moved to other European nations in these years, compared to about fifteen million who left mainly for the Americas during the first wave of globalization. One-quarter of the labor force of Greece had moved to other European countries or beyond in search of better economic opportunities. More than a million Portuguese remained abroad in this period too. By the 1970s, foreign workers made up roughly 12% of the workforce in West Germany and France. Migration would slow in subsequent years, as economic growth decelerated and authorities imposed stricter limits on how many non-European workers could come or stay within their territories.

In the Americas, the pace of immigration was considerably lower when compared to the years before World War I. The United States had imposed a number of restrictions during the inter-war period, even expelling and forcibly repatriating Mexican and Spanish-speaking/Hispanic workers during the Great Depression. In South America, the Great Depression and the wars cut off the back-and-forth migration between Argentina and Italy/Spain that characterized previous years. Until the 1980s, US immigration focused largely on admitting family members of immigrants already present and refugees feeling armed conflicts, especially in Southeast Asia. The source for the majority of American immigration was increasingly Latin America and Asia (80%) as opposed to Europe (20%), which had been the main source prior to the 1930s. In 1970, the share of the foreign-born in the United States stood at 4.7%, compared to 15% in 1910. By 2020, this share would again reach roughly 15%.

Summary

In the years after World War II, the global economy reoriented and regained a more solid foundation than it had had in the 1920s. The United States emerged as a global superpower driven by a desire to contain the perceived threat of communism. Trade policy, decolonization, the process of European unification, and immense changes in shipping and communication technologies promoted trade and movement of people. Capital flows were largely limited as a legacy of the destabilizing speculation of the 1930s.

The share of trade in global output climbed steadily in this period, while capital flows remained subdued. Migration was significantly more controlled and limited than it had been historically, but there were large movements of population, especially immediately after the war and in Western Europe in the 1950s and 1960s. Economic growth in Europe and elsewhere was partly driven by a strong urge to reintegrate. Major economies focused on mutually beneficial trade liberalization instead of harmful zero-sum, 1930s-style trade policy. New countries joined the ranks of those experiencing modern economic growth, especially in East Asia. The stability and growth would not last forever. The 1970s saw a return to instability and a slowdown in the pace of growth.

12

The Bretton Woods System

A New Regime

As early as 1941, the leaders of the United Kingdom, the United States, and the USSR foresaw their victory over Nazi Germany. They believed this to be the most likely outcome of the ongoing war. President Roosevelt and Prime Minister Churchill began, in earnest, to make appropriate plans for the post-war international order during several clandestine summits during the war.[1]

In order to construct a more stable international financial system than that which prevailed in the 1930s, the United Nations Monetary and Financial Conference was held in 1944 in Bretton Woods, New Hampshire, at the Mount Washington Hotel. Delegates from forty-four allied countries were sent to hash out the finer points of a system that had been sketched by American and British policymakers and advisors.

The Bretton Woods conference focused on several key objectives. The first was a system that would balance international integration and policy independence. Second, there was a desire to avoid the destabilizing capital flows of the early 1930s. Third, nations wanted to avoid pernicious competitive devaluations and disorderly exchange-rate management. Finally, by the 1940s, it was now widely understood that the burden of adjustment to international imbalances (i.e., a current account deficit or accumulated debt) was often laid on the deficit countries. The deflationary pressures of adjustment under fixed-exchange-rate systems were disdained by modern approaches to economic policy like Keynesian demand management, which sought to attain full employment. The requisite deflation and fiscal austerity tended to generate unemployment and slow economic growth. Consequently, policymakers sought to encourage surplus countries to share the burden of adjustment. Leaders hoped that all this would take place under the umbrella of an international organization to promote cooperation like the International Monetary Fund (IMF). The system that resulted placed the

[1] In fact, the US State Department and the Council on Foreign Relations had already begun such planning in late 1939.

One from the Many. Christopher M. Meissner, Oxford University Press. © Oxford University Press 2024.
DOI: 10.1093/oso/9780199924462.003.0012

US dollar at the center of the global financial system, an arrangement that produced many unanticipated consequences.

The Compromise

While some agreement about broad objectives existed, the compromise eventually hashed out at the Mount Washington Hotel ultimately reflected the battle between the United States and the United Kingdom for dominance of the international economy. While the United States was clearly superior in economic size and productivity, and host to the leading financial center New York, the United Kingdom maintained global reach in terms of commercial and financial networks as well as with its empire. Some view the ultimate particulars of the Bretton Woods agreement as a compromise between these two nations. Others have argued that the United States attempted to out-maneuver the British by imposing policies that would eventually weaken and isolate the United Kingdom, ultimately allowing for US hegemony. Replacing sterling with the dollar as the leading international currency was paramount. US financial interests and the State Department believed a dollar-based international financial and payments system was a prerequisite for establishing the United States as the "global hegemon."

Whatever the case may be, the conference established the system as follows. International capital flows were largely restricted, and capital accounts remained "inconvertible." Myriad forms of capital controls existed throughout the period. Capital controls were expected to limit "destabilizing speculation."[2] Although the United States insisted on open capital accounts at the Bretton Woods summit, delegates voted for current account convertibility only. This means that trading foreign currency and assets was restricted to be for merchandise and service transactions, while obtaining foreign currency for foreign investments was strictly controlled and limited. Trading in foreign currency and gold was supposed to be

---

[2] Speculation is defined as making a (financial) bet on the value of a currency relative to another. In the pre-1914 global economy, traders often believed if a leading country's exchange rate had fallen below its gold parity, then it would soon return to parity and so placed bets in favor of the currency reinforcing the trend toward parity. This stabilized exchange rates, since deviations from parity would lead quickly to a return to parity. De-stabilizing speculation would entail a bet that a currency which was falling in value relative to its parity would continue to fall away from parity. Placing such a bet would reinforce the trend leading a currency to fall further.

done by central banks and a select number of highly regulated financial institutions.

Next, a system of fixed exchange rates was reinstated. Exchange rates or "parity rates" with the US dollar were to be established as soon as possible after 1947. This was a new direction compared with previous versions of the gold standard and preceding international monetary regimes. During the gold exchange standard of the 1920s and 1930s, nations used historical parities based on a local currency price of gold. Convertibility in the inter-war period was either directly into gold or indirectly into gold via a limited set of international reserve currencies. Now countries would define their currencies strictly in terms of the US dollar. The US dollar would be the only currency defined in terms of gold. Unlike during the classical gold standard, when the parity was inviolable, the established parities could be altered in the case of a "fundamental disequilibrium." The adjustable peg allowed, in principle, for greater autonomy of monetary and fiscal policy.

Finally, the conference established the IMF to carry out international supervision and sustain cooperation. The initial proposal by the United Kingdom was that surplus countries (i.e., the United States) would contribute up to $23 billion for the Fund to leverage IMF assistance to relieve current account imbalances (i.e., deficits). The United States refused this amount, citing the possibility of unlimited liabilities and commitments and the consequent political infeasibility of such a large contribution. The original "quotas" or contributions to the IMF totaled $8.8 billion, with the United States contributing $2.7 billion and the United Kingdom putting up $1.3 billion. The IMF started with nearly $9 billion worth of resources that effectively acted as reserve cushions for member nations. The IMF could now lend to member nations in financial distress. These funds came to be called "drawing rights." In addition, the IMF provided surveillance of the macroeconomic conditions of member nations by tracking and collecting such data as to show the prevailing macroeconomic conditions.

The IMF formally came into existence in December 1945. A new era of international cooperation had begun with the express intention of ameliorating the chronic financial instability of the 1930s. The world would now be based on a dollar standard with each ounce of gold valued at $35. Capital flows, now strictly limited, would no longer threaten to destabilize the exchange rate policies of nations. Nations regained economic policy autonomy and celebrated a new spirit of cooperation. According to the plan, the process of balance of payments adjustments would be smooth.

How the System Worked (or Didn't)

The IMF began operations in 1945. More than fifteen years passed before the Bretton Woods system became fully operative. First, from the late 1940s, it was apparent that the new system of parities was already under strain. European nations had been over-optimistic and had chosen exchange rates that overvalued their exchange rates. Many countries experienced high and persistent trade deficits. Consequently, these nations soon devalued their exchange rates. Britain (1949), France (1948), and Germany (1949) all devalued their exchange rates by up to 30% in order to alleviate the pressures associated with their persistent trade deficits and the "dollar shortage." Another several dozen countries joined them in adjusting their "par values." Exchange-rate instability evidently remained an issue.

By the mid-1950s, the situation had stabilized. Strong economic growth in Western Europe and American cooperation (e.g., via the Marshall Plan, the EPU, and even German Debt Relief) eventually led to a turning of the tables. European economies moved from deficit to surplus. It took until 1958 for leading countries to declare their currencies to be convertible for current account transactions. This meant, in principle, that a currency would no longer be rationed for trade transactions. With the notable exception of France's devaluation in 1958–1959, dollar exchange rates held fairly stable in the leading countries (Figure 12.1). Par values aside, the United Kingdom and many other countries persisted in maintaining multiple exchange rates, which acted as a control on capital flows as well as a limit on current account convertibility.

Over time, the US current account deteriorated. Persistent trade surpluses in Europe and rising deficits in the United States meant that the United States was slowly stripped of its gold reserves. In 1948, the United States held about 2/3 of world gold reserves, but by 1958 it held only one-half. Rather than running a persistent and strong trade surplus, the United States seemed to be losing its accumulated "marbles."[3]

One notable success of the Bretton Woods period was the near elimination of banking crises and therefore also the complete absence of twin (currency

---

[3] This is a reference to French economist Jacques Rueff who wrote in 1961: "The unending feedback of the dollars and pounds received by the European countries to the overseas countries from which they had come reduced the international monetary system to a mere child's game in which one party had agreed to return the loser's stake after each game of marbles" (reprinted in Rueff 1972, 22 and cited in Meissner and Taylor, 2009). Rueff was an advisor to French president De Gaulle, who called for a return to the gold standard and an end to the dollar-based system.

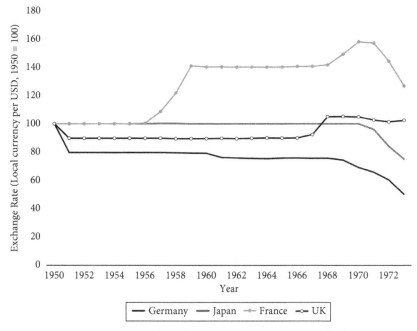

Figure 12.1 Exchange Rates (Local Currency Units per US Dollar), 1950–1973
Source: Jordà, Schularick, and Taylor (2021)

and banking) crises. Banking crises and twin crises were limited because of both capital controls and strict domestic financial market repression. The former meant that banks could not get overly indebted in foreign currency nor did nations build up massive negative net international investment positions via foreign portfolio investment inflows. Keeping a lid on foreign debt helped banks, and the financial sector more generally, from engaging in over-optimistic lending sprees based on foreign borrowing.

For the record, it should be noted that currency instability was not completely eliminated during the years between 1945 and 1971. In fact, the frequency of currency crises rose to levels even higher than during the Great Depression or after 1971 (Figure 12.2). Most of these crises involved persistent trade deficits, leading to a loss of foreign reserves and ultimately requiring a devaluation and adjustment of the IMF parity. Typically, the IMF would offer a "stabilization" or a "structural adjustment" program to a nation in such a situation, prescribing a policy of reduced government expenditure and higher taxes in exchange for financial support. This policy mix aimed to reduce the budget deficit and limit the "balance of payments deficit."

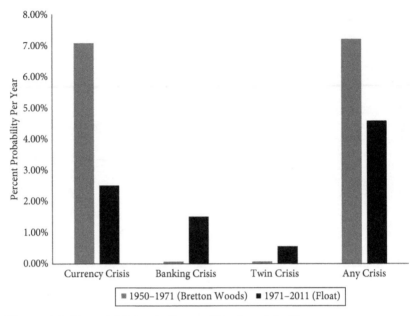

Figure 12.2 Financial Crises in Bretton Woods and the Float

Source: Author's calculations using data underlying the following *sources:* 1950–1971: Bordo, Eichengreen, Klingebiel, and Martínez-Peria (2001); 1971–2011: Laeven and Valencia (2012). Notes: Probability is calculated as the share of country-years in which all countries are in the first year of a crisis. A twin crisis occurs when a currency crisis and a banking crisis occur within one year before or after the other type of event

Fiscal austerity and tight monetary policy were not the first choices of most voters in the post–World War II era, but they were viewed as the orthodox response to an inescapable balance of payments crisis. The fact of the matter remained: rather than provide smooth adjustment, under the Bretton Woods System, most deficit countries preferred to delay adjustment. Associated austerity was postponed for as long as possible until the reserve situation became untenable. Countries frequently ignored the IMF until it became impossible to do so.

Instead of harmonious and cooperative interaction, surplus countries complained that deficit countries were living beyond their means. But surplus countries also played a role in perpetuating imbalances. Surplus nations also disdained advice from the IMF, which mandated higher consumption, higher inflation, and an eventual loss of export competitiveness. Surplus countries saw such prescriptions as detrimental to national priorities at best and at worst likely to stoke unwanted inflationary pressures.

The "adjustable peg" therefore faced several problems. First, the term "fundamental disequilibrium" was simply not a well-defined term. The term did not refer to a specific threshold or economic quantity, nor could it be defined in the same way for all countries. Surplus as well as deficit countries failed to heed the advice of a largely economically toothless watchdog like the IMF. Without the political will to adjust, the Bretton Woods system was unable to provide either the expenditure switching or the expenditure shifts needed to achieve smooth adjustments in the balances of payments. The system was fundamentally incapable of forcing adjustment in a period when domestic employment objectives took precedence over exchange-rate objectives.

The Dollar at the Center

As discussed above, the 1950s witnessed a return to economic growth in Western Europe accompanied by reserve accumulation. US gold reserves, once massive on an absolute scale, and relative to its international obligations, began to dwindle. Some economists attribute this to a "balance of payments deficit."[4] It arose due to increased short-term foreign lending to the United States. Although the United States began the post-War period as a large net creditor to the world, its current account surplus was increasingly smaller. Around 1963, US liabilities payable to official foreign entities, including central banks, exceeded American gold reserves. Figure 12.3 shows that over time the ratio of US gold reserves to US external liabilities was declining.

The Bretton Woods system was analogous to a bank operating on the fractional reserve principle. US official gold balances were like the cash reserves that modern banks hold on hand for liquidity needs of depositors. During normal times, the bank can service demand for liquidity. However, if depositors were to doubt the solvency of the bank or if a large number of people showed up at the bank one day to ask for cash (i.e., gold), then it would soon be rational for all depositors to ask for cash. In essence, as US reserve losses mounted, and US liabilities to the world rose, the credibility of the commitment to return gold for dollars declined. While the United States could never face a long line of unsettled and panicky depositors, foreign

---

[4] See Bordo (1993) for an extensive account of the Bretton Woods system and further explanation of the US balance of payments.

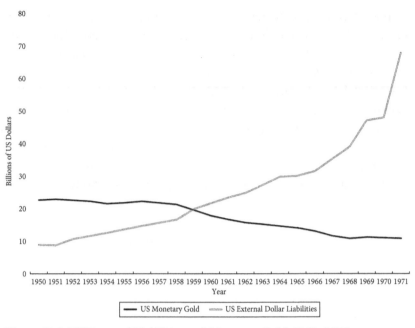

Figure 12.3 US External Liabilities and Monetary Gold, 1950–1971
Source: Author's calculations based on Bordo (1993)

central banks and government officials did raise their (proverbial) eyebrows about the increasingly fragile commitment to convert dollars to gold.

By the early 1960s, French president Charles De Gaulle, backed by economic advisors such as Jacques Rueff, began to openly question the reliability of dollar convertibility, seeking a change to the entire dollar-based system. The French were concerned with the inflationary consequences of US deficits and the reduced ratio of gold to American currency and debt in circulation. Moreover, the French were incensed at what they called America's *exorbitant privilege*. This privilege allegedly allowed the United States to borrow from the rest of the world at very low interest rates (foreigners had to accumulate dollars to back their currencies under the IMF articles of agreement). Moreover, the United States could, in principle, turn around and lend these funds out at higher interest rates. This fueled suspicion that the Americans reaped unfair economic advantage from the Bretton Woods system.

A series of initiatives emerged in the 1960s to deal with the persistent US loss of gold. To promote US exports, American embassy staff were encouraged to extoll the virtues of US exports. Gold holding by the public, already limited from the 1930s, became increasingly regulated. In order to protect exchange rate parities, the international initiative called the Gold Pool arose in 1961. This was a reserve pooling arrangement that would lend gold, short-term, to countries that were in need—major nations like France, the United Kingdom, and the United States were involved. The arrangement did not last very long, since British and American deficits were persistent, and not temporary aberrations. The French would not assume ultimate liability from serial debtors whose ability to repay in hard gold currency became increasingly unlikely.

As time passed, the capital controls that gave nations some breathing space began to weaken. Multinational corporations found ways to keep and establish dollar deposits "offshore," for instance, in the so-called Euro-dollar market. Out of the reach of US authorities, this market yielded a (higher) dollar price for gold that diverged from the official price and supplied exceptional returns. Markets were telling the world that the dollar was overvalued. Given this market, the opportunity cost of maintaining the official price of $35 per ounce became very high.

Agents attempted to speculate on the dollar by withdrawing their funds from the United States and moving to safer currencies like the mark. The US government provided incentives to keep dollar deposits onshore by taxing offshore investments with the "interest equalization tax." Discussion about enlarging the special drawing rights (SDRs) that the IMF could deploy to help deficit countries incited further instability. French and American discord torpedoed this possibility. The Americans viewed higher SDR quotas as a threat to the centrality of the dollar. The French wanted the United States to run a tighter fiscal policy before consenting to allow the United States to rely on more SDRs.

The ultimate fate of the system was decided in 1970 and 1971 amid intense speculative pressure on the US dollar and diplomatic pressure from Western allies. German policymakers complained of the imported inflation that the dollar peg brought to them. Rumors on international currency markets that the French and British would ask the United States to redeem their gold claims and for the gold to be physically transferred out of the United States were flying about in the summer of 1971. The German mark and the Dutch guilder appreciated sharply. The US Secretary of the Treasury, a sharp-tongued Texan named John Connally, remarked to the US economic partners, "The US dollar is our currency, but it is your problem." Essentially any devaluation of the dollar would mean a capital loss for those who had accumulated US assets.

The long-expected dollar devaluation came on August 15, 1971, a Sunday evening. President Nixon told a press conference that the United States would no longer honor the official price of $35 per ounce of gold. Rather than consult with allies and the IMF, the President simply announced the devaluation to the world by surprise. In addition to the devaluation, Nixon proposed a 10% surcharge on imports. In effect, the gold standard ceased to exist from this date onward. A futile attempt in 1972 to stabilize exchange rates, called the Smithsonian Agreement, failed as quickly as it had been implemented. Fundamental policy differences and internationally mobile capital made fixed exchange rates an impossible challenge. A new era of "floating" exchange rates had commenced by 1973. While some European countries would eventually manage to re-peg their exchange rates with each other by the early 1980s, the United States and its dollar would now "float" freely against its major trade partners, never again to be made convertible into gold.

Summary

Some economists argue that the key design flaw of the Bretton Woods system was the use of one global currency, the dollar, as the anchor for all other currencies. Robert Triffin famously identified a problem that has come to be called the "Triffin Dilemma." Under Bretton Woods, the supply of US dollars dictated the level of the global money supply. If the United States did not expand the supply of dollars in pace with global economic growth, deflation and unemployment would beset the global economy. On the other hand, if the United States expanded the supply of dollars, then the commitment to convert dollars to gold would be compromised since the amount of gold was largely fixed. No practical solution was available given the policy objectives enunciated in the 1940s. Getting the supply of US dollars "just right" was unlikely. Triffin's views were somewhat plausible, but not necessarily the reason for the failure of the Bretton Woods system.

Ultimately, the Bretton Woods system was simply unworkable. Member countries outside of the United States with persistent deficits failed to undertake the required harsh austerity that rebalancing would mandate. Exchange rates for deficit countries ultimately collapsed, but with costly delay. Surplus nations had no intention of easing the burden of adjustment and often complained of the imported inflation that the pegged rates of the system wrought. Finally, the key country, the custodian of the system, the United States, failed to rein in its deficits. Accelerating inflation in the United States after 1965 was the final straw. Eventually, world markets (and policymakers) demanded a devaluation of the US dollar. The United States clearly also eschewed the constraints that the Bretton Woods agreements imposed.

The system that was designed in part by the economic genius John Maynard Keynes, and which had incorporated many of the lessons of the Great Depression, was probably unworkable in the long run. Stable exchange rates promote international trade to a degree, but as time passed, financial markets found cheaper and more sophisticated ways to hedge unanticipated exchange-rate movements. Capital flows were limited with capital controls during the 1950s and 1960s, but they became increasingly obsolete and unmanageable. Nevertheless, these capital controls, plus the intense financial repression of the era, mostly eliminated the problem of twin banking and currency crises that were evident in the 19th century, the 1920s and 1930s, and which would reappear in the 1980s.

The Bretton Woods system also was built upon an implicit compromise specific to the Cold War. The United States, leading (and supporting) NATO, promised shelter from the threat of Bolshevism. In return, Western Europe consented to allow the United States to have a certain amount of financial and economic privilege, both narrowly construed in the *exorbitant privilege*, but also more broadly in terms of foreign investment and leadership in the global economy. While the world did not end on the evening of August 15, 1971, the international financial order and globalization were indeed set on a new course. This new course was ultimately charted toward greater, not less integration, but it also involved much greater instability. Nevertheless, as we shall see, the dollar remained the world's dominant international currency.

13

International Financial Flows and Financial Crises after the End of the Bretton Woods System

Following the collapse of the Bretton Woods system, international capital flows mushroomed in the late 1970s. International lending and borrowing came along with greater financial instability. The first major financial crisis was the Latin American Debt Crisis of the early 1980s. Financial crises that engulfed the global economy had been absent since the Depression, but would continue to plague the international economy in the following decades. Advanced and less developed countries (LDCs) alike were affected by these global events in 1997 and then again after 2007.

The determinants of these crises varied over the years, but cross-border capital flows were often involved. Incentive problems like moral hazard played a role, as did the structure of international lending and local policy choices. The successive waves of crises challenged the world to learn from and adapt to the new reality of financial flows with new policies.

International lending and borrowing also created slow-burn, train-wreck-in-slow-motion debt crises in dozens of the world's poorest countries. Unsustainable rises in foreign debt culminated in a powerful international movement in favor of debt relief. In these countries, odious debt—national debt piled up by despotic (and unaccountable) politicians—tended to crush the basis for economic growth for generations. Reluctant international lenders, mainly the richest countries of the world, stonewalled debt relief, despite the negative consequences of inaction for economic growth, development, and politics. Debt relief eventually was successful. This revealed, once again, the dangers and risks inherent in international lending and borrowing when institutional capacity is low and the economy is vulnerable to external shocks.

One from the Many. Christopher M. Meissner, Oxford University Press. © Oxford University Press 2024.
DOI: 10.1093/oso/9780199924462.003.0013

Prologue: Persistence and Change in the Economics of International Capital Flows

In the decades following the 1970s, international capital flows made a come-back (Figure 13.1). Having been interrupted due to war and more-or-less limited by decades of capital controls, economists and market participants alike were unprepared to understand and manage these flows. The return of capital flows led also to a return of international financial crises, but in the post–Bretton Woods era, many new unanticipated issues surrounding the economics of international finance were (re-)discovered.

Policymakers and economists drew many lessons from the inter-war period. The inter-war period demonstrated that financial crises associated with international capital flows were best avoided. Observers believed capital flows of the 1930s generated "destabilizing speculation." Currencies regularly came under speculative attack in the 1930s due to fears of imminent devaluation. Twin crises, simultaneous banking and currency crises, were often the result of domestic banks carrying foreign liabilities together with

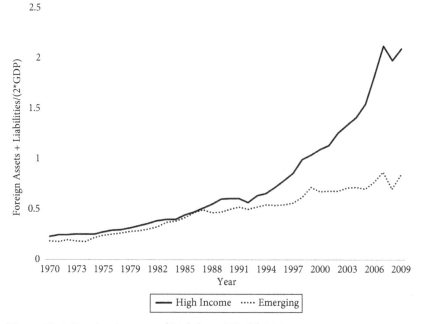

Figure 13.1 Foreign Assets and Liabilities/World GDP, 1970–2009

Source: Author's calculations based on data underlying Lane and Milesi-Ferretti (2017)

exchange-rate crashes. Moreover, several dozen sovereign debt defaults occurred in the 1930s—many in Latin America (Brazil, Chile, and Colombia, among others). The so-called economically advanced countries were not immune from currency, banking, twin, and debt crises either. Germany postponed its reparations obligations in 1931 causing allies like France and Great Britain to default on official loans and assistance inherited from World War I. Germany succumbed to fascism, in part, due to the accumulation of excessive foreign debt. The Bretton Woods regime we explored in the last chapter mandated capital controls, limiting the prevalence of international financial crises.

Indeed, it is remarkable that the years between 1945 and 1971 saw no significant banking or debt crises. Financial crises engulfing multiple countries simultaneously were unheard of. These observations point out the direct and positive impact capital controls and financial repression (i.e., heavily regulated and constrained banking systems) had on snuffing out crises. That said, currency crises did occur between 1945 and 1971, but they mainly took the form of "first generation" financial crises. These currency crises afflicted developed and developing countries alike in this period. They were usually short-lived events driven by persistent trade or current account deficits and maladapted monetary policies, culminating in sharp devaluations of the currency.

Nobel Prize–winning economist Paul Krugman studied this variety of crises theoretically. He determined that such crises were the inevitable outcome of a fiscal and monetary policy combination inconsistent with a pegged exchange rate. The typical example involves a persistent government deficit. The central bank obligingly purchases the new debt issues associated with the ongoing deficits by simply "printing money." Under a pegged exchange rate, the central bank must not and cannot expand the money supply unless external forces warrant such a change. Now note that the money supply is backed by two types of assets: domestic bonds and foreign exchange reserves. In order to maintain the peg, foreign reserves must shrink since the domestic assets held by the central bank are expanding.[1] Foreign exchange

---

[1] If the exchange rate is constant, then prices move in proportion to other countries, including the country to which a nation pegs. This is called Purchasing Power Parity (PPP), and we have seen an example in the Law of One Price earlier. PPP requires $P^*=Pe$. For example, prices in France (P^*) equal prices in the United States (P) times the exchange rate (e). If e is a constant, then P^*/P is constant. Prices in both countries move together. For the money supply, note the following. To simplify we have $M = R + B$. In words, the money supply (M) equals the total assets of a central bank, which equal

reserves serve as the "backing" for a fixed currency. They enable a central bank to intervene in foreign exchange markets and to keep the price of foreign exchange in terms of the domestic currency constant. Another view is that without reserves, the peg, the pledge to convert local currency into a currency like the US dollar, just becomes less and less credible. At some point, in the very near future, it will make sense for capital markets (banks, non-financial companies, and households) to exchange domestic assets for reserves. They expect (correctly as it turns out) that the local currency will depreciate against the reserve currency. Waiting until the currency depreciates to exchange local currency into foreign currency would lead to a large capital loss. Krugman showed that well before reserves run dry, capital markets will suddenly demand all remaining reserves from the central bank, causing the currency to crash.

Where and how did capital flow in the post–Bretton Woods era? Throughout the 1970s, countries began to progressively loosen or eliminate their formal capital controls (Figure 13.2). Prior to this, many controls had already become weakened due to evasion. With the elimination of these barriers to foreign investment, cross-border capital flows increased quickly. Banks in developed countries channeled loans to households, property developers, and non-financial companies through their subsidiaries and loans to other foreign banks. Eventually, by the 1990s, the international bond market became a principal channel by which governments, companies, and banks borrowed. Foreign direct investment (FDI), establishment of direct ownership, and control of production facilities also marked the period beginning in the 1980s. Despite the return of capital flows, rich countries, not poor countries, received the bulk of these inflows. Robert Lucas's paradox was stronger in the late 20th-century than in the late 19th-century era of globalization (see Figure 4.4).

By the first decade of the 21st century, capital flows had exploded with gross flows expanding to two to three times GDP in many advanced countries that were central to the global financial system. One set of IMF economists calculated that between 1980 and 2014 there were 152 episodes of surges and reversals of capital inflows to 53 emerging market economies. In roughly 25% of the cases, nations experienced a financial crisis. This frequency is

---

domestic assets (B or government bonds for simplicity) and foreign reserves (R, bonds issued by reliable countries with stable international currencies). If M is constant, then an increase in B implies a decrease in R.

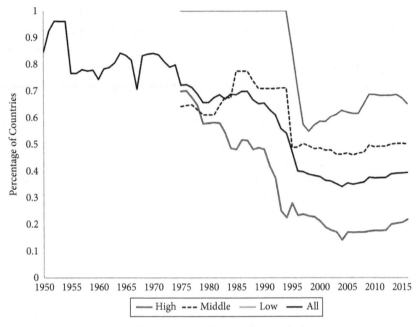

Figure 13.2 Percentage of countries with capital controls, by income status, 1950–2016

Source: Author's calculations based on data underlying the following sources: 1950–1975: International Monetary Fund Annual Report on Exchange Arrangements and Exchange Restrictions (various years); 1975–2005: Dell-Arricia, Mauro, Faria, Ostry, Di Giovanni, Schindler, Kose, and Terrones (2007); 2005–2015: Fernández, Klein, Rebucci, Schindler, and Uribe (2016)

three times higher than the average incidence of crises in the entire sample of countries.[2]

In theory, capital should flow from rich countries with slower growth prospects to less-developed, "emerging" countries with greater growth potential. However, a key hallmark of capital flows from the late 1990s onward until the global financial crisis of 2007–2008 was heavy capital flows *toward* richer countries *from* poor countries. Some of these flows were in the form of "official" flows or reserve accumulation. The majority of these kinds of flows emanated from China, other leading East Asian countries, and some oil exporters. At its peak, the People's Republic of China had accumulated more than four trillion dollars in US government bonds and other investments in the United States being held as foreign exchange reserves. Sovereign wealth

[2] See Ghosh, Ostry, and Qureshi (2016).

funds like China Investment Corporation (CIC), Government Investment Corporation (Government of Singapore Investment Corporation), Temasek (also Singapore), and the Norwegian Government Pension Fund accumulated trillions of dollars of assets issued by developed countries in the first decades of the 21st century. Meanwhile, significant amounts of gross investment from rich to poor countries continued to flow with the elimination of capital controls and financial liberalization in the so-called emerging markets.

What on balance did such international capital flows achieve? The theoretical case for free international capital flows is akin to that of free trade. By allowing capital to be reallocated from where it is abundant to where it is scarce, the global economy becomes more efficient. Rates of return converge as investment drives up the abundance of capital in receiving areas. Investment can directly raise the capital-to-labor ratio in recipient countries, driving higher income per capita. Moreover, capital flows allow for diversification of risks and what economists call risk-sharing. Having real investments in markets and countries abroad allows an investor to maintain consumption when output falls locally and would otherwise drive consumption down. The prediction here is that consumption growth should become more highly correlated with open international financial markets.

On the first issue, the connection between income per capita and capital flows, there is surprisingly little reliable evidence that the capital flows of the post–Bretton Woods era had any positive impact on per capita incomes. A range of cross-country studies has shown very mixed evidence, concluding that there is little, if any, relationship between capital flows and economic growth. One possibility is that investment was not highly correlated with capital inflows, as shown by economists Moritz Schularick and Thomas Steger.[3] Their finding only deepens the mystery of what these capital flows were actually used for. Unfortunately, there is little doubt that some of it went into the private Swiss bank accounts of corrupt rulers and other government officials. Additionally, it is possible that capital flows were directed to residential investment or else to projects with lower-than-expected returns due to corruption, cronyism, and informational "asymmetries."

As for risk-sharing, this measure improved slightly in the period following 1971. Traditional theories in financial macroeconomics predict that with open and efficient capital markets, consumption correlations across countries will equal one as agents seek to diversify and spread exposure to risks.

[3] See Schularick and Steger (2010).

Table 13.1 Output and Consumption Co-Movement and Correlation for Four
Monetary Regimes, 1880–2009.

		Gold Standard (1880–1913)	Inter war (1920–1938)	Bretton Woods (1950–1971)	Float (1973–2009)
All countries	Consumption correlation with output	0.55	0.62	0.67	0.75
	Consumption correlation with UK/USA	0.18	0.12	0.05	0.26
Core countries	Consumption correlation with output	0.68	0.5	0.71	—
	Consumption correlation with UK/USA	0.21	−0.25	0.07	—
Periphery	Consumption correlation with output	0.48	0.68	0.66	—
	Consumption correlation with UK/USA	0.18	0.25	0.05	—

Source: Author's calculations based on data underlying Barro and Ursúa (2008).

Notes: Consumption correlations are with respect to the United Kingdom pre-1950 and against the United States post-1950.

Table 13.1 shows that the correlation of local consumption with US consumption between 1950 and 1971 was about 0.05 under the Bretton Woods system and 0.26 between 1973 and 2009. This implies that closed capital markets are not as good at distributing consumption risk as liberalized international capital markets. Still, consumption correlations have been well below the value of one, which would signal perfect integration. Either the gains from capital market integration have been overstated in theory or something else impeded risk-sharing from occurring. This international diversification puzzle remains a mystery and presents a major anomaly for macro-financial theoretical models.

Another explanation for the lack of any discernible effect on economic growth from foreign capital flows is that international capital flows can sow the seeds of financial crises. Crises are economically destructive. Crises raise economic volatility, and financial crises lead to slower growth and lower incomes. A generic narrative is as follows: in the 1980s and 1990s, emerging market leaders decided to liberalize capital flows by removing the restrictive capital controls that had previously sheltered the local financial system. The advice of policy advisors from the World Bank and the IMF gave them the intellectual cover and the financial incentive to do so. This policy prescription came to be known as the "Washington Consensus" and has also been called "neo-liberalism." Fixed exchange rates were another key recommendation. Recalling the macroeconomic trilemma, fixed exchange rates required that countries necessarily had to sacrifice monetary policy autonomy. Inevitably, this policy of liberalization and adherence to "best practice" policy created current account deficits, fast inflows of foreign capital, and an accumulation of foreign liabilities. With the stage set, financial crises were sparked when capital flows suddenly reversed or stopped flowing into a country.

A sudden stop in capital flows requires a massive turnaround in the trade balance (or current account more precisely) from a deficit (negative value) toward surplus (positive). If the trade balance rises, then imports are on the decline and exports are going up. National income accounting also requires that consumption must be cut too, which may be catalyzed by a tightening of monetary policy. To repay debt, national expenditures must be lower than the value of production. During a sudden stop, a surplus is required, pronto.

The exchange rate must also depreciate. There are few other ways to boost exports rapidly. The depreciation is often very large relative to recent past movement in the exchange rate. Such turnarounds are often complicated by foreign debt. Try repaying a dollar of debt when dollars are now suddenly twice as expensive in terms of your own currency. A depreciated currency raises exports eventually, but the debt problems arise immediately. The additional revenue from exports might not be enough to repay short-term dollar debt. Nothing guarantees a country can export enough and quickly enough to cover payments on the previously incurred dollar debts. The world only needs so many tropical goods, minerals, and other primary goods from these countries at one time, and orders for local products can be slow to come in.

The Comeback of Financial Crises in the Global Economy: The Latin American Debt Crisis

The late 1970s witnessed an incredible, global commodity boom. Perhaps someone in your family remembers the high gas prices and the scarcity of fuel associated with the OPEC embargo. Maybe you have seen video footage of drivers lined up at gas stations waiting to fill up. Not only did gasoline prices rise to historical highs, but inflation in the United States and other leading countries averaged 15% to 20%. Extremely low real interest rates in the United States prevailed.

This commodity boom and the economic distortion of ultra-low interest rates led to the Latin American Debt Crisis of the 1980s. High oil/commodity prices led to large profits for international oil producers, who parked the money in New York banks. New York banks in turn redressed the low returns on their money by lending to banks in low-income countries where higher returns prevailed. Governments, firms, and banks in Latin America took these loans. International capital flows had come back with a vengeance, and these new liabilities had the potential to create a debt crisis. All that was needed was a shock to the system.

The shock that came was the sudden and unexpected rise in US interest rates at the hand of Paul Volcker. Chosen by Jimmy Carter in August 1979 to tame high inflation in the United States, this 6' 8", cigar smoking, veteran Federal Reserve economist aimed to cut the rate of money growth and establish the inflation fighting credibility of the Federal Reserve. While Volcker's reputation for slaying inflation and reestablishing the credibility of the Fed made him a lasting hero to many, the global economy would suffer in the short run. Without regard for the consequences on the fragile international eco-system of capital flows, Volcker surprised the market by raising the federal funds rate from 11.5% in mid-1979 to 17.5% by April 1980. The largest rise came in March 1980 when rates rose 3 percentage points from 14% to 17%. Almost overnight, the cost of borrowing for the entire world shot up.

The foreign loans outstanding in Latin America were not spared. Countries in Latin America, many of which had heavily borrowed on international markets in the run-up to 1981, had to quickly find more revenue to pay outstanding loans, generate projects with massively higher returns, or to default. In August 1982, Mexico defaulted on its foreign obligations. In the ensuing year, all major countries in Latin America ended up doing likewise. Borrowing was the fuel, and the interest rate shock was the spark that started the fire.

The culmination of the crisis was drawn out and economically very costly. The crisis involved large financial losses at lending banks, but the borrowing countries mainly paid the costs in terms of lost output, unemployment, and continuing economic instability. With so much debt left to be repaid (default does not mean a 100% repudiation of all debt), countries also had to sacrifice consumption for repayment of debt. This debt "overhang" limited spending on current needs by diverting real resources to repayment. The years between 1982 and the mid-1990s were a "lost decade" for many of these countries. Inflation rose, economies stagnated, political turmoil emerged, and living standards, especially of the most vulnerable, fell.

A key breakthrough deal in resolving the crisis and clearing the debt overhang came in 1989. The Brady bond deal, named after US Secretary of the Treasury Nicholas F. Brady, who negotiated it, allowed unpaid loans to be turned into marketable securities called Brady bonds. Brady bonds turned illiquid loans on banks' books into liquid securities tradeable on international capital markets. Brady bonds would not have been possible if borrowers had not agreed to the collateralization of their bonds (reserves and other assets could be forfeited in case of default) and if the United States had not offered generous guarantees to lenders in the case of default. These bonds helped reinvigorate lending and to clean up the balance sheets of the banks involved in lending.

With benefit of hindsight, it is easy to see that over-borrowing and exposure to interest rate changes were the principal causes of the Latin American Debt Crisis. Analysts at the time were more sanguine. Lenders perceived the massive oil and commodity revenues as collateral. With oil prices at record levels, this seemed like a good bet. The usual metrics for debt problems were *not* flashing critical either (Table 13.2). Typical measures include the reserve-to-debt ratio or the debt-to-export ratio. Higher reserves to debt would be correlated with a greater ability to repay with more foreign currency on hand for each dollar of debt. Higher exports to debt improve debt sustainability for a similar reason since a portion of export revenue would be used to repay foreign debt. As it turns out, none of these traditional indicators were all that high in leading borrowers in the run-up to the debt crisis. Of course, the problem is that these indicators were backward-looking and failed to take account of the possibility that interest rates would change and global demand would "tank" as it did in 1981 and 1982. The former made repayment difficult for obvious reasons while the latter decisively curtailed export revenue. Shades of the Great Depression were present. Indeed, the lost decades of Brazil, Argentina, and Mexico amounted to economic depressions in their own right.

Table 13.2 Principal Debt Ratios 1973–1980.

Country	1973	1975	1979	1980
	Debt to total exports			
Unweighted Averages	106.6	121.4	116.0	98.3
Medians	111.2	122.5	94.1	83.1
	Interest payments to total exports			
Unweighted Averages	4.5	7.3	9.3	9.8
Medians	5.1	8.0	6.6	7.6
	International reserves to debt			
Unweighted Averages	70.0	149.5	85.7	81.8
Medians	43.8	27.0	95.5	89.4

Source: Author's calculations based on data in Diaz-Alejandro (1984), Table 2.
Notes: Debt is long-term (> 1 year) public external debt. Countries in the sample are Argentina, Brazil, Chile, Colombia, Mexico, and Venezuela. Values are ratios x 100.

Bad Things Happen to Good Countries: The Unexpected European Financial Crisis of 1992

London, Black Wednesday, September 16, 1992, 10:30 a.m.: short-term interest rates in the United Kingdom now stand at 12%, two percentage points above yesterday's rate. Another hike in interest rates up to 15% later in the day is communicated to markets. The United Kingdom's chancellor, Norman Lamont, attempting to defend the pound sterling from speculative attack, faces accelerating sales of the pound and continuing losses of hard-won foreign reserves. Ultimately, the chancellor fails in defending the pegged exchange rate. The pound succumbs to speculative pressures later in the day and falls 5% overnight against the German mark, thus ending the two-year attempt to keep sterling closely pegged to the mark and other leading European currencies. Speculative attacks and large, sharp exchange-rate depreciations also occurred around the same time in Italy and the Nordic countries of Sweden, Norway, and Finland in 1992 (Figure 13.3). France was forced to widen its band of fluctuations by the summer of 1993. This was clearly an international currency crisis.

All these countries had committed in the years prior to 1992 to maintaining relatively stable exchange rates with Germany and with each other. This Exchange Rate Mechanism (ERM) was a step on the path toward

Figure 13.3 Exchange Rates versus German Mark, 1990–1995
Source: Author's calculations based on data in Jordà, Schularick, and Taylor (2021)

full monetary union in Europe. Governments had long agreed on the need to limit the trade-destruction and the economic uncertainty induced by the volatile exchange rates of the 1970s. What nearly all the policymakers failed to grasp was how precarious such pegged-exchange-rate commitments were. In the new world of open capital markets, speculative attacks, like in the 1930s could move quickly and destructively. The political costs of "defending" an exchange rate with high interest rates were immense. George Soros, now a major philanthropist but back then a razor-sharp market speculator, made billions of dollars selling the pound short in 1992.

What Soros realized was that credibility mattered as much to the durability of a pegged exchange rate as the ability to speculate did. To understand how credibility mattered in this case, a different model from Paul Krugman's "first generation crisis" is necessary. In Krugman's first-generation model, the fundamental problem is an ongoing deficit. An attack will occur at some point with a probability of one—complete certainty. In the early 1990s, economists like Barry Eichengreen and Charles Wyplosz noted that standard explanations based on deficient "fundamentals" were not apparent in the United Kingdom or France. Their preferred explanation was the "self-fulfilling" model of currency crises first developed by economist Maurice Obstfeld, among others.[4]

The self-fulfilling model says that a currency can crash out of a fixed-exchange-rate system even without a persistent deficit. In the first-generation model, a deficit was a necessary condition. Krugman's model tells us bad outcomes are determined by bad policies. The self-fulling approach demonstrated that a crisis could occur if there were an attack on the currency, but if there were no attack, no crisis will occur. The crisis is independent of macroeconomic policies, deficits, and other observable variables like reserves or debt correlated with the sustainability of an exchange rate peg.

To understand better the idea of multiple outcomes or "multiple equilibria" (in the parlance of game theory), think of the problem of credibility. Consider a recurrent theme in the Charlie Brown comic strip. Lucy frequently promised Charlie Brown she would hold the football when Charlie tried to kick it. Charlie would sprint toward the ball, but something bad would invariably happen. The joy and pleasure of schadenfreude overcame Lucy. As poor Charlie tried to kick the ball, Lucy would remove the ball. Charlie landed on his back with a thud. Lucy's promise was not credible.[5]

Similarly, policymakers who promised to maintain interest rates even with Germany could not hold to this promise. Germany had a well-known aversion to inflation and so the merest hint of inflation would lead to higher interest rates. When German reunification threatened to bring such inflation, the Bundesbank responded with tighter monetary policy. Could the United Kingdom or France keep up by also raising interest rates? Capital markets traders who gambled that the United Kingdom could follow suit would end up being served with the equivalent of Lucy's bait and switch. Those betting on stability of the sterling exchange rate ended up on the economic equivalent of their backs. Notice that the typical signals in the Krugman model for a currency crash of endless budget deficits or rising foreign indebtedness are not part of this story.

Instead, keen observers like Soros developed an intuition (and a hefty short position in the pound), that when challenged to raise interest rates, the United Kingdom would demur. Rather than wait for German interest rates to rise and for obvious gaps in policies to generate changes in the exchange rate, Soros and the markets decided to accelerate the process. By short-selling

---

[4] See Eichengreen and Wyplosz (1993) and Obstfeld (1986).
[5] Why Charlie Brown could be repeatedly fooled by this promise is unclear.

the pound at the fixed exchange rate against the mark, traders put pressure on the United Kingdom. They did so because the UK treasury stood by to sell unlimited amounts of foreign exchange for pounds at a fixed price. As traders emptied the reserves from the coffers of the United Kingdom, they were doing nothing more than buying foreign exchange with pounds at a low price and hoping to sell it later at a higher value in terms of sterling.[6] The UK treasury, faced with a choice of raising interest rates to economically pernicious levels in order to attract capital or abandoning the exchange-rate commitment ultimately opted for abandonment.

The devaluation and exit from the Exchange Rate Mechanism (ERM), by the United Kingdom, Italy, and France as well as the devaluations in the Nordics revealed that fast-moving speculative attacks were back on the scene after nearly sixty years of hiatus. As we learned in our exploration of the gold standard, credibility mattered then as it did in the early 1990s. The lesson for countries and international capital markets should have been that fixed exchange rates were fragile. Instead, many argued that the crashes seen in Europe were specific to Europe or inevitable due to the divergence in economic policies. Many countries that could have learned a lesson chose to ignore the events, continuing to peg their exchange rates and welcome capital flows from abroad. Such was the case in the most advanced emerging markets such as those in East Asia like South Korea, Indonesia, Thailand, and Malaysia. The global economic crisis of 1997 was the result.

The Next International Financial Crisis and the NICs: East Asia and Financial Contagion

The mid-1990s: the global economy is purring along. Tariffs are at historical lows. Fixed exchange rates prevail. The WTO arbitrates trade disputes. There is strong economic growth in Southeast Asia, Latin America, and the United States. Financial markets have been liberalized and stock markets are booming. Democracy is becoming more and more common, and communism has failed. The USSR has collapsed. The Eastern Bloc is now in

---

[6] Hypothetically, the short sales would give someone like Soros an obligation to repay a given quantity of pounds sterling. With the eventual depreciation of the pound, it became cheaper in terms of dollars or marks for a holder of foreign currency to repay that amount of pounds than before the depreciation. Speculators like Soros pocketed the difference, keeping their high returns in hard currency like the mark or dollars.

"transition" to capitalism. What is not to like about the so-called Washington Consensus? Macroeconomists and policymakers were so pleased that they branded this period the "great moderation." Low price volatility, low and stable inflation, and strong economic growth characterized the moment, at least in the economically advanced countries.

The sheen began to wear thin starting in late 1997 and into 1998, when a financial crisis erupted in Thailand. Soon thereafter, South Korea, Malaysia, and Indonesia fell victim to similar events. Currencies in all these nations crashed almost simultaneously (Figure 13.4). Ministers of finance, central bankers, the International Monetary Fund, and the president of the United States were called in to administer emergency policy action. How did this occur in such a promising global economic environment?

First, the balance of payments certainly played a role. Abundant foreign capital flows stopped and then reversed in the 1990s. Interest rates shot up. Exchange rates depreciated. Banks failed and governments negotiated bailouts and stabilization policies with the IMF and the US Treasury. These

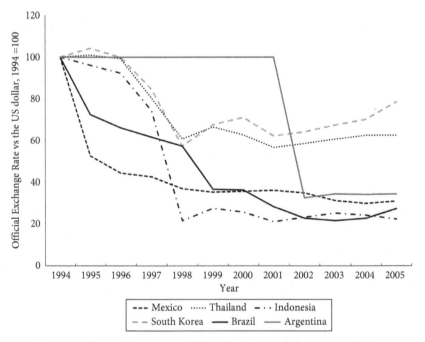

Figure 13.4 Exchange Rates versus US Dollar in Six LDCs (1994 = 100), 1994–2005

Source: Author's calculations based on World Bank (2021)

crises were a humiliating culmination of a period of strong economic growth in countries that just years earlier were the darlings of international economic policy advisors and prime examples (allegedly) of the benefits of the Washington Consensus.

Second, and once again, the financial crisis was unanticipated. Capital markets were optimistic about growth in East Asian countries. Standard indicators such as short-term debt-to-reserve ratios, and public debt growth were not anywhere close to the critical levels that typically warned economists of an impending crisis. What happened? First, the crisis was again a case of multiple equilibria. International capital markets went into a panic in late 1997 and early 1998 and, because of the panic, the crisis likely became worse.

Fixed exchange rates led to another, previously unrecognized issue. Fixed exchange rates gave rise to an incentive problem called "moral hazard." Moral hazard occurs when someone who is insured engages in excessive risk-taking. This was a familiar concept in microeconomic approaches to insurance from the late 1970s. Few policymakers had such issues on their radar screens, nor had many macro-economists raised the alarm about such incentive problems prior to the crisis.

Fixed exchange rates led local borrowers to believe they were insured. Local banks, firms, and households believed that the exchange rate pegs with the US dollar were guaranteed. As a result, these nations accumulated significant short-term debt denominated in US dollars. Why not? The cost of capital was lower when borrowing in dollars than borrowing in local currency. When capital flows reversed, reserves drained from the system as a first defense. Ultimately, policymakers found it too costly to defend the dollar exchange rate pegs. Exchange rates crashed. Debt that was once affordable was now much more costly when expressed in terms of local currency.

Government involvement in these economies conspired to make the crisis severe and international in scope. In post-mortem evaluations, many economists blamed the eventual panic on faulty corporate governance or crony capitalism. In South Korea, observers blamed the industrial conglomerates' cozy relationship with governments and state-owned banks that facilitated access to subsidized capital and funding for investments. Apparently, strong economic growth could not be expected when the government was allocating resources. Indonesia serves as another example. President Suharto, an autocrat who had ruled the country since 1967, allegedly appointed friends and close relatives to positions of power in leading economic concerns. Such cronyism was identified as justification, after the fact, for the panic and capital flow reversal.

The fact that multiple crises occurred simultaneously also highlighted financial contagion. Just like a communicable disease transmits to those in proximity of the infected, close economic linkages transmitted crises across East Asia. Economists identified four potential channels. First, a depreciation in one country could lead to an invasion of imports and losses of revenue for nations most closely linked in the region. Second, the loss of market share in competing nations on third markets like Japan, Europe, or the United States was a potential cause for economic weakness in competing nations. Third, correlated shocks to fundamentals might have kicked off the crisis. Investors may have realized that China's imminent emergence into the global economy would reduce the future economic prospects of many economies in the region through much stiffer international competition. Economic prospects were suddenly dimmer than anticipated in a range of countries. Finally, an information channel was identified. Economic theorists dubbed this a "wake-up call." Foreign investors may have blindly followed market sentiment and allocated funds toward a range of emerging Asian markets. If one country was in trouble in Asia, then under-informed investors could infer that all countries in the region could be worthy of a downgrade.

As the financial crisis worsened in early 1998, IMF and US policymakers rushed in to assist. The IMF's historical purpose was to provide resources to individual economies facing balance of payments pressure and to recommend corrective policy changes. The IMF had never faced a global crisis of this magnitude. Accordingly, the IMF response was largely modeled on individual stabilization policies in which it specialized. IMF advisors swooped in to counsel massive hikes in short-term interest rates to stabilize the currency, reductions in government spending and tax rises, government guarantees of deposits and other liabilities of the banking system, pro-competitive breakups of large industrial conglomerates, and privatization of state-owned enterprises.

While well intentioned, the IMF goals of stabilizing the currency and the financial system were not necessarily salutary for the economy as a whole. Higher interest rates and fiscal austerity could only put downward pressure on aggregate demand, raising unemployment. Bailouts and guarantees only heightened the contingent debt of governments whose resources depended on a strong economy. In addition, the IMF was much too small in terms of resources. Fortifying the reserves and extending large credits beyond a nation's quota were already contentious. Doing so for a set of large economies facing a massive simultaneous crisis was impossible. It is no wonder that the advice of the IMF and foreign advisors was widely perceived to be an intrusion on sovereignty and inconsistent with earlier plaudits that these economies had received in international circles. In the midst of crisis, governments and leaders like Indonesia's Suharto were forced from office. In Malaysia, Prime Minister Mohammed Mahathir eschewed advice from the IMF and implemented his own heterodox response. The centerpiece of his go-it-alone policy was the implementation of strict capital controls in the midst of the crisis. These controls aimed to slow down speculative pressure on the currency. The IMF did not warmly approve.

The East Asian financial crisis was a defining moment in the history of the international economy. Output losses in the East Asian economies ranged from 5% to 10% in the aftermath, and larger if calculated as a cumulative gap between actual incomes and those projected based on historical trends (Figure 13.5). The human cost was even more tragic, as economic instability led to political instability, civil disobedience, and high unemployment for years afterward. According to my own research with David Stuckler and Lawrence King,

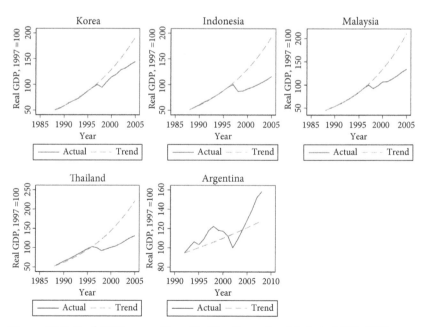

Figure 13.5 Real GDP versus Trend in Five Emerging Markets, 1989–2005
Source: Bolt et al. (2018)

health problems accompanied the economic stress and austerity of the period. There was a rising incidence of heart attacks and other stress-related causes of death in the wake of such crises.[7] What started as economic shocks ended up as financial crises, political upheavals, and public health problems.

In the aftermath of 1997, mainstream economists who assured the world that economic growth and higher living standards could be attained by following the Washington Consensus were to some extent discredited. A more nuanced look suggests that the global financial system was much less stable than it ought to have been and certainly much less so than standard textbook macroeconomic models featuring smooth adjustment would have suggested. The crisis sparked a new debate to revamp and revise the rules governing capital flows and the governance of the international financial system.

The New Financial Architecture: Prediction, Prevention, and Management

In the aftermath of the Asian financial crisis, a vigorous debate about the future of the international financial system ensued. Barry Eichengreen, one of the leading voices in this debate, boils the main issues down into three areas: crisis prevention, crisis prediction, and crisis management.[8]

Preventing crises would intuitively be the first best solution, if in fact crises are so destructive.[9] What about prediction? If we cannot prevent financial crises then surely predicting them with high accuracy would give us time to prepare, much like a weather forecast for a hurricane gives us time to evacuate. Finally, better policies to manage crises could potentially limit the severity of crises.

Predicting Financial Crises

Let us examine the challenges of predicting financial crises first. Accurate and precise forecasts for the timing of a crisis are nearly impossible. "Economic

---

[7] See Stuckler, Meissner, and King (2008).

[8] See Eichengreen (2002).

[9] Forget for now the fact that economists Franklin Allen and Douglas Gale have published an academic paper titled "Optimal Financial Crises." See Allen and Gale (1998). In fairness, their paper argues that under reasonable assumptions, central bank intervention to stop a panic leads to Pareto improvements in welfare.

fundamentals" and other observable variables matter, but these do not help predict exact timing. Financial crises are like earthquakes. Although earthquakes are more likely along major fault lines, the timing of these events is largely unknown to researchers. Random shocks matter. Indeed, since the early 1990s, economists have realized that financial crises are often driven and started by ostensibly random shocks to market expectations that are not correlated over time nor are they correlated with observables. The exact timing of these shocks is largely unknowable. The basic premise is closely related to economists' claim that the best model of the stock market says the stock market is virtually unpredictable. If it were predictable, then everyone would take advantage of the opportunity and all profits would quickly be exhausted. As one economist quipped to another who pointed out a $100 bill on the sidewalk: "There is no $100 on the sidewalk! If there were, it would already have been taken."

Financial crises cannot be predicted for another economic reason having to do with the evolutionary nature of financial markets. The vulnerabilities in the financial system that lead to a financial crisis are often eliminated in the wake of a crisis with new regulations or restrictions. Prudent regulation and economic management require this. However, savvy financial traders are not precluded from finding new ways to gamble, get over-leveraged, and hide their risk-taking from the prying eyes of regulators.

We should not believe that each generation begets a financial crisis because it fails to learn from the past. But we might believe that regulators have a hard time keeping up with financial markets. We may also infer that banks and market participants often have no incentive to internalize the potential economic costs to society of their gambles. The "public good" of strong financial architecture and regulation, which could prevent crises, is often in short supply. While crises may be a fixture of the environment for years to come, the mantra "this time is different" should probably be taken literally since the causes of financial crises are typically unique.[10] Crises are complex phenomena that require an auspicious coincidence of multiple factors, compounding the difficulty of prediction.

---

[10] "This Time Is Different" is the tongue-in-cheek title of an influential book by economists Carmen Reinhart and Kenneth Rogoff. The title refers to a phrase that, according to some, is commonly heard in the run-up to past financial crises. Market participants often argue that the most recent financial boom, bull market, or surge in lending is different in fundamental ways from the previous boom that turned to bust. An example is that many pundits argued (falsely) that "house prices have historically not declined" prior the sub-prime crisis of 2007–2008. Reinhart and Rogoff claim that most financial crises over the last eight hundred years have similar causes and are especially likely when lending and credit grows rapidly. See Reinhart and Rogoff (2009).

A significant literature in economics has devoted itself to predicting crises, but it has failed to provide robust results. The approach to finding "early warning signs" is to collect data from a sub-sample of countries and years and then apply econometric tools to find statistical correlates of crises. The usual method is to control for as many observable determinants as possible and see which ones have the greatest predictive power. One study by Graciela Kaminsky and Carmen Reinhart based on data from 1970 to 1995 proposed that crises are more likely when the growth of the money supply and interest rates are above trend. An appreciating real exchange rate and exports below trend help predict crises. In their sample, output falls below trend prior to a crisis.[11] The best predictors for banking crises are appreciation of the real exchange rate, equity price booms, and the money multiplier. The problem with this line of research is that the results seem to be heavily dependent not only on methodology but on the countries and years in the sample. This confirms the evolutionary nature of crises. The bottom line is that predicting crises in real-time can be a significant challenge. Given the reflexive nature of financial markets (a technical way of saying one person's actions depend on the actions of others), the prospects for reliable and timely prediction become even dimmer. In such markets, one actor may panic if others are expected to panic and vice versa. But an equally plausible outcome is no one expects anyone else to panic and hence no panic occurs. Again, predicting crises is ultimately like predicting earthquakes. We can say with some certainty where they are likely to occur (California), but knowing precisely when one will happen and how big it will be is nearly impossible.

Preventing Financial Crises

Numerous solutions for preventing crises were proposed after the 1990s. Most of these ideas were inspired by past events and so are likely to be helpful only insofar as the causes of crises remain stable. Let us explore some of the main solutions that were discussed.

One proposal is to abandon the policy of fixed exchange rates in favor of a floating exchange rate or a hard peg. Fixed exchange rates, many of them not exceptionally credible, fueled borrowing in foreign currency in many prior

---

[11] See Kaminsky and Reinhart (1999).

crises. Economists predicted a "hollowing out" of exchange-rate regimes toward these extremes. Floating exchange rates could limit the moral hazard inherent in foreign currency borrowing. A country could be forced to develop a more resilient domestic financial system. On the other hand, floating exchange rates bring volatility, limiting international trade and economic growth. A hard peg (e.g., a currency board, or monetary union) limits exchange-rate volatility and is less prone to speculative attack. By eschewing the local currency, countries in the CFA franc zone in West Africa, the Eastern Caribbean Currency Union, and the European Monetary Union, import the monetary credibility of the leading central bank. Similarly, Ecuador and El Salvador officially substituted the dollar for their national currencies effectively relying on the US Federal Reserve for monetary policy. Hong Kong's currency board, successfully managed since 1983 by the Hong Kong Monetary Authority (HKMA), backs the monetary base one-for-one with US dollars. These arrangements, however, remain exceptions. Over the succeeding decades, instead of moving toward the extremes, countries seemed to have opted for better management of intermediate regimes. Many economies, especially in East Asia, now have larger backing ratios, make fewer explicit commitments, and intervene more actively to protect the exchange rate from excessive movement.

Stronger supervision and regulation of the financial system is another obvious policy change. Financial and non-financial institutions should be on the frontier when it comes to accounting, auditing, and corporate governance. Proper checks and balances and greater transparency could help investors to avoid corruption and self-dealing, which inevitably occurs when information is "impacted" or murky. Attempts at regulating the balance sheets or investments of banks were instituted in the Basel I accords of 1988 and subsequent iterations. Shockingly, the rules of Basel I told investors banks would be less risky in proportion to the ratio of short-term loans they made. Of course, short-term lending is inherently risky because of the *maturity mismatch* problem. Banks lend to entrepreneurs with long-term development in mind but can pull the plug on short-term funds in a panic. Such panic induces pre-mature bankruptcies even in projects that would be economically profitable in the long run. Indeed, short-term lending was viewed as a primary cause of the Asian financial crisis.

Other deficiencies in emerging markets have been cited. These include a lack of creditor rights—specifically the ability of shareholders and lenders to monitor the day-to-day business of the firms in their investment portfolios.

Investor protections against insider trading and market manipulation are of concern. Many countries liberalized their financial systems before having adequate regulations in place. Just because there is an Open sign in the window of a shop does not mean you want to shop there!

Finally, bankruptcy proceedings should be quick, efficient, and balanced in terms of stakeholder goals. These are subpar in many emerging markets. Without such proceedings, adjudicated by impartial and uncorrupt courts, firms may be reluctant to liquidate even when it would be economically efficient to do so. This could create a buildup of risk in the economy. The solution, then, is to modernize the bankruptcy procedures in LDCs. This, however, requires modernization of the legal environment, which is not trivial.

Finally, there is the idea that capital controls can limit financial crises. Obviously inspired by experience in the 1950s and 1960s when banking crises went dormant, this approach was anathema to the spirit of the Washington Consensus dominant in the 1990s. The IMF, in particular, generally opposed such regulations. Recall that the IMF refused to deal with Prime Minister Mahathir after imposing such controls in 1998. Only recently, in the aftermath of the Global Financial Crisis of 2008, did the IMF soften its stance, recognizing that capital controls could enhance financial stability if applied properly.

The idea behind capital controls is that "hot money," or short-term financial flows that could reverse nearly instantaneously, could be limited. In Chile, the government penalized foreign capital that exited the country too quickly. The side effect of capital controls is, of course, that capital flows would be limited. Any belief in the idea that free capital mobility was beneficial would clash with this policy. There are additional problems with capital controls too. First, financial markets are often one step ahead. Sophisticated international banks and fund managers have always been able to find ways to evade capital controls, as they did in the 1960s under the Bretton Woods regime. Imposing capital controls, like Mahathir, in the middle of a financial crisis could send a signal to investors that the economy is doing poorly and thus may damage confidence. Capital controls imposed during a crisis seem to be a last resort when all else fails. Cyprus like Greece adopted capital controls in the 2010s in the midst of financial turmoil in order to limit bank deposits and other funds from leaving the country. While such controls surely helped keep capital in the country, they did nothing to promote the image that the governments in question were in control of the situation.

These economies faced ongoing turmoil and problems with excessive liabilities even after the imposition of such controls.

Management of Financial Crises

On the international scene, some economists maintain that it would be useful to have a universal lender of last resort. Some may consider the IMF to be the leading candidate for this role. However, with a total lending capacity limited to $1 trillion, and no ability to "print money," the IMF is simply not big enough, nor is it designed to play this role. Having an international lender of last resort would require a much larger institution with much greater power than most countries are willing to accept. The IMF's main mission is to lend to members experiencing balance-of-payments problems.

On the other hand, when the IMF does extend a "standby loan," it has proved useful as a "delegated monitor" for financial markets. Financial markets receive a signal that a country is on the path to recovery upon being approved for a standby arrangement. In the past, the IMF has imposed strict "conditionality" when offering such a loan. Conditionality means that in exchange for a loan, a member nation will take a number of policy actions in order to redress the crisis or imbalance. Economists believe that acceptance of these terms and conditions implies a credible commitment by the member nation. In this sense, the IMF has been called catalytic. A small amount of resources can go a long way to fostering recovery and increasing stability by instilling confidence among market participants.

Some economists advocated applying "Collective Action Clauses" (CAC) to sovereign bond contracts. A CAC may be useful when a country needs or wants to renegotiate the terms of repayment on a bond. A CAC requires the approval of a qualified majority of bondholders rather than unanimity to make such changes. Full unanimity was historically required for bonds issued in New York prior to 2003. Bondholder rights were deemed to be individual and not collective.

A CAC is helpful in renegotiating debt because a simple or qualified majority is easier to obtain than unanimity. Under unanimity, a stalwart bondholder, can thwart the entire project of renegotiation. Economically, CACs can shift the costs of lower-than-expected revenue streams onto creditors, rather than having the debtor bear the entire brunt of repaying in full in tough times. Involuntary losses for creditors with outright default or else financial penury and great economic sacrifice for the debtor are the outcomes when a debt contract cannot be renegotiated. A CAC may be a more equitable way of sharing the losses in times of economic turbulence.

Since 2003, bonds issued in New York contain CACs. Bonds under British law, issued in London, have always had them. After January 2013, all bonds issued by Eurozone members were required by the Eurogroup to have CACs. Of course, any mechanism to facilitate renegotiation would arguably create greater incentives to do just that—another example of moral hazard indeed. In fact, when debating the idea of CACs, both borrowers and policymakers worried that CACs would raise borrowing costs and would decrease the supply of loanable funds. Binding in the "rogue creditor" with a CAC was not universally seen as a cure-all. Perhaps the optimists were right. Since collective-action clauses have become more prevalent since the 1990s, there is little evidence that CACs have caused higher borrowing costs for sovereign debtors.

Another proposal for dealing with over-borrowing and sovereign default included an international bankruptcy court. Besides violating the long-cherished idea of sovereignty enshrined in modern international law, the mechanics of such a system seemed complicated from the beginning. How would a bankruptcy proceeding measure the liquidation value of a sovereign entity? How would a constraint on local authorities to limit "hiding assets" analogous to the rules which disable managers from doing so in domestic proceedings be implemented? Needless to say, this idea has not had legs. To date, there is no such court for sovereign bankruptcy.

A final idea was aimed at staunching a panicky bond sell-off. These panics can cause "bankruptcy" (i.e., default) endogenously or in a self-fulfilling way. To avoid this, economists suggested the "Universal Debt Rollover Option with Penalty" (UDROP). The UDROP would allow a sovereign debtor to stop repayment of principal for up to ninety days and to defer interest payments, potentially paying a penalty to do so. This contractual change to sovereign borrowing would help limit post-default litigation in the case of a missed interest payment or a delayed abatement in the principal outstanding. The obvious downside is that, in the case of fundamental insolvency, the day of reckoning is only further delayed. Delay is sub-optimal in this case. To date, few bonds have implemented a UDROP clause.

Would a fundamental rethink of the IMF for the realities of the 21st century be desirable? Could its powers be enhanced or its resources be enlarged so as to make it a viable international lender of last resort? Many would question the idea that an international organization should have such power, not least the world's leading shareholder in the IMF, the United States.

After the Asian financial crisis of 1997, critics of the IMF like Joseph Stiglitz decried the imposition of harsh austerity measures imposed on already poor countries in the midst of crisis. Stiglitz insulted IMF economists by calling them "third rank" economists trained at "first-rate" schools, claiming they were deaf to the realities of real-world market failures.[12]

Since the 1990s, the IMF has not grown significantly larger (relative to world GDP), nor has it grabbed unlimited powers. However, it has been somewhat sensitive to criticism, and it has implemented numerous internal reforms. The IMF has softened the baseline policy stances under conditionality for many crisis countries compared to the 1970s and the 1980s. In addition, the IMF has supported debt relief for the Highly Indebted Poor Countries and become more transparent than it once was.

The Highly Indebted Poor Countries (HIPCs) and Debt Relief

A major humanitarian and economic crisis caused by excessive foreign borrowing emerged in the 1980s and 1990s, afflicting many of the world's poorest countries. Rather than manifest itself in a panic and sudden collapse in financial markets, this crisis unfolded slowly. The process began as capital flows and international borrowing took off in the 1970s, continuing throughout the 1980s and early 1990s. Much of this borrowing was ostensibly to further the development goals of the world's poorest economies, often with the intention of exploiting natural resource endowments.

International banks, multilateral agencies, and official creditors (i.e., sovereign nations) lent, often indiscriminately, to promote economic as well as geopolitical goals. Dictators, strongmen, and autocrats were all too willing to mortgage the future of "their" countries. In doing so, these leaders often diverted funds to their private offshore bank accounts, purchased arms and munitions to engage in Cold War proxy battles for the Soviets or Americans, or even engaged in civil wars to establish control over natural resources

---

[12] Ken Rogoff, chief economist of the IMF at the time, responded with ire saying to Stiglitz, "Your ideas are at best highly controversial, at worst, snake oil" and "as a policymaker, however, you (Joe Stiglitz) were just a bit less impressive."

like diamonds or uranium. Examples of this kind of looting include the regimes under Mobutu Sese Seko, Ferdinand Marcos, Jean-Claude Duvalier, Anastasio Somoza, and Muammar Quadaffi.[13]

Once accumulated, these national debts remained "on the books" of the sovereign nations, despite the fact that those who had borrowed so recklessly were now gone, in "exile," or deceased. The term "Odious Debt" evolved in international law to describe such debts. While official leaders might have incurred the debts, the people of the country who inherited the debt burden had little say in this process due to political repression and a lack of popular representation.

The response from the international community of development activists was to propose a debt relief program. These proposals originated in the 1980s but progressively gathered momentum as prominent economists like Jeffrey Sachs, pop-culture icon Bono, and even the pope endorsed the idea. The HIPC debt relief initiative evolved from the 1980s throughout the 1990s. Official creditors, designated the Paris Club, held rounds of negotiations in the 1980s and 1990s, but the reduction in debt was minor compared to what was required.

In the mid-1990s, Jeff Sachs, a prominent development economist, as well as the IMF and other multilateral institutions, combined to reenergize the campaign for greater debt relief. The key economic argument was that the debt-to-GDP and debt-to-export ratios in many countries were not only un-sustainable, but they were also impeding economic development and growth. Social justice also required a reduction in accumulated obligations.

High debt ratios that averaged 120% of GDP in the HIPC countries im-plied a drain on fiscal resources that might have been used for education, health care, housing, and other crucial services that only the government could provide. Since the high debts had led to default or to an inability to access further loans, countries were almost literally choking on these liabil-ities. Moreover, piecemeal debt relief from individual creditors and via aid transfers was viewed as insufficient and destructive. Transfers of aid often circumvented official government ministries, preventing those most knowl-edgeable from engaging in their administrative remits.

The HIPC initiatives of the late 1990s proposed a multi-step path toward debt relief. First, nations would apply for relief from the international com-munity. At this point, economists assessed the duress of the debt burden by

---

[13] See Sarr, Bulte, Meissner, and Swanson (2011).

comparing the debt-to-export ratio to a sustainable ratio of 150%. If a country had a ratio above the threshold, then it became qualified for relief. Countries would then cooperate with the IMF and other creditors to provide a strategic plan known as the Poverty Reduction Strategy Paper (PRSP), showing how debt relief would allow for resources to be devoted to necessary social and infrastructure spending. Once the plan was approved, nations could move to a "decision point" and begin to receive debt relief. The ultimate objective at completion was to fully eliminate many types of debt. Jeff Sachs, among others, argued strenuously and relentlessly that 100% debt relief was more appropriate and consistent with social justice and the UN's sustainable development goals, given the odious nature of these debts.

As of the early 2000s, the HIPC initiative had succeeded in reducing debt in several dozen economies, largely in Sub-Saharan Africa, but also in the Caribbean basin and South Asia. By 2010, the IMF reported that thirty-two of forty HIPC countries had achieved completion and another four had reached their decision points. As of February 2020, thirty-seven countries had qualified. Such nations have seen real reductions in their debt-to-GDP ratios by as much as 90% of their pre-initiative ratios. A combination of "traditional" debt relief, multilateral involvement through the multilateral debt relief initiative (MDRI), and HIPC resources contributed by the IMF and World Bank have combined to make this possible.

The IMF calculated the total costs to creditors and multilateral institutions of debt relief in 2010 as about $76 billion. Multilateral institutions themselves provided about half of this amount. The costs would appear to be money well spent. By one calculation, participating nations have increased their spending on programs to aid reduction of poverty by up to three percentage points of GDP while at the same time reducing their interest payments by a similar amount. Education spending has increased significantly in these countries, and the framework for macroeconomic management has improved significantly, leading to greater financial stability.

Another metric of achievement is progress toward the United Nations' Millennium or Sustainable Development Goals. These established targets for poverty reduction, access to universal education, greater gender equality, better maternal and infant health care and access, and so on. Many of the HIPC countries have made substantial progress on several fronts due to debt relief.

While many of the countries classified as HIPCs remain economically disadvantaged, the HIPC initiative appears to have met with broad success.

Discussions have occurred regarding making the program a permanent facility available for countries on a repeated basis, but little appetite exists for this proposal. In effect, many economists believe that the original remit of the program was to be a one-off. The incentive costs of debt relief, referred to as moral hazard, are also troubling to many economists.

Moral hazard may be a decreasingly valid argument. A new trend of commercial litigation of sovereign entities has emerged. Historically, sovereign countries claimed to be exempt from extra-territorial judgments, but this has changed since the 1990s. Increasingly, commercial creditors are finding success in lawsuits against defaulters in New York and London courtrooms. While it is too early to say what impact this will have on the overall issuance of sovereign debt, it does appear that such lawsuits are having an impact on curtailing countries' interest in issuing new sovereign debt, at least while such litigation is unsettled, according to economists Julian Schumacher, Christoph Trebesch, and Henrik Enderlein.[14]

Summary

Leading economists in the 1980s remarked that international financial flows held the promise of better allocation of resources, stronger growth, and less economic and financial volatility. Instead, myriad market imperfections inhibited capital from flowing in the "right direction" and from being invested in projects with high social benefits. The fragility of financial markets has made financial crises a problem to be reckoned with, one not easily regulated out of existence and one that will not go away anytime soon. Still, there are undoubtedly some benefits to international capital mobility, and foreign direct investment seems to be more stable, yielding greater social returns.

Properly managed, financial liberalization can bring benefits and relieve inefficiencies in the allocation of resources. However, any such liberalization seems to require certain forms of regulation or an adequate institutional framework to provide stability. The magic recipe depends on the time and place. Canada is a country that has benefited from greater financial stability than most other nations over the long-run. A highly concentrated banking sector, sound financial regulations, an efficient, professional bureaucracy, embedded in a competitive political system, administering strong regulatory

---

[14] See Schumacher, Trebesch, and Enderlein (2021).

oversight all work to limit instability. Without returning to the world of the 1950s and strict financial repression, there must be a way to balance the benefits of international capital markets with the potential risks. On the other hand, critics may yet reply that in the 1950s and 1960s, growth was historically unprecedented, economic inequality was low, and technological advance was reasonable. Again, what is right for one period may not be right for another.

In the aftermath of the 1990s, it was claimed that the lesson learned by emerging markets was that crises are unpredictable and impossible to prevent. To fortify their financial systems, many emerging markets that had been battered by the global crises of the 1990s and early 2000s adopted an approach of extreme caution. In particular, countries like South Korea, among others, built up large war chests of international reserves so as to overcome currency speculation. Such a strategy seems to be fighting yesterday's battle and may be unsuited for future crises.

We may certainly conclude that financial crises are hard to avoid. But economists have few answers on how to avoid them. Because the answer to the question of how a country can avoid a crisis in the future is a "known unknown," policymakers and economists must remain humble while staying abreast of subtle changes to the risks incurred by markets operating in a world of scarce information. One test of success is not whether crises are avoided entirely, but whether new policies can eliminate a repeat of a particular crisis. A second test is whether management of crises has improved over time, so as to minimize the costs associated with crises. As we will see next, financial crises did not disappear in the 21st century, despite the immense quantity of ink that was spilled in pursuit of financial stability.

14

The International Economy since 2000

Hyperglobalization and Beyond

Between 1988 and 2007, the level of globalization and integration continued
to grow rapidly (Figure 14.1). Some referred to this dizzying rise as "hyper-
globalization." Levels of integration had broken historical records.[1] Despite
this rhetoric, the world economy languished far from what we might objec-
tively call a unified global economy. There remained plenty of room for further integration if only the barriers to trade could be reduced.

The return of globalization was driven by lower communication costs and
a continued push to lower trade barriers. Offshoring pushed global trade to
unprecedented levels. At the same time, the entry of a quickly modernizing
China presented new challenges and opportunities. Economic growth continued apace, dramatically lowering rates of poverty, but many countries
experienced rising income inequality. In addition, large trade imbalances
alerted the world to potential weaknesses in the global economy. The Great
Financial Crisis (GFC) that began in 2007 and 2008 once again changed the
course of evolution of the global economy.

Income Growth and Its Distribution in the 21st Century

The first decade of the 21st century started with a note of triumph. Many
economists extended themselves self-reaffirming congratulations. They
argued that globalization and enhanced market integration, driven by liberalization in the 1970s, were working to raise living standards, cut poverty,
and enhance the prospects of liberal democracy.

The accession of China into the WTO in 2001 was the culmination of the
long road to a truly multilateral international trading system. Global finance

---

[1] Recall that global capital markets and commodity markets were roughly as integrated in 1910 as
they were in the early 1980s.

One from the Many. Christopher M. Meissner, Oxford University Press. © Oxford University Press 2024.
DOI: 10.1093/oso/9780199924462.003.0014

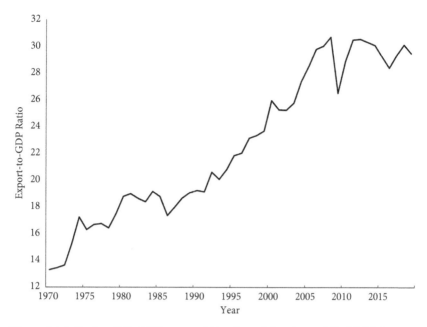

Figure 14.1 Ratio of World Exports of Goods and Services to World GDP,
1970–2019

Source: World Bank (2021)

extended its reach and depth. New initiatives for development finance in
Africa and Latin America emerged from the private sphere as well as the
World Bank, IMF, and even China. Immigration rates to the advanced nations reached levels previously attained in the early 1900s. Current account
deficits (and surpluses), one measure of reliance on international capital
markets, soared to new levels.

The decade following the Global Financial Crisis of 2007–2008 witnessed
remarkable deceleration in the process of global integration. The new hyper-
globalization had seemingly gone too far. Inequality soared to new heights.
Activists and politicians blamed job losses in traditional industries and
manufacturing on the new globalization. The relentless offshoring of high-
quality jobs led to a "hollowing out" of the labor market in economically advanced nations. Globalization was blamed not only for a rise in structural
unemployment and misfortune, but also for the rise in "deaths of despair"
and suicide among blue-collar workers, especially in the United States.[2]

---

[2] See Autor, Dorn, and Hanson (2013) and Case and Deaton (2020).

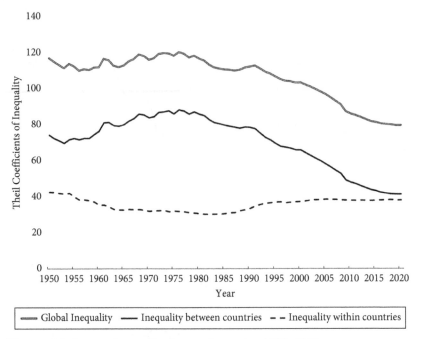

Figure 14.2　Income Inequality Across Countries, 1950–2020

Source: UNU-WIDER (2022) Theil indexes based on series "ge0" (total, within, between)

The rise of income inequality since the 1970s has been emphasized by Thomas Piketty.[3] However, Figure 14.2 shows that global income inequality has actually fallen during the second wave of globalization. It is true that "within" country inequality has risen modestly since the 1970s. However, the most significant conclusion from this figure is that between-country income inequality has *fallen*. In particular, economic growth in East Asia, especially in China, has raised the incomes of hundreds of millions of people, lifting them out of extreme poverty and driving global inequality lower. These gains have been so large that despite rising inequality inside China and the United States, among other countries, global income inequality has been continuously in decline since the late 1970s.

What happened within countries? Piketty has argued that in the United States, and to a degree in the United Kingdom and several other leading countries, inequality has taken a sharp turn upward since the 1970s. According to Piketty, the share of income going to the top 1% of income earners (tax

---

[3] See Piketty (2014).

units for the United States) has risen from about 10% to over 20% since the 1970s. In the decades after World War II, inequality had fallen from the highs attained in the 1920s. There are many potential explanations for the recent rise in the top income share, including a loss of bargaining power of workers through de-unionization, lower tax rates on high incomes and owners of capital, new technologies that increase demand for high-skilled workers faster than less-skilled workers, and globalization itself.

Recent research shows technological changes explain the rise in high-skill incomes in the US. Globalization and offshoring play a trivial role. Robert Feenstra and Gordon Hanson estimate that 99% of the rise in the relative wage of skilled (non-production) workers was explained by investment in high-tech equipment. Only a fraction of a percentage point of the rise in inequality is due to offshoring.[4] Contrary to the evidence, many still believe globalization is the culprit for the slow income growth and misfortune of manual workers in the advanced countries.

International capital flows were also implicated in the Global Financial Crisis of 2007–2008 and the follow-on Eurozone crisis of the 2010s. The crises generated sluggish growth and high unemployment, leading to further discontent with the globalization process. In the case of the GFC, local failures in regulating the banking system were probably the single largest explanation for the severity of the financial crisis.

Finally, continued immigration to the advanced countries and within the EU, as well as the movement of people into Europe from the Near East due to revolutions, wars, and natural disasters, led to further dissatisfaction. As regards immigration, recent studies show that immigrants complement local workers in the labor market, leading to higher, not lower, wages for skilled locals and to small or negligible declines for low-skill workers.[5]

Nevertheless, an epic political backlash emerged in the 2010s. Activists and other thought leaders alleged that globalization and integration were problematic. Many Western democracies took a surprising turn toward a more nationalistic and "populist" form of politics. In some Western democracies, there was even a nascent rise in approval of authoritarianism. This was surprising and unexpected because, after the collapse of the Berlin Wall in 1989 and the end of the Cold War, it was argued not only that liberal democracy was the most viable system but also that further globalization

[4] See Feenstra and Hanson (1999).
[5] See Card (1990) and Peri and Ottaviano (2012).

would itself promote democracy. The "End of History" thesis was increasingly less tenable in the 21st century.[6] Countries like China or Singapore had grown dramatically faster under non-democratic regimes than many countries in the West had. Although absolute economic performance was largely positive across the world, the relatively sluggish growth of the liberal West was generally perceived as an absolute decline. Many politicians began to portray trade and globalization as a zero-sum game. Had globalization failed to be win-win and if so, was it really to blame? Or, was it merely a convenient scapegoat?

Trade Integration and the Rise of Global Supply Chains

As we have seen, between the 1950s and the 1980s, trade integration rapidly increased, as measured by the ratio of total exports to global GDP. This period of intensified globalization relied on steep declines in transportation and communication costs. Regional trade agreements, customs unions like the European Community, and the successive rounds of tariff negotiations under the GATT lowered tariffs on many products, especially between the advanced nations. All these factors served to lower trade costs and enhance market global market integration.

Since the 1990s, new research has repeatedly shown that market integration and liberalization of product and factor markets serve to raise GDP per capita. In an early study, Jeffrey Sachs and Andrew Warner looked at episodes of liberalization and found that economies that decreased intervention in the economy and lowered the barriers to trade grew faster. Jeffrey Frankel and David Romer also found convincing evidence that economies more "open" to trade had higher levels of income even after carefully eliminating the potential for omitted factors that could explain both high income and high trade openness.[7]

Economic geographers have shown that low trade costs increase "market potential," which in turn raises incomes. Market potential is a theoretically inspired measure of how connected an economy is to other economies. Trade between markets is higher when this measure is higher. Market potential rises when it is less costly to reach global markets and when income

---

[6] See Fukuyama (1992).
[7] See Sachs and Warner (1995) and Frankel and Romer (1999).

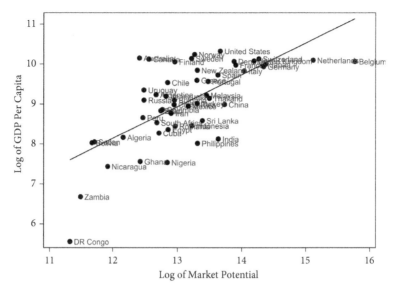

Figure 14.3 GDP per capita versus Market Potential, 2010
Source: Author's calculations based on Jacks and Novy (2018)

or demand is higher. Figure 14.3 shows incontrovertibly that greater market potential is associated with higher GDP per capita. The gains from trade are necessarily generated in this case by greater access to a wider variety of final and intermediate goods, as well as the lower cost of living, that international competition undoubtedly generates.

Global integration accelerated in the 1990s. What caused this this hyper-globalization? Economist Kei Mu Yi observed that, as of the 1990s, a given magnitude decline in international trade costs was associated with a much larger rise in trade than ever before.[8] These structural changes to the "elasticity of trade" seem to be due to offshoring.

Offshoring dates back to the maquiladoras of the 1960s and the "twin plants" of the 1980s. These arrangements allowed textiles and raw materials to be sent abroad from the United States to Mexico in the early stages of production. Cloth and rough products were subsequently sent back to the United States to be finished. Finally, these products would cross the US border again as they were exported out to global markets. This process accelerated rapidly in the 1980s as communication and air travel costs for managerial staff

---

[8] See Yi (2003).

plummeted. Today, Apple, one of the world's largest IT companies, designs its mobile phones in many countries, orders manufactured parts and components from dozens of countries, sends these parts to mainland China for assembly, and finally ships the phone to the entire world.

The largest companies in the world, and many smaller ones, now rely on complex, globally integrated supply chains or global value chains (GVCs). Final goods in the vast majority of manufacturing industries are no longer produced from start to finish in the exporting country. Instead, each step of the production process relies on low-cost suppliers from many different countries that supply various parts. In fact, by 2010, half of global goods trade consisted of intermediate products with such intermediates making up three-fourths of imports in large LDCs like China and Brazil. Imported intermediates are frequently assembled, packaged, or reworked, and then finally "re-exported." Imported content made up nearly 30% of Chinese and German exports circa 2010.

Take the automobile industry as another example. Cars and other vehicles are primarily designed in the United States, Germany, Japan, France, or South Korea. Component parts for a vehicle come from a multitude of source countries around the planet. Assembly takes place in yet another country, and the final product, a Volkswagen, Ford, Kia, or Nissan vehicle, is shipped to final destinations that may or may not have participated directly in one or more steps of this process.

This "back and forth" trade is an integral part of manufacturing today and has powerful implications for who gains and who loses from international trade. Prior to the era of offshoring, nations competed at the level of broad sectors—agricultural versus labor-intensive manufacturing, for instance, in the 19th century. Comparative advantage was defined and determined by relative productivities or costs in these broad sectors. This model had one set of implications for the remuneration of the factors used intensively in each sector, as discussed above. In the mid-20th century, nations traded varieties of finished products (e.g., Audis for Fords), and the gains from enhanced variety were significant.

With offshoring, it is difficult to say who gains and who loses from trade. Generally speaking, advanced countries have offshored semi-skilled and low-skilled jobs and tasks. There have been gains from offshoring for high-skill workers in the advanced countries. Semi-skilled workers may have fared less well. Less developed countries now specialize in semi-skilled tasks, leading to gains for semi-skilled labor in those countries.

More generally, by the 21st century, international competition was at the level of production tasks. "Offshorable" tasks were those most "at-risk" from declines in trade costs. A semi-skilled worker in an advanced economy, like a line manager or event planner, whose job cannot be offshored, will not have the same experience as those in offshored production occupations. Offshoring of a task occurs when a firm can capitalize on the comparative advantage of a location in a particular task. By doing so, a firm raises its profits and is able to economize on resources. On average, this should be welfare enhancing, bringing lower prices and enhanced varieties of goods to consumers and higher profits to firms. The job losses (and gains) by competing in tasks, however, will be highly context-specific, and they will cut across industries and sectors.

For example, design, manufacturing, assembly, and distribution can now all take place in different locations far from the country that had any incumbent advantage or which invented the particular product. The examples of Apple's iPhone or the Mattel Barbie doll are only two well-known cases. In both instances, companies originally founded in the United States hold the patents and intellectual property rights for these products (but potentially not for all the constituent components where there are licensees). A large fraction of the value added accrues to a much larger set of countries, however. In other sectors, workers in the United States today rarely weave textiles, spin thread, or cut wood for furniture. Nor do they assemble such goods. Instead, these jobs have been offshored to low-wage, low-skill-abundant countries. The United States, and other advanced nations, now increasingly specialize in the white collar/back office aspects of production, including design, marketing, distribution, logistics, insurance, and financing.

There is also the inevitable political debate about how the gains from trade have been distributed under offshoring. Some politicians claim that offshoring is directly to blame for stagnating living standards for the middle class. Research shows that we should be cautious in reaching any conclusions about the destructiveness of international trade. Most economists who have investigated the issue carefully find a much larger role for automation and skill-biased technological change in explaining the overall loss of jobs in semi-skilled manufacturing. Still, trade's impact has been more significant in some industries than others and has had a regional dimension that interacts with political cleavages in important ways. Workers in the particular states in the US South, and parts of the Midwest, once homes to significant manufacturing sectors, voted more strongly for Donald Trump, a candidate who promised policies to regenerate areas hit hardest by lost manufacturing jobs.

Bretton Woods II: China, America, and Global Imbalances

In the aftermath of the financial crises of 1997, many countries adopted a precautionary policy of foreign exchange reserve accumulation. Instead of adopting the proposals of the new international financial architecture, nations aimed to boost their trade surpluses, avoid capital inflows, and to hoard reserves. Reserve accumulation would help fortify their financial systems, manage the exchange rate from day-to-day, and defend the exchange rate from speculation in the event of an international loss of confidence like that of 1997.

Other countries also saw massive reserve growth and large trade surpluses. Among these was China, notable because of its growing size and importance in the global economy. Beginning in the late 1990s, China's trade and current account surplus ballooned. In the decade prior to 2007, the Chinese ratio of the current account surplus to GDP was typically on the order of 5% to 10%. This surplus contributed to the growing trade deficit in the United States. There, the ratio of the trade deficit to GDP was between 4% and 7% from 1999 until 2007 with a strong negative trend. Other countries that enjoyed large trade surpluses included Germany, Middle Eastern oil exporters, Japan, and several other East Asian economies. In addition to the United States, countries like Australia, Ireland, Greece, and Spain ran persistent trade deficits. The dollar value of these "global imbalances" for the largest surplus and deficit economies is plotted in Figure 14.4.

Of course, the balance of payments implies that the nations running trade surpluses were accumulating large claims on other countries while the deficit countries racked up increasing amounts of debt to the rest of the world. In 2007, US gross foreign liabilities reached nearly 140% of GDP. At the same time, the United States invested heavily abroad, offsetting a significant share of these liabilities. Throughout the period in question, the United States' net international investment position (total foreign assets minus foreign liabilities) declined from about –7% of GDP in 1999 to –25% in 2004 (Figure 14.5). This was a sizeable change in the long run dynamics of the US international position. The United States maintained its net creditor status from the 1950s until the early 1990s. From the 1990s onward, the United States became a net

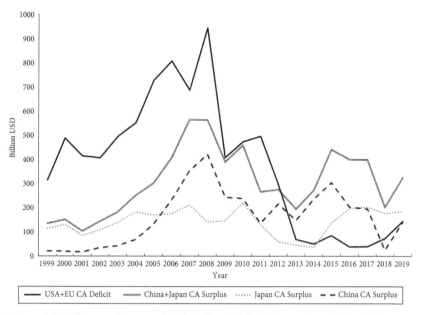

Figure 14.4 Current Account (CA) in Four Major Economies, 1999–2019
Source: World Bank (2021)

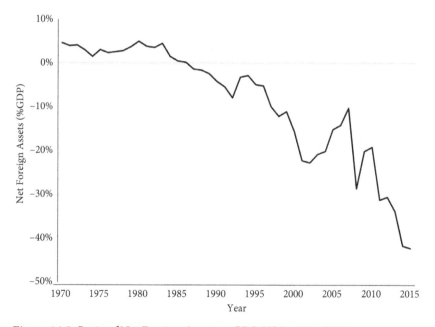

Figure 14.5 Ratio of Net Foreign Assets to GDP, USA, 1970–2015
Source: Author's calculations using data from Lane and Milesi-Ferretti (2017)

borrower, persistently owing more to the rest of the world than the world owed to the United States.

Part of the rise in US borrowing can be explained by the foreign demand for US dollars and US dollar "liquidity." The United States offered many types of investment opportunities for the rest of the world such as direct investment opportunities, corporate debt and stocks, as well as US government debt. Countries like China accumulated reserves in the form of US treasury bonds and debt issued by entities like Fannie Mae and Freddie Mac. The latter are financial entities originally created by the US government that issued debt in order to purchase and hold large volumes of US mortgages. In the case of mortgage default and loss, the US government stood by to use taxpayer funds to cover losses and ensure repayment of those holding Fannie and Freddie debt. Such debt was rated AAA and viewed as a safe investment. In 2006, China and Japan held just less than half of all US treasuries owned by foreigners (Figure 14.6). Foreign holdings of US treasuries equaled about 50% of all US debt held by the public. China's foreign reserves (with a large percentage of them in dollars) reached about two trillion dollars.

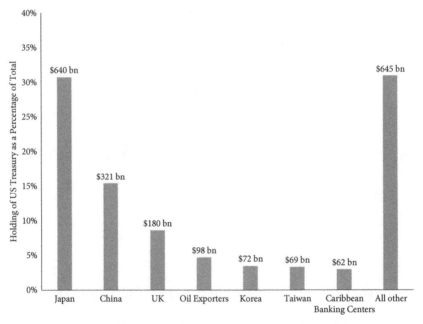

Figure 14.6 Principal Foreign Holders of US Treasury Debt, March 2006
Source: Federal Reserve Bank of San Francisco (2005)

What explains these large and rising imbalances? Some observers pointed to the undervaluation of the Chinese currency, the renminbi.[9] Some economists claimed that the exchange rate was pegged at a value too low in terms of dollars, causing US imports from China to be priced too low. An extreme view even suggested that Chinese currency undervaluation against the dollar contributed to deindustrialization and low-skill job loss in the United States. Globalization, according to this narrative, was a win for Chinese exporters and US multinationals but a loss for US-based manufacturing. Again, the evidence shows that American manufacturing jobs were in decline in the 1990s and 2000s mainly due to technological changes, not Chinese exchange rate policy.

While nominal undervaluation was cited as a problem, what matters is the relative price of imports in a common currency. From the mid-1990s, until about 2004, the renminbi was pegged to the US dollar at a rate near 8.2 yuan per US dollar. Starting in 2004, the Chinese currency appreciated in nominal terms against the dollar to about 6.8 by early 2007. This reduced the growth rate of Chinese exports. In addition, with a fixed exchange rate, arbitrage should eliminate any remaining price differentials that might be created by the nominal exchange rate. Prices of Chinese imports in dollar terms normally should have been rising. Indeed, they were. As it turns out, inflation in China was higher than in the United States in the early 2000s. Chinese inflation worked to erode any alleged competitive advantage of the exchange rate peg. Nevertheless, the inflation was not high enough to completely diminish the trade surplus.

One explanation for imbalances focuses on the "real" forces affecting the economy instead of the exchange rate. The aggregate labor supply curve of mainland China was arguably extremely elastic in this period. Increased demand for labor associated with the supersonic growth rates experienced by China in this period did not act to push up labor costs. In effect, the rural workers in China, of which there were approximately five hundred million as of the late 1990s, were under-employed in the countryside. Many of them were willing to move to the cities to find work in export industries. Because labor supply was so abundant, wage rises

[9] The renminbi is the official name of the Chinese currency. The word *yuan* refers to units of currency in which renminbi transactions are denominated. A similar confusion arises with the official currency of the United Kingdom, which is the pound sterling. When making a transaction, agents typically refer to the value as a certain number of pounds. Colloquially the US currency is referred to as the greenback, but the cappuccino you just bought cost four dollars, not four greenbacks.

were slow and not high enough to raise inflation and diminish export competitiveness.

A monetary explanation for the sustained surplus is also possible. The central bank of China, the People's Bank of China, actively sterilized the increase in real balances associated with the trade surplus. This procedure reduced the inflationary consequences of China's trade surplus. It also caused China's official foreign exchange holdings to mushroom, as we have seen. Historical comparisons are abundant. In sterilizing the inflows associated with an under-valued exchange rate, China seemingly took a page from the playbook of France in the years prior to the Great Depression. In the parlance of the 19th-century gold standard, China was not playing by the rules of the game.

Other explanations co-exist with these. One will recall that the trade balance equals the difference between national savings and investment. Indeed, aggregate Chinese savings rates were high in this period, rising from 35% of GDP in 2000 to nearly 50% by 2007. In China, households saved on average about 25% of their income in this period. Businesses saved another 20%–25% of national income. Meanwhile, US savings rates were low and declining. Whereas net savings rates to national income in the United States averaged 8%–10% from the 1950s to the 1980s, they declined from 6.5% in 1999 to about 2.5% in 2002 until 2007. What explains these trends in savings rates?

Many factors have been cited for China's high national saving rate. The lack of a social safety net and a meager public pension system meant that Chinese households could only insure themselves with personal saving. Chinese businesses also faced an environment that incentivized high levels of corporate savings (i.e., retained earnings). Economists cite China's capital controls and weak corporate governance. Another explanation focuses on the preference in Chinese households for male offspring. This trend with historical and cultural roots has continued into the present era. For every 100 women in China, there are 115 men. The unintended consequence of this imbalance is to make the marriage market intensely competitive. A surplus of men means that men must compete more intensively to find a wife. In this era of fast-rising household incomes, families enhanced the attractiveness of their sons on the "marriage market" by increasing family saving and accumulating wealth that would be transferred to the newlyweds upon signing their nuptials. Some economists believe this can explain the near doubling in the household saving rate between the 1990s and the 2000s.

Since the imbalances are global, some economists preferred to explain the rise in capital inflows to the United States as the root of the problem. In the early 2000s, US households borrowed increasing amounts to fund purchases of housing. House prices were quickly rising in value. Homeowners also took advantage of low interest rates to fund extravagant home remodels, leading some economists to characterize US consumers as using their houses "like an ATM."

This debate is not complete. It is still unresolved whether there was a massive increase in demand for loanable funds in the United States, or whether there was a large shift in the supply of loanable funds arriving in the United States from the surplus countries. The argument for the supply shift notes that US treasuries and debt issued by Fannie and Freddie (those entities which backstopped and incentivized the housing bubble of the 2000s) were viewed as liquid and ultra-safe and therefore enticing as stores of accumulated surplus funds. Some economists argued for a shortage or absence of "safe" assets in the surplus countries, stemming from low financial development, among other causes.

These trends gave impetus to a body of research focused on the implications for the international monetary system. As we have seen, global imbalances of the magnitude reported above were not uncommon in the first wave of globalization. Argentina, Canada, and Australia borrowed massively while Great Britain, France, Germany, and Belgium invested significant shares of annual income abroad. After the Great Depression, until the 1990s, imbalances of this size were rare or isolated. Many observers, unfamiliar with historical evidence, believed the global economy to be in uncharted territory. While the magnitudes were surely not surprising to those familiar with the past, the contours and causes of the new global imbalances were in many respects quite new.

In an influential contribution, economists Michael Dooley, David Folkerts-Landau, and Peter Garber argued that the imbalances were nothing short of a Bretton Woods replay. They dubbed this period "Bretton Woods II" or the "revived Bretton Woods System."[10] Indeed many of the contours were reminiscent of the Bretton Woods era pre-1971. China, along with other countries, pegged their currencies to the US dollar much like the rest of the world had in the 1950s and 1960s. China and other nations also accumulated a large volume of financial claims on the United States, as the European

---

[10] See Dooley, Folkerts-Landau, and Garber (2004).

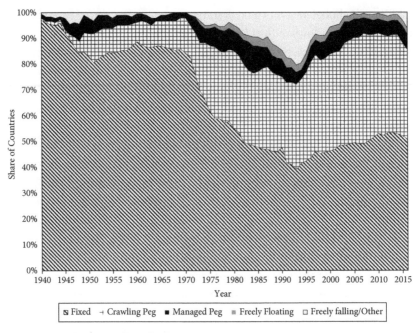

Figure 14.7 Exchange Rate Regimes, 1950–2016
Source: Author's calculations based on data underlying Ilzetzki, Reinhart, and Rogoff (2021)

exporters of the 1950s and '60s had done. Finally, the United States began running larger trade deficits as in the 1960s.

It is interesting to note, the US dollar never really lost its status as the main international currency after the collapse of the Bretton Woods I regime in 1971. After 1971, a handful of economically and financially advanced countries (Australia, Canada, Germany, Japan, and the United Kingdom) started to float their currencies. These currencies had no explicit or consistent exchange-rate target or objective. However, most countries have kept pegging their currencies (Figure 14.7) and avoided outright floating by pegging, only allowing slow-moving changes (crawling pegs) or managing their exchange rate within narrow reference bands. What is more, countries still prefer the dollar as an anchor (Figure 14.8). The dominance of the US dollar extends to reserve holding, currency denomination of corporate and sovereign debt, and to invoicing of trade flows. The US dollar is, for now, dominant. The reason? US dollar debt offers low-interest-rate financing. Currency invoicing is determined by the demands of trade partners and hedging strategies of corporations. Reserve demand remains high for financially

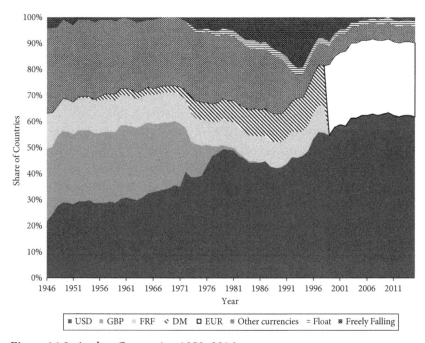

Figure 14.8 Anchor Currencies, 1950–2016
Source: Author's calculations based on data underlying Ilzetzki, Reinhart, and Rogoff (2021)

less-developed economies that choose the dollar to backstop their financial system. Ultimately, the dollar benefits from a combination of the scale of its use and the reliability of the US government debt to honor its debt. With the dollar remaining at the center and increasing its allure as hyper-globalization proceeded, it is no wonder that economists ultimately rediscovered the Bretton Woods analogy.

As part of the new system, economists also established that the United States continued to benefit from an "exorbitant privilege." In essence, it was able to borrow at highly favorable (low) interest rates by selling US treasuries. But US households, firms, and banks could invest abroad at high rates of return. Indeed, the value of this privilege was found to be on the order of 0.5% of GDP between 1981 and 2003. The implications were startling. First, it had to be the case that US-based investors possessed a peculiar talent for identifying investments with high rates of return. Second, it implied that the United States was taking on risk that the rest of the world ostensibly did not want to bear. Finally, it implied that the persistent US trade deficit was more sustainable than most thought because, year-after-year, the total returns on all US foreign investments acted to decrease the size of the US current account deficit. Economists argued that the value of US returns on foreign investments measured in dollars was high, so long as foreign currency returns measured in US dollars stayed high.[11] As the dollar traded at lower values in the period, dollar returns stayed high while interest rates paid on US liabilities (measured and denominated in US dollars) were relatively stable.

In any case, the stability of the Bretton Woods II system was of paramount interest. Economists wondered whether the tolerance for ever-increasing US indebtedness would continue unabated or whether the United States and other countries would throw in the towel, as in the early 1970s. Others, like economist Nouriel Roubini, nicknamed Dr. Doom because of his eternal pessimism, envisaged a sudden stop of epic proportions. Economists divided themselves roughly into two camps: optimists and pessimists.

The optimists argued first that the global appetite for US dollars would continue for decades. After all, Chinese economic development relied on bringing millions of rural laborers into the urban modern sector at globally competitive, low wages. So long as China had a "reserve army" of underemployed in the countryside, wages and Chinese export prices could stay low. Bringing five hundred million people or more into the cities was a process that could be sustained well into the 20-teens or longer. After that, they argued, nothing prevented India, with well over one billion people living in poverty or on very low incomes, from copycatting the strategy.

Research also highlighted that the global imbalances were self-reinforcing. Bretton Woods II was associated with elevated demand for US bonds and assets, which lowered the real rate of interest for the United States. The United States benefitted from this. Without such financing, US government and household debt would have been less sustainable. Congress members in the United States railed against China for "currency manipulation" and threatened the imposition of punitive tariffs to eliminate the "unfair" advantage. However, while such a policy might work to reduce imports from China, it would also have served to reduce demand for US treasuries and therefore to raise borrowing costs. Clearly, the threat of punishing China was not wholly credible.

On the other hand, the Chinese implicitly threatened to stop-purchasing US treasury or even to start selling, even to start selling, if the United States were to impose punitive tariffs. Such a move was also not credible. It would have meant a massive capital loss for China as US bond prices would have tumbled. China's export-driven development plans would have been stymied. China and the United States were seemingly locked into an economic embrace from which neither could escape. Some economists called this "Chimerica"—a global economic system made up of China and the United States (two very different economies)—in reference to the mythical creature composed of different animals, called a Chimera.[12]

Pessimists, like Barry Eichengreen, pointed out a range of weaknesses in the argument, however.[13] Unlike in Bretton Woods I, the United States had no commitment to maintain the value of the US dollar. Higher inflation in the United States could have eroded the real value of dollar savings in the rest of the World. Bretton Woods I was more stable because the countries that were accumulating claims on the United States were more cohesive (e.g., Germany and France). In the 21st century, not only China but also a diverse range of countries from the Middle East to South Korea and Japan accumulated US dollar reserves. Such diversity of US bondholders could lead to instability if expectations about the price of US treasuries shifted. In a panic, akin to a bank run, it was argued, a small-to-medium holder of treasuries might begin a sell-off of US bonds, leading to downward pressure on bond prices. Were other US bondholders to catch wind of this sell-off, they would rush to sell their bonds first before prices fell even further, thus exacerbating the downward trend already in motion. The panic scenario would lead to a sharp rise in US borrowing costs, a fall in the dollar, and a long recession.

Denouement? The Global Crisis and the Unraveling of Bretton Woods II

The emergence of global imbalances in the early 2000s provoked near hysteria among a certain set of economists. From the early 2000s, observers like Nouriel Roubini and the editorial staff of the *Financial Times* began to sound the alarm over a potential impending global financial crisis. Many worried about the sustained rise in the American deficit and the potential for a sudden stop in capital flows to the United States. Such a sudden stop had been the hallmark of many global financial crises since the 19th century, through

---

[12] See Ferguson and Schularick (2007).
[13] See Eichengreen (2010).

the Great Depression, and into the 1980s and 1990s. Significant superficial similarities existed. The emergent housing bubbles fueled by fast credit growth of the early 2000s in the United States as well as in Spain, Ireland, and the United Kingdom were an early warning signal for many economists. In the US case, it was argued that a housing bust and the associated financial turmoil could lead to a dramatic slowdown in capital inflows to the United States, causing interest rates to rocket upward. A major recession was likely to occur, accompanied by a sharp fall in the dollar.

Roubini highlighted the potential for mutually assured (financial) destruction. The terminology was a reference to the Cold War potential for a globally catastrophic nuclear war. This time, a global sell-off of US treasury bonds would lead to a major recession in the United States, but also major capital losses in the rest of the world. The United States was seen as just another victim of a petulant global financial market, this time with repercussions not just on the receiving country but on the entire world.

Ultimately, the crisis did not unfold in this way. In fact, the Global Financial Crisis of 2007–2008, and the follow-on Eurozone crisis, brought many largely unexpected troubles. The epicenter of the crisis was the US financial system and housing market. In the years leading up to the crisis, the US housing market took off with US housing prices rising by over 60% between late 2001 and mid-2007.

The rise in demand for housing was fueled by an increase in the supply of loanable funds. The rise in the supply of loanable funds had two main sources. The first was the rise in capital inflows to the United States (from China and other sources) which lowered US borrowing costs. The second source was a relatively new set of financial innovations called asset-backed securities (ABS) and collateralized debt obligations (CDO). Creation of an ABS or a CDO is known as "securitization."

An ABS is a packaged bundle of underlying assets sold to investors. Asset-backed securities in the housing market took the form of mortgage-backed securities (MBS) or packages of mortgages sold onward to multitudinous investors. Local US banks specialized in originating mortgage lending. Bigger banks would then purchase these loans from the original issuers. This was called the "originate and distribute" business model. The big banks would then "consolidate" or package thousands of these mortgages into a new form of asset dubbed a mortgage-backed security. Purchasers of MBS expected that the risk from buying such assets was low. After all, holding a diversified batch of home loans should have lowered the variability of returns. This notion, along with rapid increases in the value of houses, increased global demand for MBS.

In the ensuing housing frenzy, banks across the country "originated" loans and "distributed" the risks to the rest of the world. Purchasers included investment banks on Wall Street, European banks, pension funds across the world, and so on. Fannie Mae and Freddie Mac also purchased many of these new home loans; after all, they were flush with cash due to capital inflows discussed above. In the midst of this lending frenzy, world-renowned investment banks from Goldman Sachs to Merrill Lynch as well as larger commercial banks like Bank of America, Citibank, and Washington Mutual held larger and larger portfolios of such assets.

The funding model for many suppliers of MBS assets led to a key source of financial fragility. Many banks borrowed short-term at ultra-low interest rates in the global money market to acquire the seemingly endless supply of MBS being produced weekly from the US housing market. There were two strategies. One was to acquire an MBS, rapidly sell it off to institutional investors- and then repay any short-term funding outstanding. The market was global. City councils from Australia to Germany slurped up MBS in hopes the high and safe returns would help defray the costs of their pension funds. The second strategy was to hold these assets, possibly in so-called specialized investment vehicles (SIVs). These SIVs had the special property that for accounting purposes they were off the balance sheets of the big banks and hence not subject to the prudential regulations mandating high ratios of capital to loans in order to buffer shareholders and depositors from potential losses.

Moral hazard also led to eventual problems. At the same time that the US housing market boomed, financial engineers employed at the world's largest insurance company, US-based AIG, developed an insurance product for the MBSs and other ABSs. This was called a credit default swap (CDS).

The CDS insured the holders of risky financial assets like an MBS. In the (allegedly) rare event that a large MBS defaulted, insurance from AIG could be claimed. The total notional coverage offered by AIG and the CDS market more generally was on the order of five hundred billion dollars. AIG potentially had a major hole in its balance sheet, but due to its size, and complicated organizational structure, no one could figure out how big. At the end of this financial chain, global financial markets were led to believe that the Federal Reserve would work to avoid a financial meltdown in order to avoid a repeat of the Great Depression. The world's financial markets thus sleepwalked their way into a financial crisis of epic proportions.

How could the world's financial system be so unaware of the impending problem? First, it was argued that since US housing prices had never fallen in recent history, the chances of a housing crash were low. Had financial analysts cared to look at data from prior to the 1950s, or to the experience of countless other countries (even Japan in the late 1980s), this outright myth could have been easily refuted. Second, it was argued that even if the housing market did slow down, the share of loans that would go into default would not be that high. The so-called sub-prime component, the riskiest of all the housing loans, only accounted for a small percentage of overall lending.

Trouble started in the US housing market in early 2007 with a slight housing price slowdown. The slowdown led all too quickly to a reality check in global financial markets. Large international banks discovered that their recent investments in housing could actually lose value. The word "could" is important here because in many cases banks simply did not know what was going to happen. The reason for the great rise in uncertainty was that it appeared banks and investors were not highly certain about the origins of the mortgages underlying their large portfolios of MBSs, ABSs, and CDOs.

This uncertainty struck like a lightning bolt near the end of 2007 and into 2008. It soon led to hesitation in the interbank market for funding and lending. Recall that banks had become increasingly reliant on short-term money markets for international funding in the years prior to 2007. Rather than rely largely on deposits, as banks had in the past, commercial banks depended on a continuous supply of cheap funding in the money markets. A disruption would wreak havoc on their business models.

In fact, these markets "seized up" in late 2007 and 2008 as large banks like the BNP in France and Washington Mutual in the United States revealed large losses on their mortgage portfolios. Money markets could no longer adequately judge the collateral which was the basis of their short-term lending. Lending more to any institution would only come at a much higher price, if at all. Shortly, a massive debt-deflation dynamic set in. The price of short-term funding skyrocketed. Instead of a panic of depositors clamoring for funds on the doorstep of the neighborhood bank, like in the Great Depression, the international financial system faced a calamitous panic involving bank-to-bank lending. The ultimate outcome was much the same as in a classic bank run.

The interbank panic was the main source of the initial problems. It was unforeseen by regulators because, under their noses, the bank-to-bank lending market had become a crucial link in the chain of global financial intermediation. However, those responsible for financial system regulation like the Federal Reserve, for reasons that defy common sense, apparently did not keep good track of such lending at the time. No early warning system could have signaled the exact fault line because no statistical agency had focused on this central component of the modern global financial system. Prior to this, regulators had been almost completely focused on capital inflows and the repercussion of a sudden stop for US government debt sustainability. Few recognized the vulnerability in the market.

Throughout 2008, the panic began to rot the balance sheets of many investment banks, and financial losses mounted. Major banks like Bear Stearns and Lehman Brothers would ultimately fail or be sold off for rock-bottom prices. Every single other investment bank on Wall Street came within a hair's breadth of collapsing in the second half of 2008. The largest scare came when it was revealed that losses were so large and comprehensive that AIG, the company that had promised insurance to the world's banks in the case of defaults, was on the verge of bankruptcy.

In September 2008, the US Federal Reserve and the Treasury scrambled to contain total financial meltdown. In a bid to rescue the entire global financial system, the Federal Reserve activated a number of new policies to provide liquidity. These involved arcane auctions of obscure financial instruments known as the TALF and other innovative and bold moves including purchases of US treasuries with long maturities. The Federal Reserve worked in conjunction with foreign central banks to provide dollar liquidity (via swap lines) to the foreign banks that had been operating in the US financial system prior to 2008. This was an all-out effort to provide liquidity and to stave off a Great Depression–like collapse of the financial system.

The US Treasury also worked to provide an unprecedented seven hundred billion dollars of funding for banks with the Troubled Asset Relief Program (TARP), which had to be rushed through Congress. All these maneuvers worked to save many banks and to prevent another Great Depression, but only barely. By early 2009, the financial system had stabilized. The US economy hit bottom in late 2009 with an unemployment rate peaking at 10%. A massive fiscal stimulus and ongoing liquidity support from the Fed dubbed "quantitative easing" (QE) kept the US and global economy afloat, with US growth returning in the third quarter of 2009.

In Europe, meanwhile, a similar financial implosion occurred. Housing booms in Ireland, Spain, and the United Kingdom had also been driven by ultra-low global interest rates and weak financial regulation. The booms turned to bust in 2008–2009, leading to Great Depression–like scenarios in Spain and Ireland. Unemployment in these two countries peaked in 2012 at 27% and 16%. respectively. Both countries were locked into the European Monetary Union, unable to take (monetary) policy action to offset the crashes.

The United Kingdom also suffered a recession, but it fared somewhat better than Ireland and Spain, having retained its own currency and monetary autonomy. Still, a wave of banking failures and near failures buffeted the British economy. The Northern Rock bank suffered from a spectacular old-fashioned bank panic with depositors from Southampton to Newcastle queueing for hours at local branches to claim deposits in the failing lender. No banking panic had occurred on such a scale in the United Kingdom since the mid-19th century. The Northern Rock strategy in the run-up to 2007 was to borrow in short-term money markets to fund mortgage lending. When global markets collapsed in late 2007, a liquidity crunch doomed the strategy causing the bank to fail.

Countries in the EMU had a challenging time, similar to those on the gold standard in the 1930s. Ireland and Spain, among the many other countries that had abandoned their own currencies and joined the European Monetary Union, faced a more severe recession than the United Kingdom did. These countries could not lower their interest rates nor use monetary policy to save their banking systems. As part of the so-called Eurozone, monetary policy was decided by the European Central Bank (ECB). The ECB was initially very slow to react to the crisis. In fact, the ECB, worried about inflation, raised interest rates in mid-2007 and again in mid-2008 to 4.25%. By 2009, the Fed had lowered rates to near 0%, but the ECB kept policy rates at about 1%. The ECB also raised rates in April and July 2011, earlier than warranted by the sluggish recovery. The dilemma for the ECB was that Spain and Ireland required lower rates, but Germany and the larger Eurozone were less affected, and the financial crisis was not expected to be as bad. The ECB believed the overall situation required tighter monetary policy.

The economy and the financial outlook in Europe went from bad to worse in 2010. In October 2009, news broke that the Greek deficit had been under-reported. Instead of running at an already high 6% of GDP, the deficit actually stood at 12.5%. Financial markets reacted swiftly with a sudden stop. Financial contagion soon affected Ireland, Spain, Portugal, and Italy. Governments in Spain and Ireland, which had borrowed massively in order to cover banking losses and support their weakened economies, faced a surge in borrowing costs. Interest rates skyrocketed to 16% in Greece and hovered around 8% to 10% in Spain, Ireland, and Portugal. Other major countries such as France and Belgium also faced higher borrowing costs, showing that financial contagion affected neighboring countries too.

Soon a so-called doom loop set in, where banking sector problems hurt government finances and vice versa. Banks in these countries (Spain and Ireland mainly), already in a precarious state due to the real estate crashes there, were the prime holders of government debt. As debt yields rose and bond prices fell, bank assets took a hit. These losses pushed more banks to the brink of collapse. Governments that attempted banking sector rescues, by issuing more debt, faced higher risk premia as market confidence faltered.

With nowhere else to turn, these countries begged the ECB for relief. However, EMU regulations expressly forbade the ECB from "bailing out" sovereign borrowers. The possibility that Greece and other countries could leave the Eurozone in a bid to devalue their currencies, an unprecedented move that would unravel the entire monetary union, led to worry that accumulated debts in Euros would be unpaid. Lending country banks, largely in France and Germany, were now at risk of failing too. Financial markets continued to panic.

The crisis was eventually managed (some would say mishandled) by the "troika" involving the European Commission, the IMF, and the ECB. Angela Merkel, German chancellor, took the lead in a bid to salvage the monetary and political union. In Greece, the troika brought resources from the European taxpayers and the IMF to provide debt relief. The contours of the "bailout" were that foreign banks would not lose money and the Greek debt would be rescheduled. In exchange, the troika imposed harsh fiscal austerity on Greece and Ireland too. The ultimate consequence for Greece was a Great Depression–style economic collapse, with unemployment reaching nearly 30%.

Calm returned in July 2012. In a devastatingly delayed reaction, ECB President Mario Draghi declared the ECB would do "whatever it takes" to maintain the Euro. Draghi loudly and clearly promised to ease monetary policy throughout the Eurozone, should conditions require it. Financial markets regained lost confidence in the wake of this announcement. Nevertheless, many European economies, especially those which had experienced the largest credit booms, were mired in recession for many years.

While the Global Financial Crisis of 2007 unfolded in ways that were unexpected, in hindsight, similarities to other systemic financial crises can be highlighted. First, financial intermediation always entails maturity mismatch and the possibility of panic. The financial meltdown in the United States made this point obvious. Because the Federal Reserve was proactive and the US dollar provided the most liquid and safest refuge for international capital, the dollar did not depreciate as many had expected. Instead, the dollar appreciated massively in 2008, especially against the euro and the pound. This was one major difference between the typical emerging market crisis of the late 20th century and 2007, highlighting that the United States still played a key role in the global financial system and was not (yet) just another vulnerable international borrower. The fact that the United States can print dollars, the currency in which its liabilities are issued, marks one difference between the United States and other borrowers.

As for Chimerica, rebalancing proceeded rather smoothly. China allowed the renminbi to appreciate against the dollar by roughly 20% during the global financial crisis. China's real exchange rate has nearly continuously risen (i.e., appreciated) between 2000 and 2019 due to rises in Chinese wages and prices (Figure 14.9). US demand for imports fell significantly during the GFC. The net result was a large decline in the US trade deficit, but nothing like a typical sudden stop occurred.

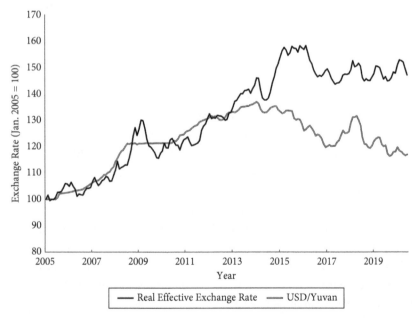

Figure 14.9 China: Real Effective Exchange Rate and USD/Yuan, 2005–2020
Source: FRED Economic Data (2021)

In Europe, capital inflows in many countries prior to 2008 had boosted real estate markets to unsustainable heights. Unsustainable borrowing sprees are, as one famous macroeconomist put it, unsustainable. Several countries in Europe did experience sudden stops of capital inflows that led to housing crashes and banking system collapse (e.g., Cyprus, Ireland, Spain, and Greece).

As was the case in the 1930s, countries without the escape valve of currency depreciation languished in seemingly never-ending depression. The founders of the Eurozone firmly believed in sound finance and market discipline and neglected to build in policy mechanisms to ensure financial stability. The ECB was unable to target monetary policy to countries facing rising debt costs and the associated recessionary environments. Banking regulation was handled at the country level, whereas monetary policy was by design international. The ECB, ultimately responsible for financial stability in the Eurozone, could not, by law, adequately regulate member nation banks. Moral hazard characterized by an epic borrowing binge was the inevitable outcome, as has often been the case.

Summary

In the last fifty years, the Great Divergence between Asia and the West began a dramatic reversal, as China and other East Asian nations regained international market share and developed economically. The consequences were astounding. Hundreds of millions of people escaped poverty. Globalization was a cause and effect in this process in what for years has become a feedback loop between economic growth and trade integration.

The global economy burgeoned in the 1980s, morphing into "hyper-globalization" by the 1990s. The key drivers were declines in trade costs and a change in production processes. Communication and travel costs fell, and new trade agreements reduced uncertainty about overseas investments. The GATT, and later the WTO, provided an umbrella of free trade based on reciprocity and non-discrimination. Market liberalization in China had an enormous impact on the magnitude and the nature of international trade. Global value chains extended across the planet. Countries became richer and trade and integration expanded even more.

Global financial market integration raced ahead as well. As new economies emerged, the financial opportunities were immense. Surprisingly, however, capital flowed "uphill" from poor countries, exacerbating the Lucas Paradox already identified in the late 1980s. At the same time, by the early 2000s, immense amounts of capital flowed between the most advanced countries as banks borrowed and lent internationally, recycling funds and fueling unsustainable housing market booms. The GFC brought the problem of financial turmoil, the likes of which had not been seen since the 1930s, to the world's most advanced economies.

The movement of people across international borders also rose steadily beginning in the 1980s. The global elite of the world traveled by private jet or with the help of the rapidly expanding commercial airline industry, providing the managerial support to international operations and boosting trade connections at the same time. In Europe, the freedom of movement guaranteed by the EU led to the large movement of populations from the less dynamic to the more dynamic economies. Unskilled workers, documented and undocumented, arrived in many countries, including Spain, the United States, the United Kingdom, Canada, and Australia. The refugee crisis in Europe and the Near East of 2015–2016 led to millions of new residents with low skills as they fled the economic despair and horrors of war. Leading economies like Australia, New Zealand, the United Kingdom, the United States, and Canada sourced global talent in order to staff the executive offices of the financial, IT, medical, and R&D sectors.

A political backlash in the wake of the financial crises and ensuing recessions blamed immigrants, especially unskilled workers, for low wages and weak recoveries. Offshoring and unfair trade practices, especially the currency and industrial policy of China also provoked political ire. The rise of anti-immigrant rhetoric and tougher restrictions, calls for trade restrictions and fewer trade agreements, and restraints on global financial activity led to new challenges for the global economy. It is now very reasonable to ask: will the global economy and integration continue to grow, or is the second wave of globalization about to wither away into senescence?

15

Prospects for the Global Economy
in the 21st Century

As we have seen, the global economy has expanded enormously since the 1980s. Many mainstream economists and other "globalists" have approved of hyperglobalization. They believe market integration raises welfare today as it has in the past. These cheerleaders and advocates argue that greater integration lowers prices for consumers, raises real incomes, increases the variety of products available, improves productivity, diversifies the economy, limits risk, and enhances the efficiency of labor markets.

At the same time, this process of deep integration has been blamed by many others for a number of short-term economic problems. The economic issues they identify include heightened income uncertainty, loss of jobs in traditional occupations, intellectual property theft, environmental degradation, loss of tax revenue, financial instability, and the erosion of health, labor, and safety standards.

There are also arguments about the political and social gains from integration. Immigration may increase diversity, but some lament the loss of cultural and civic cohesion. Global capital markets and monetary integration lead to a loss of policy autonomy. Commodity market integration allegedly homogenizes the range of products available, leading to a loss in overall global diversity. Trade agreements subject smaller nations to the whims of larger nations and trading blocs. In light of these debates, how should we analyze the process of integration from a (crude) cost-benefit analysis? What do these debates tell us about the prospects for globalization in the coming years?

Rodrik's Globalization Trilemma

Do economies lose their autonomy due to globalization? The answer is yes, according to Harvard economist Dani Rodrik. Rodrik has long been a

One from the Many. Christopher M. Meissner, Oxford University Press. © Oxford University Press 2024.
DOI: 10.1093/oso/9780199924462.003.0015

skeptic of the process of un-mitigated international integration. Rather than quibble with the abstract logic of textbook economic orthodoxy, Rodrik cites a number of real-world problems. Rodrik emphasizes unequal bargaining power between nations, overreach of international organizations like the WTO, EU, and IMF, externalities not mitigated by the market, and imperfect information. All these are typically beyond the scope of traditional, oversimplified economics textbooks and models. Rodrik argues vociferously that globalization may have gone too far and that a new paradigm is appropriate.

One way to illustrate the tradeoffs inherent to globalization is with reference to a governance trilemma. In Rodrik's view, there are three possibilities and only two of them can be attained at any one time. The three possibilities are representative democracy at the nation-state level, sovereignty of the nation-state, and deep economic integration. Some examples are in order. The first wave of globalization witnessed high integration and sovereignty, but democracy was uncommon prior to World War I. The Bretton Woods period limited integration, especially in capital markets. Many nations were much more democratic and were able to attain sovereignty, allowing for policies suited to the social preferences of a country. The recent period of globalization has brought heightened integration. Democracy is widely (though not universally) prevalent. There is erosion of sovereignty when the IMF dictates fiscal and financial policy after financial crises, when the WTO binds nations to supra-national dispute resolution tribunals, or when "footloose" capital and firms threaten to leave a country if the rate of taxation becomes too high.

How have nations changed their choices in response to rising globalization over time? In the first decades of the 20th century, many nations extended the franchise. By the 1930s, it was clear that either integration had to be reduced to regain political and policy autonomy or that nations would have to suffer under the harsh gold-standard rules of the game.

In the early 21st century, the EU and the common market promoted integration within Europe. While member nations retained democracy, they seemingly lost local autonomy over market regulation in many dimensions. More widely, signatories of free trade agreements and regional trade agreements were often asked to surrender authority to supra-national bodies designed to arbitrate labor and trade disputes. This is referred to as Investor-State Dispute Settlement (ISDS). ISDS allows international panels to rule on disputes between foreign businesses and local jurisdictions, overriding long-established national regulations.

Another question we might ask about the Rodrik trilemma is whether, from a normative perspective, it is sensible for democratic nations to worry about the loss of sovereignty that seems to accompany integration. On the one hand, the loss of autonomy seems to defy centuries of tradition developed in the wake of the Treaty of Westphalia. That treaty, and international norms that developed afterward, established the primacy and legal sovereignty of the nation-state. Article 2 section 7 of the United Nations charter enshrined the norm of state sovereignty by disallowing the UN from intervening in "matters which are essentially within the domestic jurisdiction of any state."

On the other hand, the axiom of national sovereignty can and has been challenged from a humanistic, internationalist perspective. The Westphalian paradigm arguably engenders rivalry between states, often for the benefit of local elites who claim to speak for their citizens—otherwise known as "subjects" in the distant past. If a humanist perspective is taken, then the natural rights of humankind are universal. A properly designed regime of global regulation accommodates the rights and welfare of all of humanity rather than favoring one nation over the other.

The spirit of "globalism" has many supporters. International figures such as the secretary general of NATO, Javier Solana, and former British prime minister Tony Blair advocated for a new doctrine in the international community, claiming that national sovereignty had quite justifiably become obsolete by the late 20th century. The ultimate answer to this question is in the realm of moral and ethical philosophy. There is unlikely to be an objective set of numbers that tells us whether the costs are greater than the benefits of one part of the trilemma versus the other. Instead, communities will have to decide whether their collective preferences are in-line, or not, with one corner or the other of the trilemma.

Several key indicators suggest that globalization since 2010 is slowing down and potentially reversing itself. Figure 15.1 shows that between 2011 and 2020, world exports barely grew, and they are far below the pre-2008 GFC trend level. The determinants of this slowdown in trade are not well known at this point. Some economists speculate that there has been a rise in non-tariff trade barriers. In recent years, nations have also resisted signing up for new trade agreements. The United States dropped out of negotiations for the Trans-Pacific Partnership (TPP) and the Trans-Atlantic Trade and Investment Partnership (TTIP) early in the Donald Trump administration. In the United Kingdom, the EU membership referendum was approved in 2016. "Brexit" undoubtedly will lower integration for the United Kingdom

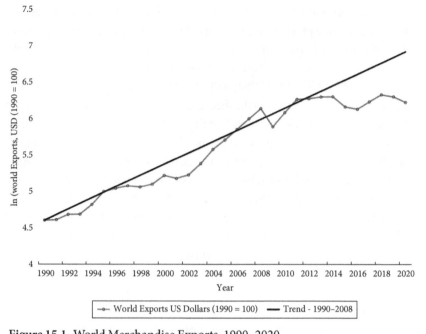

Figure 15.1 World Merchandise Exports, 1990–2020

Source: Author's calculations using data from World Trade Organization (2021). Notes: Solid black line represents the trend using the average growth of world exports pre-2008

and somewhat for the EU. In approving Brexit, UK voters cited high immigration and administrative overreach of the EU as reasons for voting for approval.

Can we call this a backlash? This is not the first time in history that international integration has been singled out as the cause of economic malaise and fueled the fire of political discontent. In fact, the first wave of globalization witnessed a series of policy changes that attempted to limit trade, immigration, and capital flows. Farmers in Europe were threatened by cheap American wheat and food. They hijacked the political system to introduce higher tariffs. While few formal restrictions on the movement of people across borders existed prior to 1914, many American workers protested that foreign immigrants contributed to lower wages. In California, Anti-Chinese riots in the 1870s led to the Chinese Exclusion Act. Politicians seeking electoral advantage from wedge issues and local groups (the Ku Klux Klan is an example) argued Southern and Eastern European immigrants, most of whom were not protestant Christians, were a threat to standard American values. In late 19th century Great Britain, a bastion of liberalism, business people argued that local firms were being starved of capital due to The City's penchant for promoting foreign bonds and stocks over domestic issues.[1] Another Briton, Joseph Chamberlain, led a popular campaign for "tariff reform," calling for higher tariffs for Great Britain and an end to "free trade."

Globalization as a Survivor: Three Case Studies

Globalization went into retreat during the two world wars of the 20th century and during the Great Depression. However, as we have seen, globalization is a survivor, making a strong comeback since the 1950s. There are several ways to view this. One is that globalization is completely random. It might arise sometimes, but other times people might prefer less integration. Another view is that there is a pendulum in preferences. Rising globalization begets a backlash, and the world may sway between two extremes perpetually. A final view, based on the very long run, is that globalization is nothing more than the urge to trade and improve the quality of life. These goals are a significant part of our shared humanity. In this view, globalization over the long run has been rising and will continue to rise in the future. If there are bumps along the way, we may conjecture that the bumps arise because of market and political failures. These are short-run hiccups. Political and economic solutions can and will eventually be found to resolve these issues and globalization can proceed.

Let us contemplate the argument that globalization will endure by way of three examples from the recent period of globalization. All three examples can be interpreted by opponents to argue that globalization has gone too far and is surely finished. But these three examples can also be seen as

---

[1] A colorful, if not mistaken, illustration of the feeling is given by CK Hobson (1914) and cited in Chabot and Kurz (2010): "A few years ago the British public was startled by a new cry . . . the cry that capital was being driven abroad . . . Foreign investment was regarded as a new and portentous phenomenon, without precedent in the history of the country, as a running sore, sapping the life blood of British industry . . . The matter was discussed in Parliament. A well-known statesman made the discovery that all the great ships going westward across the Atlantic were carrying bonds and stocks in ballast . . . Other speakers lamented the increase in unemployment and the stagnation of trade, which they attributed to the unparalleled outflow of capital." Incidentally, in the early 2000s, ships returning to China from North America were not carrying American stocks and bonds in ballast (most of those transfers are electronic nowadays). Instead, they often carried material like used-paper and used-plastics for recycling in mainland China.

manifestations of economic and political failures that have obvious and practical solutions. Global integration brings gains and losses. Often the distribution of these gains and losses creates political cleavages, leading to disputes. If humanity is willing to pay attention to evidence-based assessment, and sufficient cooperation can be brought to bear, it is likely we can continue to reap the benefits of globalization. Effective methods for compensating wage or job losses, or mitigating economic harm, are well known but mostly very poorly implemented. Globalization falters when governance fails. If this is true, integration has not yet met its ultimate demise. We should be aware that policy responses to support globalization may require constant upgrading. Economies must be adaptable.

The "China Shock"

China's recent economic rise has been viewed as a threat by some and an opportunity by others. China has for millennia been a relatively large, unified, and prosperous economy. But, from the 1700s, China fell behind economically. Its influence on the global economy and in international relations has been under-sized for generations. The economy stagnated for most of the 20th century, suffering from revolution, imperialism, a painful civil war, and then an overly centralized command-and-control economy. From the late 1970s, China initiated a major economic reform program, unleashing the power of the market. Progressively, the Chinese economy liberalized a number of sectors, becoming a manufacturing platform for leading industrial nations. Its economic fortunes improved dramatically.

In 2001, the WTO admitted China as a full member. WTO membership was supposed to limit the chances that the United States and other trade members could arbitrarily decide to impose discriminatory retaliatory tariffs on China. With this reduction in uncertainty, processed exports of final and component goods surged. China's exports grew at an annual average of 20% between 2001 and 2007, while economic growth averaged 13%. With exports outpacing the growth of GDP, China soon became one of the most integrated countries in the world, as its reliance on exports (and imports) surged. This was surprising, given that large countries typically tend to be less reliant on trade than small economies are.

China's export surge has been implicated in the loss of manufacturing jobs in the United States. Before that, one economist wondered, "Are your wages set in Beijing?"[2] The truth is that skill-biased automation, the loss of labor's bargaining power, and other shocks of domestic origin have had a strong role in American wage and employment dynamics. Studies show that trade is at most responsible for the loss of 10%–20% of the US manufacturing jobs that have been lost since the 1970s. Trade with China is responsible for only a fraction of this portion.

Focus a bit more on the issue of trade "competition" with China for a moment. Trade with China has indeed had a dramatic impact on some specific sectors. American producers in the sectors that were most likely to be in direct competition with China, such as those that required low-skill, manual labor, found it hard to compete with the low prices offered by Chinese suppliers. Wages and costs were too high in the United States for many of these sectors to remain competitive. Comparative advantage dictated that many US jobs, and those in Europe in these sectors, would be shed and even offshored. China emerged as a global export powerhouse. There is further evidence that the localities in the United States (and in Europe) most affected by this 21st-century-style competition experienced relative increases in poverty rates, unemployment, drug use, and divorce. Political disillusion followed. Unfair trade with China was often cited as the cause.

This, of course, is only part of the story. As trade theory would predict, some gain and some lose from international trade. Trade is based on comparative advantage, and some sectors benefit while others lose. Chinese workers have, of course, gained from liberalization and the new opportunities to sell into the world's largest and richest markets. In the United States, unskilled labor in some manufacturing sectors has been hit hard by China's entry into global markets, as we have seen.

There are also benefits to trade. As it turns out, US exports as a share of GDP have surged too, almost doubling between 1995 and 2011. The winners from trade with China and the rest of the world are those who are engaged in services, but gains have also come to the natural resources sector and the farm sector. Research by economists Robert Feenstra and Akira Sasahara has shown that US export growth in these years created two million new jobs in manufacturing.[3] So, while imports made an impact on certain sectors, the *net* loss in manufacturing jobs due to trade was not a devastating blow. Feenstra and co-authors describe this process as a textbook reallocation of resources along the lines of comparative advantage.

[2] See Freeman (1995).
[3] See Feenstra and Sasahara (2018).

The politics of this shock are decidedly darker than the economics. While trade has grown significantly, it is still a relatively small share of US output. The share of exports in GDP averaged about 10% in the 2000s. The jobs and livelihoods depending on and exposed to international trade are rarer than you might think. Still, political campaigns in the United States can, and have, successfully blamed international trade for the woes of the American worker, at the same time stoking the insecurity of the electorate. Such a tactic has likely won votes despite its lack of correspondence with the facts and the data.

The "China Shock," then, illustrates two problems that have more to do with governance and policy than with international trade itself. First, information about the true impact of globalization has not been widely stressed or emphasized. Special interests and extreme outliers have been able to dominate the policy process and the public discourse about the impact of trade. This is a problem that says much more about democracy and institutions than about the economics of globalization.

Second, it is impossible to discount the job losses that likely stem from the "China Shock." However, the best solution for such a problem is not necessarily higher tariffs on our trade partners. Reallocation is painful and takes time, but retraining, jobs programs, educational subsidies, and safety net expenditures for those hardest hit are likely to be much less costly and even more effective than tariffs in redressing the problem. These policies are always contentious, though, as they require new taxes or spending cuts in other areas. Such change can indeed be difficult. Again, this is a commentary more on the state of policy-making and equity than about the net benefits of globalization.

Grexit, Investment, and the Rodrik Trilemma

The debt crisis in Greece reveals that integration can exacerbate market frictions. One solution is to solve the underlying problems rather than blame globalization. Over the past two centuries, Greece has frequently been a delinquent debtor. Greece has borrowed vast sums only to default on its creditors on four separate occasions since 1800. The most recent debt crisis occurred in 2012. The debt crisis was also accompanied by a severe banking crisis. Unemployment skyrocketed to nearly 30%. The life of ordinary Greek citizens became increasingly miserable in countless other ways. During the crisis, withdrawals of cash from the bank were limited. Medical patients suffered due to massive budget cuts in the public health system. There was a near takeover of the government by reactionary and extremist political parties.

The Greek crisis illustrates Rodrik's trilemma. Foreign powers and un-elected officials from the EU arguably humiliated Greece and brought it to its knees in the wake of 2010. After endless negotiations with the European Commission, the IMF, and the European Central Bank (the "Troika"), Greece was finally forced to adhere to a regime of harsh fiscal austerity. The agreement obliged the government to raise taxes, cut government spending, and even stay in the Eurozone to continue receiving liquidity support and debt relief. The impact on economic growth was decidedly negative. Fiscal expansion and exchange-rate devaluation are two typical safety valves in these types of situations, but they were unavailable to Greece.

As the cuts imposed by the Troika kicked in, the general population of Greece voiced its lack of support for the chosen route to financial stability. The prime minister of Greece called for a national referendum in late June 2015 on the terms of the Troika's bailout. The referendum did not pass. In fact, 61% of voters showed their support for alternative policies. Despite losing the referendum, the Greek government was undeterred and ultimately agreed to the strict terms of the Troika bailout. The former finance minister Yanis Varoufakis claimed the punitive plan was comparable to the Treaty of Versailles.

Although unlikely to lead to another world war, the bailout was indeed a bitter economic pill to swallow. The direct negative impact of fiscal contraction was bad, but the loss of autonomy was a major shock. The willingness to override the will of the people as expressed in the referendum provides a striking example of Rodrik's argument. Democracy had not died in Greece, as the referendum illustrates. Neither had integration been eliminated. The submission to the will of the Troika shows how sovereignty can easily be lost.

Was joining the EU and the European Monetary Union a mistake for Greece? Can the severe economic depression in Greece after 2012 be blamed on the deep integration associated with these choices? It is arguably the case that the root cause of the crisis was corruption and malfeasance in the Greek government. After all, these were the causes of the excessive borrowing in the run-up to the crisis. After the fact, the European banks, which were all too willing to lend, ostensibly expected a bailout should trouble occur. This type of moral hazard is clearly a market failure. Both of these deficiencies could have been eliminated with better governance and stronger economic regulation.

What about the loss of autonomy? Surely this was a heavy price to pay for integration into the EU. A pair of counterfactuals illustrate the problems with this argument. First, it is very likely that the financial crisis would have been at least as deep had the Greeks stayed in the euro but not adopted austerity. In fact, it is likely that the Greek prime minister chose to ignore the referendum because of this possibility. Second, abandoning the euro and eliminating austerity may not have led to a quick fix either. A new Greek currency would have immediately depreciated against the euro. Greece's debt was payable in euros, and it was sizeable relative to total Greek GDP. Reinstating a local currency means this debt would have become instantly more expensive in terms of local Greek currency. A severe decline in aggregate demand or a major default would likely have occurred. Neither would bring immediate relief to the Greek economy. Once again, it is quite unreasonable to argue that the economic and political challenges Greece has faced since 2010 are due to globalization or integration per se. Greece's issues have more to do with a failure of governance and lax financial regulation than with globalization.

Brexit, Immigration, and the European Union

It is not an understatement to say that the British were always extremely hesitant about their membership in the EU. Historically, Great Britain has always been skeptical of economic entanglement with other European nations. The fight against Napoleon in the early 19th century was a battle for independence and autonomy from a continent-based regime willing to impose its will on those defeated. Later, at the monetary conference of 1867 in Paris, the British delegate said that Britain would never change its monetary standard to silver or bimetallism and that joining a global monetary union was impossible. In the 20th century, this skepticism held fast. In 1950, Robert Schuman announced plans for a European Coal and Steel Community. Britain reacted by telling French officials that a European "High Authority" would undermine UK sovereignty.

The United Kingdom did eventually join the European Community in 1973, sixteen years after the Treaty of Rome was signed. Still, Prime Minister Margaret Thatcher negotiated significant limitations on British involvement in the European project, negotiating the right to "opt out" of many European initiatives, including the European Monetary Union and other social legislation.

In 1993, the UK government approved the Maastricht Treaty without a referendum. A popular vote would likely have failed. Almost immediately, the Referendum Party was established. The main platform was a call for a referendum on EU membership. British resistance to EU membership hardly abated over the years, with campaigners like Nigel Farage of the UK Independence Party (UKIP) placing intense pressure on the main political parties to call a referendum on EU membership.

The relentless UKIP campaign emphasized the alleged loss of British autonomy to faceless, unelected bureaucrats from Brussels. EU laws, standards, and acts were allegedly meted out to member states without input from members. Accountable leadership at the EU level was missing, leading to a democratic deficit. The UKIP and others further claimed that EU health and safety standards and labor laws constrained the sovereignty of Britain. They were not only incompatible with British social preferences, but they also jeopardized the economy. The guaranteed freedom of movement for people within the EU was also a key issue. British campaigners for an exit referendum argued that low-wage workers from the newly admitted member states in Eastern Europe flooded the British labor market, working for low wages and taking jobs from the British. Worse yet, it was argued that many European citizens came to Britain simply to enjoy better social welfare benefits and medical coverage under the National Health System (NHS) without meaningfully contributing to the tax base.

In May 2015, following a victory in the general election, conservative party Prime Minister David Cameron offered a referendum on EU membership as part of a campaign pledge. The election would be held in the summer of 2016. On June 23, a rainy summer Sunday, British voters exercised their right to have their voices heard. The referendum passed, to the world's astonishment. A slim majority of 51.9% of those voting approved of British exit (Brexit) from the EU. Turnout was high at 72% of the electorate. Voters that were more likely to vote in favor of Brexit were typically older, from the North, living in rural areas, and places that had lower percentages of immigrants in their district. The UKIP and conservative pundits declared a victory for British sovereignty. A protracted, controversial, and acrimonious series of negotiations with the EU followed. The United Kingdom ceased to be in the EU as of March 2019.

Were campaigners for Brexit right? Those who supported the "remain" side would beg to differ. Not only would EU exit lead to lower trade with the EU and much lower national income, but there was also no basis in reality for many of the strong allegations made by Brexiteers. On the key question of immigration, research shows that immigrants to Britain took jobs no longer viewed as desirable by the British. Not only that, but immigrants acted as complements to British workers, raising wages, especially of skilled workers. Other factors such as health and safety, fishing quotas, and financial regulations could have been negotiated within the EU.

The final analysis of the economic benefits of EU membership and the losses from Brexit will not be known for certain for some time. However, the referendum initially led to a sharp drop and sustained losses in the UK stock market. The pound sterling–dollar exchange rate fell to historic lows. Trade with the largest and richest trading bloc in the world, the EU, is in jeopardy and set to decline. Economists have calculated the weekly losses to the British economy at 350 million GBP.

The disillusion with the EU was no doubt intense in certain areas of the United Kingdom. However, it stands to reason that the disillusion had much more to do with the lack of economic opportunity created by slow British productivity growth and poor incentives given by a locally mismanaged welfare and social security system than with being part of the EU. Campaigners for Brexit used misleading statistics and dubious analysis to support their claims that the UK economy was hamstrung by EU regulations. Moreover, there are serious and believable allegations that the Russian secret service maliciously intervened in surreptitious ways to influence swing voters on social media. Such a factor could have made all the difference in such a close vote. In summary, the Brexit decision should be seen more as revealing a victory for manipulative politicians and special interests than as a verdict on the downside of integration and globalization.

Epilogue

It is now the autumn of 2023. The global economy remains prostrate. Donald Trump is no longer president of the United States. The United States administration is attempting to un-do Trump's quadrennial, most of which he devoted to dismantling long-standing alliances and torpedoing global engagement. A lack of trust is pervasive, domestically and internationally. The American Republican party shows few signs of wishing to return to something like the post-war era. Instead, many favor a nationalistic approach to international economic relations. Voters are also suspect of Democratic leaders who promote trade agreements and further giveaways, especially in regards to labor standards and the environment. The Biden administration has not repealed many of Trump's tariffs.

China, the world's second-largest economy, remains full of economic potential. The challenges it faces are rebalancing its economy toward more consumption and lower (mis-) investment. China's property economy is collapsing with a gigantic thud due to the insolvency of one of the largest property developers, Evergrande. The consensus is that the Chinese government will not allow this to derail economic growth, nor to engulf the real economy. The next several decades will see further economic growth as it modernizes its industries, energy grid, and its consumption patterns. Given its size, China will always exert a significant influence on the global economy.

In Europe, growth remains slow. Germany's longtime leader, Angela Merkel, has retired, and a future of political uncertainty awaits. Post-Brexit Britain is suffering from fuel and food shortages due to a scarcity of truck drivers and the red tape that impedes free trade and movement between the United Kingdom and its largest trade partner, the EU. Dissatisfaction with the COVID response has also been high. Europe is also too large to lose global relevance, but it could continue to suffer from internal distractions. Immigration from Africa and the Middle East will present policy challenges.

As for the global economy, a lot depends on the willingness of world leaders to continue pushing an agenda of less-restrictive trade in goods and services. Several trade agreements, notably a revision to the Trans-Pacific

Partnership (TPP), are in the early stages of negotiation. China continues its drive to fund infrastructure throughout the world and aims to strengthen the global economy by bolstering its international supply chains. It remains to be seen whether global trade partners can bend Chinese policies to be less interventionist and state-led or whether the world will have to learn to live with such policies. One likely scenario is greater involvement of governments in the advanced economies (e.g., via industrial policy) with the goal of helping to level the playing field.

The global technologies of the future also matter. A number of new technologies promise to radically reshape the global economy, but it is hazardous to guess exactly how. These innovations include 5G telecommunications, hyper-sonic air travel, hyper-loops, high-speed railways, electric vehicles, autonomous driving technology, quantum computing, enhanced energy/battery storage, mRNA vaccines, CRSPR gene splicing, genetic engineering, fintech (blockchain, crypto, and digital currencies, and many other IT applications to finance), and many others. World leadership in terms of trade agreements, financial stability, and the environment will also remain important. Cooperation on these fronts seems difficult in light of the every-nation-for-itself response to COVID-19 and vaccines.

Regarding the environment, the single largest long-run threat to the global economy and humanity remains anthropogenic climate change. At the very least, the costs of adaptation will be significant and unevenly distributed. At worst, humanity faces an existential threat. Climate change, like a global pandemic, requires a cooperative, global solution. Economists have proposed a carbon tax, emissions trading, incentives to invest in new technologies, and border taxes for countries that rely too heavily on carbon emissions for production. The latter takes aim at solving the climate problem but also obviously has an impact on the global economy. A global carbon tax that values carbon emissions at a price close to its social marginal cost seems like the least bad way to limit climate change. Achieving global agreement and coordination on this has, so far, been impossible. One hopes that bold leadership can and will encourage the adoption of new policies that will lessen the costs and enable the world to overcome these issues. No one can know for sure whether humanity will succeed.

There is, however, one thing that is certain and some cause for optimism. Global cooperation and coordination to this global problem is the only path to overcome these issues. For humans, as a species, one of our most distinguishing characteristics is the urge to engage in trade. But trade is a form of cooperation, and humans cooperate better than most other species. Based on the long run of history, our innate sensibilities, and our continued awareness of what is at stake, we must be cautiously optimistic about the future of the global economy and the challenges that it will inevitably and continuously bring.

References

Accominotti, O. (2009). "The Sterling Trap: Foreign Reserves Management at the Bank of France, 1928–1936." *European Review of Economic History* 13(3), 349–376.

Accominotti, O., and Eichengreen, B. (2016). "The Mother of All Sudden Stops: Capital Flows and Reversals in Europe, 1919–32." *Economic History Review* 69(2), 469–492.

Accominotti, O., and Flandreau, M. (2008) "Bilateral Treaties and the Most-Favored-Nation Clause: The Myth of Trade Liberalization in the Nineteenth Century." *World Politics* 60 (2), 147–188. doi:10.1353/wp.0.0010.

Acemoglu, D., Johnson, S., and Robinson, J. A. (2001). "The Colonial Origins of Comparative Development: An Empirical Investigation." *American Economic Review* 91(5), 1369–1401.

A'Hearn, B., and Venables, A. (2011). "Internal Geography and External Trade: Regional Disparities in Italy, 1861–2011." CEPR discussion paper 8655.

Åkerman, S. (1976). "Theories and methods of migration research." In *From Sweden to America: A History of the Migration: A Collective Work of the Uppsala Migration Research Project,* edited by H. Runblom and H. Norman, 19–76. Minneapolis: University of Minnesota Press.

Allen, F., and Gale, D. (1998). "Optimal Financial Crises." *Journal of Finance* 53(4), 1245–1284.

Austin, G. (2008). "The 'Reversal of Fortune' Thesis and the Compression of History: Perspectives from African and Comparative Economic History." *Journal of International Development: The Journal of the Development Studies Association* 20(8), 996–1027.

Autor, D., Dorn, D., and Hanson, G. H. (2013). "The China Syndrome: Local Labor Market Effects of Import Competition in the United States." *American Economic Review* 103(6), 2121–2168.

Bairoch, P. (1972). "Free Trade and European Economic Development in the 19th Century." *European Economic Review* 3(3), 211–245.

Baldwin, R. E., and Martin, P. (1999). "Two Waves of Globalisation: Superficial Similarities and Fundamental Differences." In *Globalisation and Labour*, edited by Horst Siebert, 3–29. J.C.B. Mohr for Kiel Institute of World Economics.

Barro, R. J., and Ursua, J. F. (2008). "Macroeconomic Crises since 1870." Brookings Papers on Economic Activity, Economic Studies Program, The Brookings Institution, vol. 39 (1 Spring), 255–350.

Bernanke, B. (2002). "Remarks by Governor Ben S. Bernanke at the Conference to Honor Milton Friedman at the University of Chicago, Chicago, Illinois." Downloaded on December 29, 2022 from https://www.federalreserve.gov/boarddocs/speeches/2002/20021108/.

Bernanke, B., and James, H. (1991). "The Gold Standard, Deflation and Financial Crises in the Great Depression: An International Comparison." In *Financial Markets and Financial Crises*, edited by Glenn Hubbard, 33–68. Chicago: University of Chicago Press.

Bernhofen, D. M., and Brown, J. C. (2004). "A Direct Test of the Theory of Comparative Advantage: The Case of Japan." *Journal of Political Economy* 112(1), 48–67.

Bolt, J., Inklaar, R., de Jong, H., and van Zanden, J. L. (2018). "Rebasing 'Maddison': New Income Comparisons and the Shape of Long-Run Economic Development." Maddison Project Working paper 10.

Bordo, M. D. (1993). "The Bretton Woods International Monetary System: A Historical Overview." In *A Retrospective on the Bretton Woods System: Lessons for International Monetary Reform*, edited by M. D. Bordo and B. Eichengreen. 3–108. Chicago: University of Chicago Press.

Bordo, M. D., Eichengreen, B., Klingebiel, D., and Martínez-Peria, S. (2001). "Is the Crisis Problem Growing More Severe?" *Economic Policy* 16(32), 52–82.

Bordo, M. D. and Kydland, F. E. (1995). "The Gold Standard as a Rule: An Essay in Exploration." *Explorations in Economic History* 32(4), 423–464.

Bordo, M. D., and Rockoff, H. (1996). "The Gold Standard as a 'Good Housekeeping Seal of Approval.'" *Journal of Economic History* 56(2), 389–428.

Bourguignon, F., and Morrisson, C. (2002). "Inequality among World Citizens: 1820–1992." *American Economic Review* 92(4), 727–744.

Burns, A. F., and Mitchell, W. C. (1947). *Measuring Business Cycles*. New York: National Bureau of Economic Research.

Campante, F., and Yanagizawa-Drott, D. (2018). "Long-Range Growth: Economic Development in the Global Network of Air Links." *Quarterly Journal of Economics* 133(3), 1395–1458.

Capie, F. (1978). "The British Tariff and Industrial Protection in the 1930's." *Economic History Review* 31(3), 399–409.

Card, D. (1990). "The Impact of the Mariel Boatlift on the Miami Labor Market." *ILR Review* 43(2), 245–257.

Case, A., and Deaton, A. (2020). *Deaths of Despair and the Future of Capitalism*. Princeton: Princeton University Press.

Chabot, B., and Kurz, C. J. (2010). "That's Where the Money Was: Foreign Bias and English Investment Abroad, 1866–1907." *Economic Journal* 120(547), 1056–1079.

Chiswick, B., and Hatton, T. (2004). "International Migration and the Integration of Labor Markets." In *Globalization in Historical Perspective*, edited by M. Bordo, A.M. Taylor, and J. Williamson, 65–120. Chicago: University of Chicago Press.

Clark, G. (1987). "Why Isn't the Whole World Developed? Lessons from the Cotton Mills." *Journal of Economic History* 47(1), 141–173.

Clemens, M. A., and Williamson, J. G. (2004a). "Wealth Bias in the First Global Capital Market Boom, 1870–1913." *Economic Journal* 114(495), 304–337.

Clemens, M. A., and Williamson, J. G. (2004b). "Why Did the Tariff–Growth Correlation Change after 1950?" *Journal of Economic Growth* 9(1), 5–46.

Clingingsmith, D., and Williamson, J. G. (2008). "Deindustrialization in 18th and 19th Century India: Mughal Decline, Climate Shocks and British Industrial Ascent." *Explorations in Economic History* 45(3), 209–234.

Council on Foreign Relations. (2009). Symposium on a Second Look at the Great Depression and the New Deal. Downloaded on December 29, 2022 from https://www.cfr.org/event/why-second-look-matters.

Crafts, N., and O'Rourke, K. H. (2014). "Twentieth Century Growth." In *Handbook of Economic Growth*, 2nd ed., edited by S. Durlauf and P. Aghion, 263–346. New York: North Holland.

Crafts, N., and Venables, A. (2003). "Globalization in History. A Geographical Perspective." In *Globalization in Historical Perspective*, edited by M. D. Bordo, A. M. Taylor, and J. Williamson, 323–370. Chicago: University of Chicago Press.

David, P. A. (1985). "Clio and the Economics of QWERTY." *American Economic Review* 75(2), 332–337.

De Long, J. B. (1998). "Trade Policy and America's Standard of Living: A Historical Perspective." In *Imports, Exports, and the American Worker*, edited by S. M. Collins, 349–388. Washington, DC: Brookings Institution Press.

De Long, J. B. and Eichengreen, B. (2003). "The Marshall Plan: History's Most Successful Structural Adjustment Program." In *Postwar Economic Reconstruction and Its Lessons for the East Today*, edited by R. Dornbusch, W. Nolling, and R. Layard, 156–189. Cambridge, MA: MIT Press.

de Zwart, P. (2016). "Globalization in the Early Modern Era: New Evidence from the Dutch-Asiatic Trade, c. 1600–1800." *Journal of Economic History* 76, 520–558.

Diamond. J. (1997). *Guns, Germs, and Steel: The Fates of Human Societies*. New York: W. W. Norton.

Diaz-Alejandro, C. (1984). "Latin American Debt: I Don't Think We Are in Kansas Anymore." Brookings Papers on Economic Activity, vol. 1984 (2), 335–403.

Dincecco, M. (2009). "Fiscal Centralization, Limited Government, and Public Revenues in Europe, 1650–1913." *Journal of Economic History* 69(1), 48–103.

Dooley, M. P., Folkerts-Landau, D., and Garber, P. (2004). "The Revived Bretton Woods System." *International Journal of Finance & Economics* 9(4), 307–313.

Eggertsson, G. B. (2008). "Great Expectations and the End of the Depression." *American Economic Review* 98(4), 1476–1516.

Eichengreen, B. J. (1992). *Golden Fetters: The Gold Standard and the Great Depression, 1919–1939*. New York: Oxford University Press.

Eichengreen, B. (1996). "Institutions and Economic Growth: Europe after World War II." In *Economic Growth in Europe since 1945*, edited by N. Crafts and G. Toniolo, 38–70. Cambridge: Cambridge University Press.

Eichengreen, B. (2002). *Financial Crises: And What to Do about Them*. Oxford: Oxford University Press.

Eichengreen, B. (2010). *Global Imbalances and the Lessons of Bretton Woods*. Cambridge, MA: MIT Press.

Eichengreen, B., and O'Rourke, K. (2009). "A Tale of Two Depressions." *VoxEu*. Downloaded January 30, 2022 from https://voxeu.org/article/tale-two-depressions-what-do-new-data-tell-us-february-2010-update.

Eichengreen, B., and Sachs, J. (1985). "Exchange Rates and Economic Recovery in the 1930s." *Journal of Economic History* 45(4), 925–946.

Eichengreen, B., and Wyplosz, C. (1993). "The Unstable EMS." *Brookings Papers on Economic Activity* 1, 51–143.

Estevadeordal, A., Frantz, B., and Taylor, A. (2003). "The rise and fall of world trade, 1870–1939." *Quarterly Journal of Economics* 118(2), 359–407.

Esteves, R., and Khoudour-Castéras, D. (2009). "A Fantastic Rain of Gold: European Migrants' Remittances and Balance of Payments Adjustment during the gold Standard Period." *Journal of Economic History* 64(9), 951–985.

Federal Reserve Bank of San Francisco. (2005). "Who Are the Largest Holders of U.S. Public Debt?" Downloaded October 21, 2021 from https://www.frbsf.org/education/publications/doctor-econ/2005/july/public-national-debt/.

Federico, G., and Tena-Junguito, A. (2019). "World Trade, 1800–1938: A New Synthesis." *Revista de Historia Económica-Journal of Iberian and Latin America Economic History* 37(1), https://doi.org/10.1017/S0212610918000216.

Feenstra, R. C., and Hanson, G. H. (1999). "The Impact of Outsourcing and High Technology Capital on Wages: Estimates for the U.S., 1979–1990." *Quarterly Journal of Economics* 114(3), 907–940.

Feenstra, R. C., and Sasahara, A. (2018). "The 'China Shock,' Exports and US Employment: A Global Input–Output Analysis." *Review of International Economics* 26(5), 1053–1083.

Ferguson, N., and Schularick, M. (2006). "The empire effect: the determinants of country risk in the first age of globalization, 1880–1913." *The Journal of Economic History*, 66(2), 283–312.

Ferguson, N., and Schularick, M. (2007). "'Chimerica' and the Global Asset Market Boom." *International Finance* 10(3), 215–239.

Fernández, A., Klein, M. W., Rebucci, A., Schindler, M., and Uribe, M. (2016). "Capital Control Measures: A New Dataset." *IMF Economic Review* 64(3), 548–574.

Fishlow, A. (1985). "Lessons from the Past: Capital Markets during the 19th Century and the Inter-War Period." *International Organization* 39(3), 383–439.

Flandreau, M. (1996). "The French Crime of 1873: An Essay on the Emergence of the International Gold Standard, 1870–1880." *Journal of Economic History* 56(4), 862–897.

Flandreau, M. (2003). "Caveat Emptor: Coping with Sovereign Risk under the International Gold Standard, 1871–1913." In *International Financial History in the Twentieth Century: System and Anarchy*, edited by M. Flandreau, C. L. Holtfrerich, and H. James, 17–50. Cambridge: Cambridge University Press.

FRED Economic Data. (2021). St. Louis, MO: Federal Reserve Bank of St. Louis. Downloaded November 17, 2021 from https://fred.stlouisfed.org/.

Flynn, D. O. and Giráldez, A. (1995). "Born with a 'Silver Spoon': The Origin of World Trade in 1571." *Journal of World History* 6(2), 201–221.

Frankel, J. A., and Romer, D. H. (1999). "Does Trade Cause Growth?" *American Economic Review* 89(3), 379–399.

Friedman, M., and Schwartz, A. J. (1963). *A Monetary History of the United States: 1867–1960.* Princeton: Princeton University Press.

Freeman, R. B. (1995). "Are Your Wages Set in Beijing?" *Journal of Economic Perspectives* 9(3), 15–32.

Fukuyama, F. (1992). *The End of History and the Last Man.* New York: Free Press.

Galofré-Vilà, G., Meissner, C. M., McKee, M., and Stuckler, D. (2021). "Austerity and the Rise of the Nazi Party." *Journal of Economic History* 81(1), 81–113.

Ghosh, A. R., Ostry, J. D., and Qureshi, M. S. (2016). "When Do Capital Inflow Surges End in Tears?" *American Economic Review* 106(5), 581–585.

Gibson, C. J., and Lennon, E. (1999). "Historical Census Statistics on the Foreign-Born Population of the United States: 1850–1990." US Census Bureau. Working Paper POP-WP029.

Giorcelli, M. (2019). "The Long-Term Effects of Management and Technology Transfers." *American Economic Review* 109(1), 121–152.

Goldin, C. (1993). "The Political Economy of Immigration Restriction in the United States, 1890 to 1921." NBER WP 4345.

Gourinchas, P. O., Rey, H., and Truempler, K. (2012). "The Financial Crisis and the Geography of Wealth Transfers." *Journal of International Economics* 88(2), 266–283.

Graham, F. D. (1967). *Exchange, Prices, and Production in Hyper-Inflation: Germany, 1920–1923*. New York: Russell & Russell.

Grossman, R. S. (1994). "The Shoe That Didn't Drop: Explaining Banking Stability during the Great Depression." *Journal of Economic History* 54(3), 654–682.

Harari, Y. N. (2015). *Sapiens: A Brief History of Humankind*. New York: Harper Collins.

Hobson, C. K. (1914). *The Export of Capital*. London: Constable and Company.

Hatton, T. J., and Williamson, J. G. (1998). *The Age of Mass Migration: Causes and Economic Impact*. Oxford: Oxford University Press.

Head, K. (1994). "Infant Industry Protection in the Steel Rail Industry." *Journal of International Economics* 37(3–4), 141–165.

Hersh, J., and Voth, H. J. (2022). "Sweet Diversity: Colonial Goods and the Welfare Gains from Global Trade after 1492." *Explorations in Economic History* 86(2), 1–9.

Huberman, M. (2012). *Odd Couple: International Trade and Labor Standards in History*. New Haven: Yale University Press.

Huberman, M., and Meissner, C. M. (2010). "Riding the Wave of Trade: The Rise of Labor Regulation in the Golden Age of Globalization." *Journal of Economic History* 70(3), 657–685.

Huff, G., and Caggiano, G. (2007). "Globalization, Immigration, and Lewisian Elastic Labor in Pre–World War II Southeast Asia." *Journal of Economic History* 67(1), 33–68.

Ilzetzki, E., Reinhart, C., and Rogoff, K. (2021). "Rethinking Exchange Rate Regimes." NBER WP 29347.

International Monetary Fund. (various years). Annual Report on Exchange Arrangements and Exchange Restrictions. Washington, DC: International Monetary Fund.

Dell'Arricia, G., Mauro, P., Faria, A., Ostry, J. D., Di Giovanni, J., Schindler, M., Kose, A., Terrones, M. (2008). "Reaping the Benefits of Financial Globalization." International Monetary Fund Occasional Paper Number 2008/07.

Inwood, K., and Keay, I. (2013). "Trade Policy and Industrial Development: Iron and Steel in a Small Open Economy, 1870–1913." *Canadian Journal of Economics/Revue canadienne d'économique* 46(4), 1265–1294.

Irwin, D. (1998). "The Smoot-Hawley Tariff: A Quantitative Assessment." *Review of Economics and Statistics*, 80(2), 326–334.

Irwin, D. (2017). *Clashing Over Commerce: A History of US Trade Policy*. Chicago: University of Chicago Press.

Jacks, D. S. (2006). "What Drove 19th Century Commodity Market Integration?" *Explorations in Economic History* 43(3), 383–412.

Jacks, D. S. (2014). "Defying Gravity: The Imperial Economic Conference and the Reorientation of Canadian Trade." *Explorations in Economic History* 53, 19–39.

Jacks, D. S., Meissner, C. M., and Novy, D. (2008). "Trade Costs, 1870–2000." *American Economic Review* 98(2), 529–534.

Jacks, D. S., and Novy, D. (2018). "Market Potential and Global Growth over the Long Twentieth Century." *Journal of International Economics* 114, 221–237.

Jia, R. (2014). "The Legacies of Forced Freedom: China's Treaty Ports." *Review of Economics and Statistics* 96(4), 596–608.

Jordà, Ò., Schularick, M., and Taylor, A. M. (2013). "When Credit Bites Back." *Journal of Money, Credit and Banking* 45(s2), 3–28.

Jordà, Ò, Schularick, M., and Taylor, A. M. (2017). "Macro-Financial History and the New Business Cycle Facts." In NBER Macroeconomics Annual 2016, vol. 31, edited by M. Eichenbaum and J. A. Parker, 213–263. Chicago: University of Chicago Press.

Jordà, Ò, Schularick, M., and Taylor, A. M. (2021). *Jordà-Schularick-Taylor Macrohistory Database*. Downloaded October 10, 2021 from https://www.macrohistory.net/database/.

Jones, M. T., and Obstfeld, M. (2000). "Saving, Investment, and Gold: A Reassessment of Historical Current Account Data." In *Money, Capital Mobility, and Trade: Essays in Honor of Robert A. Mundell*, edited by G. A. Calvo, R. Dornbusch, and M. Obstfeld, 303–364. Cambridge, MA: MIT Press.

Kaminsky, G. L., and Reinhart, C. M. (1999). "The Twin Crises: The Causes of Banking and Balance-of-Payments Problems." *American Economic Review* 89(3), 473–500.

Kandel, W. (2011). "The U.S. Foreign Born Population: Trends and Selected Characteristics." Congressional Research Service Report 41592.

Keeling, D. (1999). "Transatlantic Shipping Cartels and Migration between Europe and America, 1880–1914." *Essays in Economic & Business History* 17(1), 195–213.

Laeven, L., and Valencia, F. (2012). "Systemic Banking Crises Database: An Update." IMF Working Paper No. 12/163.

Lane, P. R., and Milesi-Ferretti, G. M. (2001). "The External Wealth of Nations: Measures of Foreign Assets and Liabilities for Industrial and Developing Countries." *Journal of International Economics* 55 (December): 243–262.

Lane, P. R., and Milesi-Ferretti, G. M. (2017). "International Financial Integration in the Aftermath of the Global Financial Crisis." IMF Working Paper Number 2017/115.

Lehmann, S. H., and O'Rourke, K. H. (2011). "The Structure of Protection and Growth in the Late Nineteenth Century." *Review of Economics and Statistics* 93(2), 606–616.

Lindert, P. (2004). *Growing Public: Social Spending and Economic Growth*. New York: Cambridge University Press.

Liu, D., and Meissner, C. M. (2015). "Market Potential and the Rise of American Productivity Leadership." *Journal of International Economics* 96(1), 72–87.

Maddison, A. (2010). Maddison Database 2010. Gronigen Growth and Development Centre. https://www.rug.nl/ggdc/historicaldevelopment/maddison/original-maddison.

McGrattan, E. R., and Prescott, E. C. (2004). "The 1929 Stock Market: Irving Fisher Was Right." *International Economic Review* 45(4), 991–1009.

Meissner, C. M. (2001). "A New World Order: The Emergence of an International Monetary System, 1850 to 1913." PhD diss., University of California, Berkeley.

Meissner, C. M., and Taylor, A. M. (2009). "Losing Our Marbles in the New Century? The Great Rebalancing in Historical Perspective." In *Global Imbalances and the Evolving World Economy*, edited by J. S. Little, 53–130. Boston: Federal Reserve Bank of Boston.

Michaels, G., and Rauch, F. (2018). "Resetting the Urban Network: 117–2012." *Economic Journal* 128(608), 378–412.

Miller, R. (1976). "The Making of the Grace Contract: British Bondholders and the Peruvian Government, 1885–1890." *Journal of Latin American Studies* 8(1), 73–100.

Mitchell, B. R. (1998a). *International Historical Statistics: The Americas 1750–1998*. 2nd ed. New York: Stockton Press.

Mitchell, B. R. (1998b). *International Historical Statistics: Europe 1750–1993*. 4th ed. New York: Grove's Dictionaries.

North, D. C., and Weingast, B. R. (1989). "Constitutions and Commitment: The Evolution of Institutions Governing Public Choice in Seventeenth-Century England." *Journal of Economic History* 49(4), 803–832.

Nunn, N. (2008). "The Long-Term Effects of Africa's Slave Trades." *Quarterly Journal of Economics* 123(1), 139–176.

Nunn, N. and Qian, N. (2010). "The Columbian Exchange: A History of Disease, Food, and Ideas." *The Journal of Economic Perspectives* 24(2), 163–188.

Obstfeld, M. (1986). "Rational and Self-Fulfilling Balance of Payments Crises." *American Economic Review* 76(1), 72–81.

Obstfeld, M., and Taylor, A. M. (2005). *Global Capital Markets: Integration, Crisis, and Growth*. New York: Cambridge University Press.

Odell, K. A., and Weidenmier, M. D. (2004). "Real Shock, Monetary Aftershock: The 1906 San Francisco Earthquake and the Panic of 1907." *Journal of Economic History* 64(4), 1002–1027.

Officer, L. (1996). *Between the Dollar-Sterling Gold Points: Exchange Rates, Parity, and Market Behavior*. New York: Cambridge University Press.

O'Rourke, K. H. (2000). "Tariffs and Growth in the Late 19th Century." *Economic Journal* 110(463), 456–483.

O'Rourke, K. H., and Williamson, J. G. (1999). *Globalization and History: The Evolution of a Nineteenth Century Atlantic Economy*. Cambridge, MA: MIT Press.

O'Rourke, K. H., and Williamson, J. G. (2002). "When Did Globalisation Begin?" *European Review of Economic History* 6(1), 23–50.

Ottaviano, G. I., and Peri, G. (2012). "Rethinking the Effect of Immigration on Wages." *Journal of the European Economic Association* 10(1), 152–197.

Perri, F., and Quadrini, V. (2002). "The Great Depression in Italy: Trade Restrictions and Real Wage Rigidities." *Review of Economic Dynamics* 5(1), 128–151.

Piketty, T. (2014). *Capital in the 21st Century*. Cambridge, MA: The Belknap Press of Harvard University Press.

Polanyi, K. (1944.) *The Great Transformation: The Political and Economic Origins of Our Time*. Boston: Beacon Press.

Pomeranz, K. (2000). *The Great Divergence: China, Europe, and the Making of the Modern World Economy*. Princeton: Princeton University Press.

Reinhart, C. M., and Rogoff, K. S. (2009). *This Time Is Different*. Princeton: Princeton University Press.

Reinhart, C., and Rogoff, K. (2021). "Dates for Banking Crises, Currency Crashes, Sovereign Domestic or External Default (or Restructuring), Inflation Crises, and Stock Market Crashes (Varieties)." Downloaded October 19, 2021 from https://carmenreinh art.com/dates-for-banking-crises/.

Richter, F. (2020). "These Are the Top 10 Manufacturing Countries in the World." Downloaded October 9, 2021 from https://www.weforum.org/agenda/2020/02/countr ies-manufacturing-trade-exports-economics/.

Ritschl, A. (2013). "Reparations, Deficits, and Debt Default: The Great Depression in Germany." In *The Great Depression of the 1930s: Lessons for Today*, edited by P. Fearon and NFR Crafts, 110–139. Oxford: Oxford University Press.

Rodrigue, J.-P. 2020. *The Geography of Transport Systems*. 5th ed. New York: Routledge.

Rodrik, D. (1995). "Getting Interventions Right. Right: How South Korea and Taiwan Grew Rich." *Economic Policy* 10(20), 55–107.

Romer, C. D. (1990). "The Great Crash and the Onset of the Great Depression." *Quarterly Journal of Economics* 105(3), 597–624.

Rueff, J. (1972). *The Monetary Sin of the West*. New York: Macmillan.

Sachs, J. D., and Warner, A. (1995). "Economic Reform and the Process of Global Integration." Brookings Papers on Economic Activity, 1995(1), 1–118.

Sarr, M., and Bulte, E., and Meissner, C. M., and Swanson, T. (2011). "On the looting of nations." *Public choice* 148, 353–380.

Scheidel, W. (2014). "The Shape of the Roman World: Modeling Imperial Connectivity." *Journal of Roman Archaeology* 27, 7–32.

Schonhardt-Bailey, C. (1991). "Specific Factors, Capital Markets, Portfolio Diversification, and Free Trade: Domestic Determinants of the Repeal of the Corn Laws." *World Politics* 43(4), 545–569.

Schularick, M., and Steger, T. M. (2010). "Financial Integration, Investment, and Economic Growth: Evidence from Two Eras of Financial Globalization." *The Review of Economics and Statistics* 92(4), 756–768.

Schumacher, J., Trebesch, C., and Enderlein, H. (2021). "Sovereign Defaults in Court." *Journal of International Economics* 131, 103388.

Sokoloff, K. L., and Engerman, S. L. (2000). "Institutions, Factor Endowments, and Paths of Development in the New World." *Journal of Economic Perspectives* 14(3), 217–232.

Sotiropoulos, D. P., Rutterford, J., and Keber, C. (2020). "UK Investment Trust Portfolio Strategies before the First World War." *Economic History Review* 73(3), 785–814. https://doi.org/10.1111/ehr.12994.

Spiegel International. (2012). "Europe Could Economize Itself to Death." Downloaded December 29, 2022 from https://www.spiegel.de/international/german-press-review-editorialists-argue-in-favor-of-austerity-measures-a-829936.html.

Statistisches Reichsamt. (1936). *Statistisches Handbuch der Weltwirtschaft*. Berlin: Verlag für Sozialpolitik, Wirtschaft und Statistik.

Stone, I. (1999). *The Global Export of Capital from Great Britain, 1865–1914*. New York: St. Martin's Press.

Stuckler, D., Meissner, C. M., and King, L. P. (2008). "Can a Bank Crisis Break Your Heart?" *Globalization and Health* 4(1), 1–4.

Temin, P., and Wigmore, B. A. (1990). "The End of One Big Deflation." *Explorations in Economic History* 27(4), 483–502.

Tena-Junguito, A., Lampe, M., and Tâmega-Fernandes, F. (2012). "How Much Trade Liberalization Was There in the World before and after Cobden-Chevalier?" *Journal of Economic History* 72(3), 708–740.

United Nations Industrial Development Organization (UNIDO). (2021). "World Manufacturing Production: Statistics for Quarter II 2021. New York: United Nations.

United Nations, Department of Economic Affairs. (1948). Public Debt, 1914–1946, Lake Success, New York: United Nations Press.

United States Bureau of the Census. (1960). Historical Statistics of the United States: Colonial Times to 1957. Washington D.C.

UNU-WIDER. (2022). World Income Inequality Database (WIID). Version June 30, 2022. https://doi.org/10.35188/UNU-WIDER/WIID-300622.

Voigtlaender, N., and Voth, H. J. (forthcoming). "Highway to Hitler." *American Economic Journal: Applied Economics*.

Willcox, W. F. (1929). *International Migrations*, vol. I: Statistics. New York: National Bureau of Economic Research.

Williamson, J. G. (1996). "Globalization, Convergence, and History." *Journal of Economic History* 56, 277–306.

World Bank. (2021). World Development Indicators. Downloaded October 21, 2021 from https://data.worldbank.org/indicator/NE.EXP.GNFS.ZS.

World Trade Organization. (2021). World Trade Organization Data Portal. Site visited October 21, 2021. https://timeseries.wto.org/.

Yi, K. M. (2003). "Can Vertical Specialization Explain the Growth of World Trade?" *Journal of Political Economy* 111(1), 52–102.

Index